Conflict and Order

Conflict and Order

The Police and Labour Disputes in England and Wales, 1900–1939

JANE MORGAN

CLARENDON PRESS · OXFORD
1987

Oxford University Press, Walton Street, Oxford OX2 6DP

Oxford New York Toronto
Delhi Bombay Calcutta Madras Karachi
Petaling Jaya Singapore Hong Kong Tokyo
Nairobi Dar es Salaam Cape Town
Melbourne Auckland

and associated companies in
Beirut Berlin Ibadan Nicosia

Oxford is a trade mark of Oxford University Press

British Library Cataloguing in Publication Data

Morgan, Jane
Conflict and order: the police and labour disputes in England and Wales, 1900–1939.
1. Labour disputes—England—History —20th century 2. Police—England —History—20th century
I. Title
331.89'0942 HD5366.A6

ISBN 0–19–820128–1

Library of Congress Cataloging in Publication Data

Morgan, Jane.
Conflict and order.
Bibliography: p.
Includes index.
1. Labor disputes—England—History—20th century.
2. Labor disputes—Wales—History—20th century.
3. Police—England—History—20th century. 4. Police—Wales—History—20th century. I. Title
HD5366.A6M67 1987 331.89'2942 87–11027

ISBN 0–19–820128–1

Set by Wyvern Typesetting Limited, Bristol
Printed in Great Britain
at the University Printing House, Oxford
by David Stanford
Printer to the University

For Ken

Preface

In this book I consider the role of the police in the course of labour disputes in England and Wales between the industrial troubles at the start of the present century and the outbreak of the Second World War. After analysis of the broad features of the labour history of the period, six chapters cover the police directly. Chapters 3 to 5 illustrate the growth of Home Office influence over the provincial police, the effect of this in the use of troops, and the decline of accountability, locally and nationally. Chapters 6 to 8, by contrast, cover the operational side. The first two of these deal with the growth of police powers in handling picketing and related disorder; the last covers the executive functions of controlling meetings and marches by the unemployed, and the impact on civil liberties. In this way, a comprehensive coverage of all aspects of the part played by the police in the industrial history of England and Wales between 1900 and 1939 is offered. The book does not deal with the situation in Scotland or in Northern Ireland where police organization was very different. Its sole concern is the police system that obtained throughout England and Wales. Nor is the attention focused on the contemporary aspects of policing which have aroused such controversy in the 1980s, with its ethnic disturbances and the year-long miners' strike. Although the emphasis in this book is wholly historical, naturally readers may wish to draw their own inferences as to how far history repeats itself, whether as tragedy or farce.

In writing this book I have incurred many lasting obligations. I am much indebted to the very great help of Miss Mary White and Mr John Allen of the Home Office Noters Section, especially to Mr Allen for his help with the references; Mr Denis Brett, librarian of Bramshill Police College; and the staff of the Public Record Office at Kew, and the Bodleian Library in Oxford. I am grateful to the chief constables of Liverpool, Manchester, and the West Midlands, for permission to consult police sources, and to the staff of the county record offices in Glamorgan, Monmouthshire, and

Carmarthen. Hywel Francis kindly directed my attention to important material in the South Wales Miners' Library, Swansea. I have greatly benefited from the academic advice of Dr Roger Hood, Mrs Jenifer Hart, Dr Mark Freedland, Dr Paul Thompson, and Dr Michael Brogden; from helpful academic discussions with Dr Victor Bailey, Dr Robert Reiner, and Dr Barbara Weinberger; and especially from the encouragement of all my colleagues at the Centre for Criminological Research. Professor Sir Henry Phelps Brown and Dr Geoffrey Marshall placed me greatly in their debt by reading through the entire manuscript, and making many helpful and wise comments and criticisms. Professor Dai Smith offered valuable advice on illustrations; Rosemary Edney and Kaye Bewlay provided expert typing skills. Finally I am grateful to my husband and two children for all their support.

Centre for Criminological Research, Jane Morgan
Oxford
January 1987

Contents

List of plates

Between pages 148 and 149

Abbreviations

ADM	Admiralty
AEU	Amalgamated Engineering Union
BUF	British Union of Fascists
CAB	Cabinet
CCR	Civil Constabulary Reserve
CID	Criminal Investigation Department
CIGS	Chief of Imperial General Staff
DCIGS	Deputy Chief of the Imperial General Staff
DORA	Defence of the Realm Act
FBI	Federation of British Industry
GHQ	General Headquarters
GHQGB	General Headquarters Great Britain
GOC	General Officer Commanding
GOC in C	General Officer Commanding in Chief
HO	Head Office
ILP	Independent Labour Party
MEPO	Metropolitan Police
MFGB	Miners' Federation of Great Britain
MH	Ministry of Health
NCCL	National Council for Civil Liberties
NUPPO	National Union of Police and Prison Officers
NUR	National Union of Railwaymen
NUWCM	National Unemployed Workers' Committee Movement
NUWM	National Unemployed Workers' Movement
OMS	Organization for the Maintenance of Supplies
Parl. Deb.	*Parliamentary Debates*
PP	Parliamentary Papers
QMG	Quartermaster-General
STC	Supply and Transport Committee
SWMF	South Wales Miners' Federation
TGWU	Transport and General Workers' Union
TUC	Trades Union Congress
UAB	Unemployment Assistance Board
UDC	Urban District Council
WO	War Office

1
Introduction

IN his report on the inquiry into the riots at Brixton in 1981 Lord Scarman laid emphasis on the main principles governing the policing of a free society which he saw as relevant to his investigation—consent and balance on the one hand, independence and accountability on the other. By this he meant that, if the police were to secure the assent of the community which they needed to support their operations, they must strike an acceptable balance between the freedom to operate without political or other constraints, and their ultimate liability to the consent of the community. Scarman thus provided an updated version of the three elements of the function of the police as defined by Sir Richard Mayne at the time of the founding of the Metropolitan Police in 1829—the prevention of crime, the protection of life and property, and the preservation of public tranquillity.

The conflict which can arise between the duty of the police to maintain order and their duty to enforce the law, and the priority which must be given to the former, have long been recognized by the police themselves. This was reflected again in the miners' strike of 1984–5, as was the inherent complexity of reconciling the principles of independence and of public accountability. Lord Scarman laid down that the exercise of the role of the police has to be as independent and unconstrained as is the exercise of professional judgement by a doctor or lawyer. Police freedom is as vital to a community as is medical or academic freedom. Nevertheless, there remain limitations of a permanent kind on the powers of the police. First and foremost, there is the law itself: the police officer must act within the law. Then there is the factor of constitutional forms of accountability: the police are ultimately servants of the community. They enforce the law on behalf of the community; indeed they cannot effectively operate without the support of the public, in all its social, cultural, and ethnic diversity. This basic principle of accountability has its traditional institutional forms. Outside London, the chief constable is both independent and accountable for his activities to a local police authority. In London, the Metropolitan Police are differently placed. The Commissioner of the Metropolitan Police is accountable, not to a local police authority, but to the Home Secretary, and through him to parliament itself. But, however expressed in institutional terms, the problem of reconciling police independence and public consent survives today as it has done ever since the modern law-enforcement agencies were created in the past century.

The supreme touchstone for the achievement of this delicate balance of principles has always been the handling of social discontent, especially working-class and labour unrest, by the police. It is in this crucial area, so central to British history since the advent of industrialization in the late-eighteenth century, that the subject of police accountability has been put to the ultimate test. The bitter course of the miners' strike in 1984–5 showed how far the police are, in the view of some on the left at least, from attaining Scarman's ideals. That strike shed new light on the high degree of centralization in the direction of police operations, and the gulf that now obtains between police activities at times of national emergency and the principles of democratic accountability, either nationally or locally. In mining and other areas, chief constables appeared to pay scant heed to their local police committees. Nationally, parliament could exercise little control over the determination of police policy, while the Home Office seemed intent on deflecting such questions as might emerge. In place of influence from elected public representatives, a growing commitment is being seen to police autonomy, with the police increasingly dependent on their own hierarchical and disciplinary structures and bureaucratic controls, mediated behind the closed doors of the Home Office. In terms of labour troubles, the miners' strike also starkly revealed the assumption of apparently novel powers by the police over picketing, the banning of meetings and marches, and discretion in interpreting the laws on obstruction, threatening behaviour, breach of the peace, watching and besetting, and riotous assembly. Instances of police violence and assault have been reported—and fully recorded in the media—which tends to suggest a sanctioning, from above, of a wider definition of reasonable force. Police powers, so some of their critics feared, were being remorselessly extended and put to political use, with potentially ominous consequences for civil liberties in Britain.

In fact the problems revealed by the miners' strike of 1984–5 are very far from being new. Bitter disputes relating to the policing of picketing and industrial disturbances, the control of meetings and marches, and the revamping and growing centralization of a national police response to labour troubles have recurred repeatedly throughout Britain's history as a major industrial power. In particular, similar problems have emerged, time and again, since the latter decades of the nineteenth century. From the 1880s onwards, and especially in the decades down to the eve of the Second World War, Britain underwent successive waves of industrial confrontation which placed new strains on its police system and the principles that governed it. Here—notably in the three decades down to the outbreak of world war in 1914, and then again in the twenty years of depression and unemployment after 1918—was the true making of the British working class. Its creation was not located in the frontier years of working-class crystallization between 1790 and 1830. Rather was it a product of Britain's industrial maturity over a half a century later, and its subsequent devastating and remorseless industrial decline. The consequences of these waves of labour unrest were powerful for almost every aspect of British politics, society, and culture, and the police were inevitably caught up within the maelstrom in a decisive manner.

Between the late-nineteenth century and the 1930s there developed some crucial changes, still only imperfectly understood, in the evolution of the British police. There was the emergence of a police force more clearly nationalized in the face of large-scale industrial disorder, more directly subject to the edicts of central government, and freer from local or national democratic accountability. These basic themes are clearly detectable throughout the period 1900–39. In addition, there was a steady extension of police powers to deal with disorder, and an increase of their resources for riot control. In the late 1920s civil servants such as Sir Edward Troup might still pronounce complacently on the delicate, and very English, balance that had informally emerged between central direction and local accountability, appropriate for an unwritten constitution.[1] But the realities of the development of

[1] Sir E. Troup, 'Police Administration, Local and National', *Police Journal*, 1 (1928), 5.

the police were very different, with immense consequences for the rights of free citizenship within the British democracy.

The importance of the role of the police during this vital period has been increasingly recognized by scholars in a diversity of disciplines over the past years. A variety of academic and other approaches have been adopted, many of them flowing directly from the civil tumults in Britain and Northern Ireland from the late 1960s onwards. Sociologists, criminologists, lawyers, political commentators, and social theorists have all had their say. Amongst these the first named have made an especially influential contribution to the discussion of the function of the police. Such sociologists as Robert Reiner, Michael Banton, and Peter Manning have tended to emphasize the broad consensus which they see as emerging in public attitudes to the police in Britain from the early nineteenth century down to the 1950s.[2] This is contrasted with the far more hostile attitudes visible in the United States or France. Banton, for example, began his pioneering social study of the police with: 'The idea that it can be instructive to analyse institutions that are working well in order to see if anything can be learned from their success . . .'.[3] Reiner has written that, 'Although they have certainly never acted with kid gloves, there is no doubt that the British police developed a tradition of containing industrial disputes and political demonstrations with minimum force when contrasted with the experiences of other countries'.[4] He believes that the achievement of the first century of policing in Britain was that:

> From a widely hated and feared institution, the police had come to be regarded as the embodiment of impersonal, rule-bound, authority, enforcing democratically-enacted legislation on behalf of the broad mass of society, rather than any partisan interest, and constrained by tight legal requirements of due process.[5]

From the later 1950s onwards Reiner see this consensus coming to an end, and police legitimacy increasingly coming under fire, in accordance with the social, ethnic, and religious conflicts of a divided and perhaps declining society. Nevertheless, he believes

[2] R. Reiner, *The Politics of the Police* (1985); M. Banton, *The Policeman in the Community* (1964); P. Manning, *Police Work* (1977).

[3] Banton, *Policeman*, p. vii.

[4] Reiner, *Politics*, p. 55.

[5] Ibid. 61

that the broad picture of consent and consensus, embodied in enduring folk symbols such as the friendly (and unarmed) village 'bobby', survived intact from the earlier period, and the majority of scholars seem to accept this view. This applies also to Roger Geary's *Policing Industrial Disputes, 1893 to 1985* (1985), although it is noticeable that his book, unlike his earlier unpublished thesis, had to take account of the events of the 1984–5 miners' strike, which ran counter to the 'victory without violence' theme which provided the main pivot of his argument.

This sociological view, however, rests on broad, and largely untested, historical interpretations. In particular it is transcendently clear that the fundamental historical data have gone unexamined, and that the historical dimension, so vital for an understanding of this problem, has often been ignored. Sociological treatments, resting on broad assumptions about social evolution at the present time, necessarily do not look at historical evidence first hand. Too often an over-simple view, born of legend or cliché, is adopted. Even someone as authoritative or impartial as Reiner makes some assumptions which appear to fly against the available documentary evidence. For instance, his belief in the police strategy of 'minimal force' in handling labour disputes, the working-class view that police are non-partisan and politically impartial, the process of working-class incorporation into British social and political structures which makes the very concept of a police force more naturally acceptable to them, all appear suspect when placed under the harsh light of historical investigation into the contemporary sources available for the earlier record of the police in relation to labour unrest. At the very least these assumptions and hypotheses need to be subjected to the most intensive and detailed scrutiny.

The historical method, therefore, is absolutely vital in understanding the range of forces which governed the approach of the police to labour and industrial questions. In practice, those historians who have turned to this theme have too often been limited or superficial in their approach. As a rule, police history and labour history have been considered in quite separate compartments. Academic scholars have seldom considered the two together, as part of the same process of the organizational response to social change.

Police historians, for their part, tend to be too internal and institutional in their approach. They focus on machinery and organization, and can show insufficient awareness of the wider public response to the expanding role of the police. Until the 1970s their view of police history was to see it as part of the inevitable march of progress towards a more ordered and civilized society. By the same token, a police force is seen as politically and socially neutral, and rooted in the inherent consent of the entire community. Historians such as Reith, Radzinowicz, Ascoli, Tobias, and Critchley have portrayed the evolution of the police almost in Whiggish terms, the true goal in view being an efficient, centralized, nationally directed police force on utilitarian lines.[6] Opposition to such a force is believed to have died away between the 1850s and the 1960s, as the benefits of order and social peace gradually became obvious. From the late 1960s, however, another, very different, school of police historians has arisen, one which emphasizes conflict rather than consensus. In this approach the police appear more as a reassertion of the power of the state over a new and threatening conjuncture of social forces. Allan Silver, in a sophisticated account in 1967, argued that the manufacturing and moneyed classes saw the police as a force which circumvented the need for direct social confrontation with 'the dangerous classes'.[7] Robert Storch has termed the police 'domestic missionaries', intended to impose forms of social control on the workers.[8] In a more ideological form, as adopted by E. P. Thompson or Tony Bunyan among others, the police are seen as a mechanism for maintaining the dominance of a bourgeois ruling class against the interest of the various elements of those working-class groups who constituted between them the vast majority of the population.[9]

[6] C. Reith, *British Police and the Democratic Ideal* (1943); L. Radzinowicz, *A History of English Criminal Law*, iv (1968); D. Ascoli, *The Queen's Peace* (1979); J. J. Tobias, *Crime and Police in England, 1700–1900* (1979); T. A. Critchley, *A History of the Police in England and Wales, 900–1966* (1967).

[7] A. Silver, 'The Demand for Order in a Civil Society: A Review of Some of the Themes in the History of Urban Crime, Police and Riot', in D. J. Bordua (ed.), *The Police: Six Sociological Essays* (1967), 1–24.

[8] R. D. Storch, 'The Policeman as Domestic Missionary: Urban Discipline and Popular Culture in Northern England, 1850–1880', *Journal of Social History* (Summer 1976), 481–509; id., 'The Plague of Blue Locusts. Police Reform and Popular Resistance in Northern England, 1840–1857', *International Review of Social History*, 20 (1975), 61–90.

[9] E. P. Thompson, *Whigs and Hunters* (1975); T. Bunyan, *The Political Police in Britain* (1976).

In some ways, paradoxically, these two opposed schools of police historians tend to share common assumptions and methodologies. Both tend to focus on the emergence of a centralized police force, the waning powers of such bodies as local watch committees, the amalgamation of local police forces, or the encroaching impact of the Home Office inspectorate. The centrists or the right accept these processes, the left condemn them. Both take them as given. Both tend to underrate or overlook vital historical processes which complicate the story, and which continue to contribute to the evolution of the British police as an institution. Historians such as Victor Bailey, Michael Brogden, and Clive Emsley have shown that both schools tend to embody questionable assumptions.[10]

While police historians may be felt to have their limitations, scholars of the British labour movement, on the other hand, have traditionally paid scant attention to the role of the police. At worst, the police are a monolithic class enemy. At best, they are an irrelevance. Seldom are the police placed alongside the trade unions, or other working-class bodies, in dynamic historical terms. Scholars such as Henry Pelling, Hugh Clegg, or Eric Hobsbawm, who have contributed so richly to an understanding of the industrial, political, or cultural evolution of the British labour movement, have shown little interest in the role of the police in the industrial confrontations that they have chronicled for British history between the 1890s and the 1930s. The same tends to apply to historians of more local developments as well, although such recent works on Welsh labour history as those by Merfyn Jones for the North Wales quarrymen[11] or Hywel Francis for the South Wales miners[12] have shown a welcome tendency to see the police as part of the industrial scene whose conflicts they record. But in general, while police historians tend to be unaware of the dynamics of the working-class movement, for labour historians the police are the ghosts at the feast, a conspicuous absentee in their accounts, however comprehensive in other respects.

In fact, the growth of the police force in Britain and its involvement in the world of organized or unorganized labour is inextric-

[10] V. Bailey (ed.), *Policing and Punishment in Nineteenth Century Britain* (1981); M. Brogden, *The Police: Autonomy and Consent* (1982); C. Emsley, *Policing and its Context, 1750–1870* (1983).

[11] R. M. Jones, *The North Wales Quarrymen, 1874–1922* (1981).

[12] H. Francis, *Miners against Fascism: Wales and the Spanish Civil War* (1984).

ably bound up with the story of civil disturbance and protest in modern British society. The historical perspective, above all, enables one to understand the police response to social crisis and national emergency during the maturity and economic decline of industrial Britain. In this way, the manner in which the police have been integrated in the social and political evolution of this country can be fully understood. Again, applying an historical perspective to the relations of the police and the labour movement shows up the essential continuity of the relationship between the police and the political structure. As Tom Bowden has written, it domonstrates 'that the public order function of the police is an enduring one, and is not simply one more facet of the politically tense age in which we live'.[13]

Previous work, such as that by Bowes, Bowden, Ronald Kidd, first secretary of the National Council for Civil Liberties (NCCL), or Sarah Mainwaring White, while stimulating in many ways, tended to present too simple a model of unified government and of police strategy as a mode of repression.[14] In the years immediately before 1914 the problem of dealing with industrial protest, meetings, and marches was seen, as in the nineteenth century, basically as a concern for the police and police authorities rather than for the central government. There was little political support for a coherent, or coercive national policy towards picketing or demonstrations. Yet tensions existed in abundance. Police determination to deal with labour difficulties or confrontations was hedged about by important constraints imposed by their local authorities and the magistracy.

The First World War marked a vital watershed in this story. With the onset of large-scale national strikes from 1918 onwards, and the emergence also of nationally organized demonstrations by the unemployed, the government became increasingly drawn into the maintenance of the peace and the suppression of what it saw as disorder. Chiefs of police were encouraged to build on the powers they had enjoyed under the Defence of the Realm Regulations during the First World War, and later under the Emergency

[13] T. Bowden, 'Guarding the State: The Police Response to Crisis Politics in Europe', *British Journal of Law and Society*, 5 (1978), 70.

[14] S. Bowes, *The Police and Civil Liberties* (1966); Bowden, 'Guarding the State', pp. 69–88; R. Kidd, *British Liberty in Danger* (1940); S. Mainwaring-White, *The Policing Revolution* (1983).

Regulations enforced during the states of emergency in 1921 and 1926. They now began to take their own initiative in dealing with such matters as picketing and unemployed meetings and marches—but with the direction and guidance of the Home Office and within the context of a police force that was becoming increasingly centralized in its form, even if still some way short of the Ministry of Police system operating in some continental countries. The police started to legitimize powers they had been taking *ad hoc* to cope with nation-wide labour disorders, for many of which they would previously have sought the authority of local councils or the justices of the peace. The passage of the Public Order Act in 1936, officially endorsed by the Labour Party in view of the anti-Semitic outbursts at the same time, marked in many ways the culmination of this process. Yet many of the causes for concern relating to the police handling of labour in a public order context still remained unresolved at the time of the Second World War.

Apart from the police force itself, the other major institution to loom large in these pages is, of course, the Home Office. The expansion of central government from the 1870s onwards, naturally, did not leave the Home Office itself unaffected. It also felt the galvanizing impact of internal reform and departmental overhaul. As young men of ability entered the department, through the open examination system, the Home Office emerged with enhanced authority, and its personnel with fresh dynamism. At times of social or industrial crisis, key officials of the Home Office were more prepared to challenge or goad other government departments, and to assert their authority or influence over local authorities.

The Home Office in this period can all too easily be seen as simply a faceless, monolithic, bureaucratic structure. Internal departmental tension is less easy to delineate than, in, say, the Treasury, the Foreign Office, or the Board of Trade. Nevertheless, human faces can be given to the personnel in the Home Office machine. The 'official view' can be broken down in terms of ministerial edict, or the decisions of individual civil servants. In particular, the role of two immensely authoritative permanent under-secretaries at the Home Office—both statesmen—Sir Edward Troup, who served from 1908 to 1922, and his successor, Sir John Anderson, who served from 1922 to 1932, is crucial in understanding the governmental response in the turbulent decades of the early twentieth century.[15]

Sir Edward Troup was the first, and most important, of a new breed of able young civil servants who galvanized the Home Office at the turn of the century. He entered the department in 1880 as a successful candidate in the first open examinations as a junior clerk.[16] He rapidly rose up the departmental ladder of promotion, and, long before he became permanent under-secretary in 1908, had clearly emerged as the dominant personality and intellect within the Home Office. He was obviously one of the outstanding bureaucrats of his day. He was said by a later admirer to have 'touched nothing which he did not illuminate'. Sir Harold Scott noted Troup as: 'A rather silent, heavy Scot, with little sense of humour.'[17] At the same time he acknowledged Troup's decisive role in setting the standards and creating the administrative machinery for the Home Office, both to carry through the immense legislation passed by the Liberal government in 1906–14 and also to deal with the onset of widespread and alarming labour disturbance.

He was followed in 1922 by another remarkable Scottish administrator, Sir John Anderson. He was already a figure of considerable stature, having been president of the Board of Inland Revenue in 1919 at the extraordinarily youthful age of 39, and then becoming under-secretary for Ireland at Dublin Castle in 1920. He moved to the Home Office in 1922 as a figure of immense prestige and authority. Here, 'Honest John' or 'Jehovah' as he was sometimes called (an indication of an almost God-like wisdom and clarity of judgement) exerted an enormous influence. He was not particularly interested in the formulation of policy, and was far less obviously the personal director of departmental policies than Troup had been. It is notable that, while Troup produced an endless stream of personal memoranda between 1908 and 1922, Anderson wrote very few indeed and usually contented himself with initialling, or providing terse verdicts on, the memoranda of

[15] For helpful general accounts, see J. Pellew, *The Home Ofice, 1848–1914* (1982); Sir E. Troup, *The Home Office* (1925); Sir F. Newsam, *The Home Office* (1954); A. L. Dixon, 'The Home Office and the Police between the Two World Wars' (MS in Bramshill Police College, 1966); J. W. Wheeler-Bennett, *John Anderson, Viscount Waverley* (1962).

[16] Pellew, *The Home Office*, p. 33.

[17] Sir H. Scott, *Your Obedient Servant* (1959), 28.

others. Penal policy, for instance, was not an area that fired his imagination. He did take a close interest in police matters, but this important area fell mainly to F Division of the Home Office, under Arthur Dixon, remodelled in 1922 following the report of the Desborough Committee. It was Dixon, assisted by Carew Robinson, who dealt with the minutiae of police operations between 1922 and 1932.[18] Sir Leonard Dunning, chief inspector of constabulary from 1922 to 1930, was also a highly active personality in this sphere. Anderson, it seems, was so eminent and authoritative a figure in the bureaucratic machine that the nuts and bolts of Home Office policy were invariably delegated to others. Even so, the impress of his personality and ideas was indisputable. More than Troup (whose experience, after all, was confined to the Home Office throughout his career), Anderson, with his wide background in a range of important departments, was a crucial influence at the highest level of decision-making.

He moved on in 1932 to the new challenges offered by the governorship of Bengal, and his immediate successors, Sir Russell Scott (permanent under-secretary, 1932–8) and Sir Alexander Maxwell (who served 1938–48), perhaps lacked his unique authority. It was, therefore, these two remarkable Scottish civil servants, Troup and then Anderson, who were above all crucial in the Home Office's perceived policy of increasing its powers of direction between 1908 and 1939, in imposing its authority over local police authorities, upholding the position of chief constables in the face of local political opposition, and in strengthening the police as a uniform standardized instrument, capable of responding, flexibly but decisively, in the face of industrial unrest. The process of growing Home Office direction—exalting the power of central government, many felt, at the expense of civil liberties and the freedom of the individual citizen—is a vital connecting theme in the history of the police in the present century. It was in large measure the regime of Troup and Anderson that was responsible.

The purpose of this book is to consider the interaction of the labour movement, the police, and the Home Office in the first four decades of the twentieth century, projecting them against a background of political and industrial change unique in British history. In doing so it hopes to shed vital new light on a crucial but neglected aspect of the modern British experience. An immense

[18] Dixon, 'The Home Office', pp. 25 ff.

array of primary materials is available for the historian of this theme. The public records are there in profusion, not only the familiar papers of the Home Office and the Metropolitan Police, which of course must be used, but also those of the ancillary departments such as the War Office and the Admiralty, or alternatively of the Ministries of Health and Labour, which equally bear intimately on key aspects of the police presence in coping with labour difficulties. While some, well-publicized gaps remain in the public records, notably on the surveillance role of the police during strikes and the unemployed marches in the 1920s and 1930s, the great bulk of the public archive remains and beckons to the historian of the police. In addition to materials housed in the Public Record Office at Kew, many files in the Home Office, not normally available to researchers under the 'hundred-year rule', have been used. Again, a wealth of local police records is available, especially the minutes of local watch committees in boroughs and standing joint committees in counties; historians are becoming increasingly aware of their value for social history as perceptions of crime and disorder loom as ever more important priorities for an understanding of British society. The local newspaper press is also a vital source, as are the files of the labour press, political, industrial, or agricultural. For the labour movement itself, apart from such familiar materials as the records of the Trades Union Congress (TUC), individual unions, the Labour Party, and other political organizations, a fascinating area opening up is that of oral history which often gives new insights into the attitudes of working people towards the police and the law enforcement agencies generally, as well as the attitudes of rank-and-file policemen, usually themselves of working-class stock, often caught up in resistance to protests by trade-union or unemployed workers, perhaps against their will.

This book has, inevitably, many contemporary overtones, especially with the outcome of the miners' strike of 1984–5 still fresh in the mind. But its purpose is essentially historical, focusing on the period 1900–39 above all. By concentrating on the historical dimension, this study hopes to ask new questions, not only on more formal aspects of the role of the law and its enforcement agencies in the handling of British industrial relations in this stormy period, but on broader themes of the nature of government by consent, and the values such an idea contains. By implication, it opens up wider aspects of the encroachment of central government upon popular liberties and social relationships, which has grown remorselessly since the Victorian heyday of Millite Liberalism in the 1850s. The tension in a police force that is technically efficient and is at the same time subject to forms of political and social control, acceptable to all classes and groups within a highly stratified and divided society, is an enduring one. It remains a theme of anxious, even passionate, controversy at the present time. The record of the interaction of the police and the British labour movement in this turbulent period takes us to the heart of a crucial aspect of the evolution of modern Britain.

2

Trade Unions and the Community in Twentieth-century Britain

IN the early years of the twentieth century trade unions inspired in the British public a mixture of respect qualified by fear.[1] It was widely acknowledged that the unions were established clients of the later-Victorian social and legal order, whose status was apparently protected in law by Disraeli's Conspiracy and Protection of Property Act of 1875. On the other hand, the expansion of trade unionism, especially in such heavy industrial occupations as the coal mines, from the late 1880s until the outbreak of world war in 1914 aroused growing apprehension amongst employers, publicists, and the political parties. Trade-union membership in Britain grew steadily from around three-quarters of a million at the end of the 1880s, to over two million by 1901, and over three million by 1911. By now some white-collar workers such as postal employees, clerks, or schoolteachers were joining manual workers in becoming unionized. The proportion of the working class in employment who were enrolled as members of unions rose similarly from a mere 6 per cent in 1888 to 17 per cent in 1910. With a further huge upsurge of membership, especially amongst unskilled occupations such as dockers, seamen, and other transport workers from 1910 onwards, British trade unions accounted for well over four million within their ranks (almost a quarter of the work-force) by August 1914. During the four years of war that followed union membership continued to soar upwards, roughly doubling during the war years, to reach a peak of over eight million by the start of 1919.

Here, then, were immensely powerful organizations, backed by

[1] The outstanding work on this theme is E. H. Phelps Brown, *The Origins of Trade Union Power* (1983). Also important for the general history of trade unionism in the period are H. Clegg, A. Fox, and A. F. Thompson, *A History of British Trade Unions since 1889*, i. *1889–1910* (1963); H. Clegg, *A History of British Trade Unions since 1889* (1985); E. H. Phelps Brown, *The Growth of British Industrial Relations* (1959); H. Pelling, *A History of British Trade Unionism* (2nd edn., 1971); C. Wrigley (ed.), *A History of British Industrial Relations, 1875–1914* (1982).

mass membership and substantial funds; a union like the Miners' Federation of Great Britain (MFGB) numbered 761,000 by 1914, with a quarter of a million coming from the thriving South Wales coalfield alone. Inevitably, perhaps, in the swirling social changes of later-Victorian and Edwardian Britain, the position of trade unions, constitutionally, legally, and in terms of public order, aroused increasing anxiety. The miners' national lock-out of 1893 showed how a mighty union in a staple industry now had the power and organizational control to exert something close to a stranglehold over the entire British economy, and to paralyse the constitutional and social system. Major disputes in the later 1890s, like the engineers' lock-out of 1897–8 and the six-month strike by 100,000 South Wales miners in 1898, aroused much alarm. Further, it was noticeable that these unions, old and new, were showing a far more aggressive and class-conscious type of leadership. The engineers, the very model of mid-Victorian craft unionism, with their bowler-hatted, watch-chained officials, now claimed the Independent Labour Party (ILP) socialist, George Barnes, as their general secretary. The Welsh miners had begun to reject the traditional leadership of old nonconformist Liberals like 'Mabon' and to follow the creed of younger, socialist militants, often from across the English border. In their turn, employers' organizations became far more aggressively anti-union in the mid- and later 1890s, especially the shipowners' Associations with their provocative use of 'free labour' in Britain's ports, and encouragement of legal action against trade-union picketing in labour disputes. The strike on the Taff Vale railway in 1900 led to the railway company successfully pursuing a civil action against the notoriously moderate railway servants' union for damages incurred in the course of the strike: total costs of £23,000 resulted, with an apparent threat to the very right of the free withdrawal of labour. Episodes like these had a major galvanizing effect upon trade-union militants and socialist zealots, and encouraged a mass affiliation by union after union to the infant Labour Representation Committee between 1901 and 1903. In 1909 the massive MFGB was to join them and to crusade for nationalization of the mines.

By the early years of the Edwardian period trade unions were widely condemned by their opponents as potentially dangerous or even subversive. In December 1902 E. A. Pratt denounced them in

The Times for 'ca' canny' methods which disrupted production and lay at the root of Britain's comparative industrial decline.[2] More ominously, anxiety about the unions' alleged threat to law and order, by such methods as mass picketing, began to be widely expressed. It was clear that, in the general election of 1906, underlying such traditional themes as free trade, temperance, and church schools, the status and responsibilities of trade unions were a fundamental issue. The defence of their unions, at a time of mounting trade uncertainty, was a powerful factor in promoting working-class support for the Liberal and Labour Parties in the electoral landslide which brought the Liberals to office by a huge majority. The legislative changes that followed did not allay public disquiet or dampen debate. The Trade Disputes Act 1906 did reverse the Taff Vale judgment in the House of Lords, but it did so in a very remarkable manner. The Labour Party's own bill, which gave the unions complete immunity in civil actions—a unique status which the unions continued to enjoy down to the 1980s—was taken over by the Liberal government in place of its own, more qualified, measure. The special legal protection that the unions now enjoyed added to the concern felt by employers and Conservative politicians. So, too, did the political links of the unions with the Labour Party, brought out into the open by the Osborne case in 1909 which declared illegal the levy from general union funds to finance the Labour Party. There was the increasing complication that the government itself, far from standing aside as an independent arbitrator at best in industrial conflicts, was now being sucked in as an employer of labour, and the controlling element in an increasingly integrated, national economy. At a time of mounting class hostility, occasional trade recession, and much local unemployment, the government found itself often in the front line of industrial confrontation. Far from the Trade Disputes Act 1906, therefore, leading to a new era of industrial peace, it heralded twenty years of conflict between unions, employers and government, which endured until the 1926 general strike, and which coloured the outlook of the police and political authorities throughout this turbulent period.

Between 1910 and 1914 the alarm aroused by the activities of the unions rose to a new pitch of urgency. During these years there

[2] E. A. Pratt, *Trade Unionism and British Industry: A Reprint of 'The Times' Articles on the Crisis in British Industry* (1904).

was a series of unusually long, often violent, nation-wide strikes, with the ideology of syndicalism or industrial unionism sometimes to the fore.[3] The cockpit of these quasi-revolutionary disturbances was, inevitably, the mining industry, especially in South Wales. The vicious rioting in the Rhondda valleys around the Cambrian pits in Tonypandy in November 1910 seemed to go far beyond any previous labour dispute for its uninhibitedly violent nature. Originating in a dispute over wage rates in 'abnormal places' where hewing coal was difficult, it led (as will be shown in detail later) to mass rioting; extreme counter-violence by the local Glamorgan constabulary afforced by the Metropolitan Police from London; the dispatch of troops to the Welsh mining valleys by Winston Churchill, the Home Secretary, and the creation of a new legend of class warfare that endured for generations. Tonypandy marked the dawn of a fresh era of class confrontation, spurred on by militant local leaders like Noah Ablett and his fellow Marxist authors of the *Miners' Next Step*, a quasi-syndicalist pamphlet published by the Unofficial Reform Committee in Tonypandy in 1912.

In that same year there was a national miners' strike in March–April on behalf of a national minimum wage. The Asquith government rapidly surrendered and passed legislation to authorize the principle of such a wage structure on a district basis. This new evidence of powerful union strength, nationally and in local coalfields, was mirrored in a national railway strike in August 1911, in the course of which two men were shot down and killed by troops at Llanelli while many violent clashes between police and strikers also took place in other areas. Coming at a time of a foreign policy crisis over the Agadir affair, the railway strike again demonstrated the clear capacity of a major union to paralyse or disrupt the entire economy. Amongst the dockers, in July–August 1911 a strike of 75,000 transport workers caused the closure of the Liverpool docks; the situation was resolved by the widespread use of troops during a virtual general strike in the Merseyside area. Two men were shot dead and scores seriously injured during widespread disturbances. A London dock strike in May 1912 also caused widespread apprehension, although in this case the Port of London Authority was able to defeat the strike and to compel the continued use of blackleg labour. Admittedly a city like Liverpool was a rare case of turbulence, with its unique sectarian difficulties

[3] See B. Holton, *British Syndicalism, 1900–1914* (1976).

and tensions, but these transport strikes fitted into a wider picture of union conflict and confrontation. The years 1913 and 1914 were somewhat calmer, even in South Wales and Liverpool, although strikes by engineers and building workers in early 1914 showed that ideas of industrial unionism and more aggressive forms of socialism than Keir Hardie or Ramsay MacDonald ever visualized were still present. The 'unrest' of the post-1910 years was far from spent. Even on the very eve of world war in August 1914 Britain was threatened with another national railway strike on behalf of a 48-hour week. The existence since that spring of a 'Triple Alliance' between miners, railwaymen, and transport workers, although in reality a non-revolutionary and strictly qualified gesture, aroused yet more alarm at the spectre of a controlled upsurge by a united workers' movement.

The causes of the unrest of 1910–14 were many and profound. To some degree, they were rooted in local circumstances and situations. The peculiar ethnic and sectarian divisions of Liverpool played their part in the troubles in the docks there in 1911. Jim Sexton, the dockers' leader, was both a union official and a prominent Irish Catholic. In South Wales the huge wave of English immigrants, bringing in new ideologies to challenge the old ethos of Celtic Lib–Lab nonconformity, helped swell the 'unofficial' rank-and-file movements. But there were more general nation-wide factors at work, too. Socialism, perhaps syndicalism, played some part, notably amongst transport workers, railwaymen, and some miners. But this was not the dominant cause of unrest. It was above all a time of immensely rapid growth of trade-union organization, especially amongst the unskilled labourers. Here was, indeed, a far more impressive phase of 'new unionism' than the early 1890s, on which the Webbs laid much emphasis. One factor was the advantage gained by the unions from their status as approved societies in administering benefit under Lloyd George's National Insurance Act of 1911. In addition, there were economic difficulties in many industries, resulting from a rapid rise of prices and fluctuations in employment especially amongst service workers. The miners suffered from the problems of a low-productivity, labour-intensive industry. The adverse cost position of employers such as coalowners and railway companies made them resistant to new wage demands.

Overall, though, the labour unrest was a sign of the workers' growing strength and prosperity. The period 1911–14 was a time of a general improvement in real wages and of a prolonged boom in the older staple industries; and 1913 was the last generally thriving year that British industry as a whole was to enjoy until the period immediately after 1945. As a result of these events, therefore, many middle-class or right-wing contemporaries saw the unions' unbridled economic power and capacity for destroying the civil fabric in very alarmist terms. Some historians, indeed, have tried to link the labour unrest of 1910–14 with the disturbances of the suffragettes and the Irish nationalists as part of the alleged 'strange death' of Edwardian Liberalism. In reality, the rise of aggressive unionism had no overt connection with these political developments. It was partly the result of growth and new opportunities. When the unions balloted their individual members, after the Trade Union Act 1913 had reversed the Osborne judgement and legalized the political levy, in union after union the links with the constitutional Labour Party were strongly endorsed. Only three small unions out of sixty-three voted to reject a political fund.[4] Without doubt, the unions had reached a new plateau of economic power by the time a still greater crisis engulfed the nation in August 1914.

During four years of total war the unions increased their membership and their strength still further. By the start of 1919 they had reached a peak of over eight million members. The war enormously enhanced the power of the unions within a labour market newly geared to meet the needs of wartime production and distribution. The unions were seen to be vital in winning the war. During the war years, indeed, the unions seemed almost to be bound to the government and the employers' organization, the newly founded Federation of British Industry (FBI), in a vast, tripartite, corporate relationship. Bargaining over pay claims was increasingly conducted on a national basis, rather than by sectional councils. The pre-war pattern of adversarial hostility between capital and labour seemed to be left behind, in the optimistic assessment of some observers. In March 1915 most unions (with the MFGB a significant exception) struck up a pact with the government, the so-called 'Treasury Agreement' under which strikes would be forgone during the war, in return for the

[4] See R. McKibbin, *The Evolution of the Labour Party, 1910–1924* (1974), 72 ff.; H. Pelling, *Popular Politics and Society in Late Victorian Britain* (1968), 162.

protection of collective bargaining procedures and some remarkably vague promises about government control of munitions firms and checks on wartime profiteering. Lloyd George at the Ministry of Munitions found himself much engaged in summit diplomacy with the engineers and other key unions in arranging for the 'dilution' of skilled work-forces with non-unionized unskilled or semi-skilled workers, often women. The 'badging' of workers at government and private ordnance plants and shipyards was another theme requiring frequent contact between the government and union leaders. At the plant level, the Whitley Committee of 1917 proposed a series of works committees to provide a system of joint consultation at workshop level. Trade union leaders even entered the government. Arthur Henderson served in Asquith's Coalition government from May 1915 and in Lloyd George's wartime Coalition from December 1916 to August 1917, being succeeded by George Barnes, another TUC stalwart. These ministers served as the voice of the unions rather than as spokesmen of the parliamentary Labour Party. They and their members could point to wartime circumstances in which money wages went up, working conditions generally improved, and the status of the unions was everywhere enhanced.

Yet the anxiety that surrounded the position of the unions did not disappear during this wartime consensus. Indeed, in the long term it greatly intensified. Developments like the Whitley Councils were a partial response. There were several labour disputes which reminded the public of the potential power of the unions. There was a brief official strike by the South Wales miners in July 1915. Munitions workers were discontented over wage scales, and rising food prices and rents. Many troubles involving shop stewards in engineering plants occurred in Clydeside, in Sheffield, and elsewhere in early 1916 and May 1917 over the restrictions imposed on workers under the Munitions of War Acts.[5] The strike of May 1917, provoked by the 'trade card' scheme for protected occupations, led to the arrest of eight strike leaders and the loss of 1.5 million working days. By 1917, indeed, the appointment of a committee of inquiry to investigate on a regional basis the prevalent industrial unrest testified to the new alarm being felt

[5] See C. Wrigley, *David Lloyd George and the British Labour Movement* (1976); J. Hinton, *The First Shop Stewards' Movement* (1973); I. McLean, *The Legend of Red Clydeside* (1983).

beneath the surface veneer of the Treasury Agreement and the apparent wartime consensus. There were powerful workshop movements like the shop stewards amongst engineering and shipyard workers, protesting at the eroding status of skilled men and at food shortages; there was the revived rank-and-file movement amongst Welsh miners which threatened a new revolt against the MFGB leadership as well as against the capitalist employers. In addition, the ideological inspiration provided by the Bolshevik revolution in Russia in 1917; the spread of war weariness and bitterness at the endless conflict; the domestic encouragement offered by the growing strength of a union-dominated Labour Party—all gave the unions new stimulus for action, at times neo-revolutionary. The strike within the Metropolitan Police force itself in the summer of 1918 illustrated the new militancy amongst the unions and the disruptive mood even within the most apparently loyalist organizations. Clearly, then, the widespread anxiety at the potentially explosive power of the unions was only intensified by the years of war.

The immediate post-war period, from the armistice in November 1918 to the autumn of 1921, saw the most prolonged phase of union militancy and class confrontation ever experienced in Britain.[6] No less than 178,000,000 working days were lost in industrial disputes in the four years that followed the end of the war. Further, there was a class-consciousness and solidarity—and apparent co-ordination of strategy between major unions—unknown before. The General Council of the TUC, created in 1921, inspired much enthusiasm on the left. From 1918 onwards the impact of labour, with its apprehended threat to the social order, the financial system, and the constitution, dominated political and industrial debate. Lenin, for one, imagined that the onset of revolutionary socialism in Britain was now imminent, so perfectly developed did the economic symptoms of class war here appear to be. Pockets of Communist strength in Clydeside or the Welsh mining valleys gave credence to his views. In fact, the initial surge of union power was related to over-ambitious assessments of its strength in the aftermath of wartime gains. Miners claiming a 30 per cent wage advance and a national wages pool, transport and railwaymen with similarly far-reaching claims, were foremost in

[6] See K. O. Morgan, *Consensus and Disunity: The Lloyd George Coalition Government, 1918–1922* (1979), 46–79.

the post-war industrial crisis. Workers reacted strongly to the reconstruction of industrial relations involving a shorter working week and a change from local to national agreements on wages and hours. In addition, the unions felt legitimately disappointed with the policies of a post-war coalition government under Lloyd George which had come to office amidst claims that it would perpetuate the alleged social unity and consensus mood of wartime but which soon showed its moral commitment to employers and the capitalist order in its zeal for decontrol and its stern defence of the private ownership of major industries. The National Industrial Conference of 1919 was abortive, almost a fiasco, whereas the government's apparent betrayal of the miners by refusing to grant coal nationalization after the publication of the Sankey Commission reports in 1919 led to immense and growing bitterness.

The post-war years, then, were a period of unusual class conflict. It will be shown in detail in later chapters how it strained the forces of law enforcement in many areas and led to the widespread use of the military and naval forces to aid the police and special constables. The Lloyd George Coalition's calculation of the troops available to serve in Germany, the Middle East, or in putting down republican opponents in Ireland was profoundly affected by the need to use the military to curb the workers at home. There were many dangerous strikes in different industries in the spring and summer of 1919, including a most violent episode in Liverpool in August 1919 during a second police strike. The national railway strike of September–October 1919 threatened a breakdown of the entire economic life of the nation. It led the government to respond in determined manner, with emergency procedures to keep supplies moving and to the eventual passage of the Emergency Powers Act 1920. Troubles in the docks and many other industries rumbled on throughout 1920, with younger union leaders like Ernest Bevin of the transport workers thrusting their way to the forefront. The 'councils of action' in August 1920, directed against the possible dispatch of British arms to Poland, illustrated the power of the unions in possibly influencing the course of foreign policy as well.[7]

But the miners were the real touchstone of the revolutionary

[7] L. J. Macfarlane, 'Hands Off Russia: British Labour and the Russo-Polish War, 1920', *Past and Present* (Dec. 1967), 126–52.

mood.[8] In 1919–21 there was one crisis after another in the mines: localized pit strikes in Yorkshire in the summer of 1919 after the rejection of nationalization by the government; a nation-wide pit stoppage in October–November 1920, which Lloyd George narrowly managed to frustrate by rapid concessions; then a much longer pit strike, following decontrol and the withdrawal of subsidies to the coal industry, which lasted from April to July 1921. This caused widespread tension and a vigorous military response by the government. In the end it resulted in a pyrrhic victory for the coalowners since the miners were starved or coerced back to work, embitterd and frustrated. In the key episode of 'Black Friday' (15 April 1921) the Triple Alliance with the railwaymen and dockers collapsed when the National Union of Railwaymen (NUR) refused to back up the miners in a general strike. It would not strike on behalf of a profits pool which the MFGB executive itself had proposed should be dropped. Thereafter, the threat of nation-wide stoppage subsided. The miners were left to face wage cuts and victimization on their own. The MFGB lost members heavily from a peak of 945,000 in 1920 to 783,000 by 1926, and a further rapid fall to only 529,000 by 1930. 'Company union' movements sprang up in Nottinghamshire, North Wales, and other mining areas. In retrospect, the claims by union leaders that the purposes of these miners' strikes were basically economic, in defence of decent wage levels and the living standards of union members and their families, rather than being inspired by ideological considerations, seem entirely reasonable. For all the violent rhetoric of miners' leaders like Arthur Cook, the miners sought a living wage rather than any upheaval in the social order. The switch to district settlements for miners had led to wage cuts of up to 40 per cent for workers in Durham and South Wales. But, in the highly-charged atmosphere of post-war Britain, with widespread fears of Bolshevik subversion and the police authorities and politicians anxious about left-wing propaganda and the possible sabotage of British industry, these desperate troubles seemed only to confirm the pre-war apprehensions about the new might of the organized workers as an unacknowledged, unbridled estate of the realm.

From 1922 onwards the temper of industrial relations began to cool. A lock-out of engineers, foundry-workers, and boilermakers

[8] See M. W. Kirby, *The British Coalmining Industry* (1977) 49 ff.

in March–June 1922, basically over the craftsman's traditional right to control his own job and working practices, was the last major confrontation and resulted in a clear victory for the employers. The major reason for the growing industrial calm, without doubt, was the prolonged recession and unemployment which afflicted British industry from the summer of 1920 onwards. With over a million unemployed year after year, thereafter unions lost membership and their funds and morale were sapped. There were swingeing pay reductions in trade after trade. Much union energy was spent in internal consolidation, such as the formation of the Amalgamated Engineering Union in 1921, the giant Transport and General Workers' Union (TGWU) in 1922 (with Ernest Bevin as general secretary), and the General and Municipal Workers in 1924. In addition, unions were active in backing the wholly constitutionalist, moderate aims of the Labour Party, for which MacDonald served as the party's first prime minister in 1924. There were some periods of industrial conflict still. There was a six-month lock-out of shipyard workers in 1923. In March 1924 a nation-wide strike by dock workers and London tramway workers brought a period of temporary confrontation between a major union, the TGWU, and a Labour government. But on balance the industrial unrest had died away since the red days of 1921.

The great exception, as always, to this picture of growing industrial peace was the situation in the coal mines. Here, in an industry suffering acutely from declining markets and foreign competition from the United States, Germany, France, and Poland, the MFGB and the Coalowners' Association were even more deeply embroiled in conflict. The miners' leadership took a marked shift to the left in 1924 when Arthur Cook from South Wales, a former Communist, succeeded Frank Hodges as general secretary. A more intransigent figure, though, was the Yorkshire president of the MFGB, Herbert Smith. The coalowners, for their part, were impelled towards a wholly negative strategy by the prominent part played within their deliberations by Welsh and Scottish coalowners coming from two coalfields peculiarly labour-intensive and dependent on a shrinking export trade. On 'Red Friday' (31 July 1925) the miners once again exerted their enduring industrial strength, insisting on the reorganization of production methods rather than more wage cuts, leading to a temporary subsidy to the mining industry from Baldwin's Conservative government. Again an elected government had surrendered in the face of a threat of a general embargo on coal movements, orchestrated by the General Council of the TUC. However, the crisis in the mines continued. The Royal Commission under Herbert Samuel, while making many criticisms of the managerial inadequacies of the coalowners, also proposed wage cuts which would lead to a 10 per cent decrease in the overall wages bill in the industry. Baldwin then refused to renew the subsidy to the coal industry when it ran out in April 1926 and on 2 May abruptly broke off negotiations with the TUC General Council and its representative committee.

Almost by default it seemed, on 3 May the MFGB led the British trade-union movement into its first and only general strike against the elected government of the day.[9] The TUC General Council was unprepared for battle, and distinctly less well equipped than the government, with its overt emergency measures for maintaining supplies and organized strike-breaking through the machinery of the Organization for the Maintenance of Supplies (OMS). Nevertheless, the calling out of millions of workers, including all transport workers in 'the first wave' from 4 May, had a dramatic impact on economic life. It would have been even more powerful had the TUC Strike Committee called out all manual workers, including such key operatives as power station workers. The government responded with the full panoply of law enforcement, with police and special constables backed up by battalions of troops, many warships, and marines, and thousands of civilian volunteers drawn from the loyalist middle class. On 12 May, despite ample evidence of a largely solid response in mining and other communities, the TUC called off the strike. The unions generally returned to work, leaving the miners to fight on alone until their solitary strike petered out in early November, amidst much local victimization. The MFGB, its leaders deeply divided by the strike, had been largely destroyed as a fighting force for a decade to come. The government made much of its attempt to conciliate the unions thereafter, but the passage of the Trade Disputes Act 1927 imposed new curbs on picketing and declared certain categories of strikes to be illegal. 'Contracting in' was substituted for 'contracting out' in

[9] The best account is G. A. Phillips, *The General Strike* (1976); see also A. Bullock, *The Life and Times of Ernest Bevin*, i, (1960), 316ff.

terms of the payment of the political levy to the Labour Party (which had been a peaceful bystander during the days of May). The general strike was almost an accidental episode, which the TUC met with extreme reluctance. But such an event added immensely to the pervasive fear of the uncontrollable economic muscle of the organized workers. At the time it reinforced right-wing fears for public order which the unions were widely believed to be threatening.

After 1927 there was a time of much greater tranquillity. The unions were manifestly defeated, as the Trade Disputes Act 1927 amply confirmed. Some of the members of the General Council now sought new forms of peaceful dialogue with the employers' representatives in the Mond–Turner talks of 1928.[10] Union after union was losing membership in the mass unemployment and industrial stagnation of the period. After the supreme economic crisis of 1931 the situation became even worse. In 1932 national unemployment was over 22 per cent; it was 41.2 per cent amongst coal-miners, 48.5 per cent amongst iron and steel workers, 59.5 amongst shipbuilders. The total level of unemployment stayed at close to two million until 1936, when the impact of rearmament helped a slow recovery. In older 'depressed' communities, like Merthyr Tydfil or Dowlais in South Wales, 50 or even 60 per cent of the insured male labour force was 'on the dole', mostly on a long-term basis. Entire communities in South Wales, Yorkshire, Durham, Cumberland, and Scotland slumped into hopeless stagnation and decay, their entire social fabric wasting away. The measures introduced by the government aroused enormous popular resentment and anger, especially the 'means test' imposed in assessing individuals or households for unemployment relief. The amended Unemployment Insurance Acts of 1934–5 also aroused intense popular condemnation.

In this grim period union leaders like Ernest Bevin and Walter Citrine emerged as a new type of industrial statesman, with ready access to government and central to the revival of the Labour Party after the trauma of 1931. Citrine in particular, who was to stay as general secretary of the TUC from 1926 to 1946, symbolized a new kind of undogmatic social philosophy, one which jettisoned all the

[10] Bullock, *Bevin*, pp. 392–405. For the response of one particular union, with some reputation for militancy after 1918, see J. E. Mortimer, *History of the Boilermakers' Society*, ii. *1906–1939* (1982), 187–202.

syndicalism and most of the socialism of the past. He looked forwards to a more constructive style of trade unionism which emphasized modernization and productive efficiency, the skills of the professional negotiators rather than the brute, despairing force of workers' solidarity. In 1935 he duly received a knighthood.[11] For all his authority, however, fear of the power of the unions continued to linger after the general strike in the official mind, and amongst the police and their superior officers. The emergency procedures which were thought to have brought victory in 1926 were kept in constant repair. It was known that there were whole communities, such as Maerdy in the Rhondda valley, which were virtually autonomous socialist republics, with revolutionary tribunes such as the Communist miners' agent, Arthur Horner.[12] There were many indications in the 1930s of surviving union power with the related background of frustrated class-consciousness amongst the workers. In 1935 South Wales exploded yet again with mass support for 'stay-down stoppages' in Monmouthshire pits against the encroachment of 'company unions'. Confronted with the raw power of a mobilized radical community, coalowners and police had to surrender. There were also three bitter national strikes, two in cotton and one in wool, in 1929–31, at the very depth of the depression. Although these were defeated, there was a legacy in the creation of a new national amalgamated textile union. Strikes took place even within the newer consumer-orientated growth industries such as the high-technology car plants of Longbridge, Coventry, and Cowley. Here, deskilled miners and steelworkers (sometimes Welshmen from mining communities) re-emerged as militant spokesmen for the transport workers and the engineers.

The class tensions of the 1930s, then, took many forms, often with political overtones. The National Unemployed Workers' Movement (NUWM), which organized 'hunger marches' from the early 1920s onwards, had clear links with leading Communists like Wal Hannington.[13] There were violent disturbances in 1931–2 when the NUWM claimed a national membership of close to

[11] Clegg, *History*, pp. 462–71; Citrine's memoirs, *Two Careers* (1967), are somewhat opaque.

[12] H. Francis and D. Smith, *The Fed* (1980), 154, for a vivid portrait of Maerdy.

[13] P. Kingsford, *The Hunger Marchers in Britain, 1920–1940* (1982); J. Stevenson, 'The Politics of Violence' in G. Peele and C. Cook (eds.), *The Politics of Reappraisal, 1918–1939* (1975), 146 ff.

100,000. In Belfast, Birmingham, Manchester, and London there were mass demonstrations against the operations of the means test, later supplemented with attacks on the regulations of the Unemployment Assistance Boards. A hunger march, starting in Glasgow and taking in unemployed men from the north and Midlands on the way to London, led to violent clashes with the police in Hyde Park and Trafalgar Square at the end of October 1932, as will be seen. Thereafter, the NUWM somewhat petered out, not least because it was viewed with much distrust by the Labour Party and the TUC. But there were other working-class movements in the mid-1930s to remind the authorities of the interaction between social protest and political ideology. The provocation afforded by Fascist demonstrations in the working-class areas of the East End of London and troubles such as the 'Cable Street battle' that led to the Public Order Act 1936; the inspiration rekindled in mining and other areas by the threat of international Fascism during the Spanish Civil War—these gave new momentum to the age-old fears aroused by the unions. These fears were shared by a powerful government minister like Neville Chamberlain, for all his experience of industrial relations in Birmingham.

The reality of much of the history of the 1930s on the industrial front was very different. The unions were generally in peaceful, constructive mood, as symbolized by the *apparatchik*, Citrine. They were more intimately bound up than ever before with a Labour Party now under the moderate leadership of men like Attlee, Greenwood, Dalton, and Morrison. There had been a steady recovery in union membership, from 4,392,000 at the worst of the depression at the end of 1933, to 6,613,000 at the end of 1939. Significantly, seven of the top ten unions, in terms of their proportion of the relevant work-force, were in service industries. Unionism had increased steadily amongst white-collar clerical and administrative workers. The Union of Postal Workers, to take one example, increased its membership from 98,000 in 1931 to 137,000 at the end of the decade.[14] In this and other unions women increasingly became unionized, especially amongst textile workers and shop assistants, with the result that women trade unionists numbered almost a million by the outbreak of the Second World War. Women union leaders like Anne Loughlin and

[14] A. Clinton, *Post Office Workers: A Trade Union and Social History* (1984), 445 ff.

Florence Hancock became national figures.[15] The pragmatic gradualism of men like Bevin and Citrine was in the ascendant; even the miners were led now by moderate figures like Ebby Edwards MP and James Griffiths. The violent turmoil of Tonypandy and Liverpool in 1910–11, the class tensions of 1919–21, even the general strike, seemed to be distant memories. The new system of national collective bargaining had survived the rigours of the depression, and proved compatible with industrial peace.

Nevertheless, on the eve of a Second World War the political and police establishment had far from come to terms with the growth of a powerfully mobilized trade-union movement. Fear of the unions—anxiety over their capacity for industrial disruption, social turmoil, and civil disorder—was, then, a central theme in British history throughout the early twentieth century, from Taff Vale to the Second World War. Containing the threat that the unions were felt to represent, reconciling consent with control in the conduct of industrial relations, provided a fundamental challenge in dictating the parameters of public order in modern Britain. Without ever quite erupting into the regular violence of labour relations in France, Italy, or the United States, the class polarizations of British industry were a constant preoccupation of governments and communities, with bitter legacies that endure to the present time.

[15] S. Lewenhak, *Women and Trade Unions* (1977), 221 ff.

3

Localism, Centralism, and Industrial Confrontation, 1900–1918

THE industrial confrontations of the early twentieth century had a dramatic impact on the organization and structure of the police in England and Wales. At the turn of the century, and indeed down to 1918, the police remained, as always, under local control. The major strikes of the 1910–14 period saw repeated attempts by the Home Office to achieve national co-ordination by the police to meet the challenge of nation-wide trade unions. But they were frustrated by the essential localism of the police system. Troops were used freely by the government in a policing role in this period; the experience of wartime reinforced their use in this way. But that merely evaded the central issues of the direction of the police and the tension between a national and a local view of the service. In this chapter it will be shown how the government came to see the need for far more leverage over provincial police authorities, in the face of the alarming new industrial challenge. The outcome would determine how far the spirit of localism could be eroded and something approaching a national police force—a concept totally new in British history—built up instead.

The essential foundation of the police system in England and Wales is the office of constable, a historical legacy of the British common-law tradition. Since the Justices of the Peace Act in 1361 constables had been the executive agents of the justices, who were themselves appointed by the Crown. A local system of policing was seen to be compatible with the recognition of the principle that maintaining the King's Peace must be ultimately the concern of the government itself. In the nineteenth century, when the police were reorganized by Peel and others, while some voices were raised in support of a state police force, successive governments felt that a national gendarmerie on continental lines would never be accepted in Britain. Thus the police remained under local control.

Separate police systems emerged for the metropolis, the City of London, the counties, and the boroughs. The Metropolitan Police

Act 1829 set up the force in the metropolis, while an Act of 1839 reorganized the force in the City of London. This was paralleled by the creation of permanent police forces in the provincial cities and boroughs under the Municipal Corporations Act 1835. Four years later the counties were empowered to establish similar forces (and both boroughs and counties were so required in 1856). By the mid-nineteenth century, therefore, there were four main forms of police organization, each operating under a separate act of parliament.

The predominant feature of this sprawling system was its diversity. The way in which these different forces were administered and controlled varied immensely, as did their size. Only the Metropolitan Police were under the direct control of the Home Secretary, who was responsible for the appointment of the Commissioner and Assistant Commissioners. The City of London force was controlled by the Common Council of the City through its police committee. The provincial forces were controlled by local authorities, who were responsible for their management and efficiency. The nature of the police authority, however, varied between counties, and cities and boroughs. In the latter, the watch committee, a committee of the town council, with no separate existence from that body and no separate funds, was charged with the appointment, promotion, and discipline of the force. The head constable of the city or borough police force had no statutory position. He was merely another constable chosen by the watch committee from among his peers, and has been described as 'merely the superintending and executive officer of the watch committee'.[1] By the end of the nineteenth century there were 127 city and borough police forces, many of them very small, where tight control was exercised by the watch committees over policing activity. In the fifty-eight large rural county areas, by contrast, there was a significant difference. Here, the county police were under the control of the quarter sessions but the chief constable had a statutory position under the County Police Act 1839. He was appointed by the justices, with the approval of the Home Secretary, who also had power to make regulations for the county forces. Once in office, the chief constable had considerable authority over his force. He was the counterpart of the watch committee in the borough with regard to the appointment, promotion,

[1] Quoted in Critchley, *History*, p. 143.

and discipline of his men. The justices had no sanction over him other than dismissal, an event practically unheard-of in the nineteenth century. In practice, the power of appointment to the chief constableship in a county was an opportunity for county magnates to appoint county men, usually with military backgrounds, men who had a social outlook similar to their own. At the end of the nineteenth century only 12 per cent of county chief constables had risen from the ranks, as against 93 per cent in the cities and boroughs. Of forty-four county chief constables in England, thirty-three were ex-army personnel, while only three had risen up from the ranks; in Wales, eight out of twelve were of military background.[2] An extreme case was Captain Lionel Lindsay, who had succeeded his military father as chief constable of Glamorgan in 1891 and who had previously commanded the gendarmerie in Egypt in the time of Wolseley.

In 1888, under the Local Government Act, control of the county police passed from the justices to the standing joint committees, consisting half of justices, half of elected county councillors. Chief constables now feared that their autocratic methods would be criticized or curbed. However, in most counties there was little change in the personnel amongst those in charge of the police. Only men with a sizeable income could afford the time to attend meetings of standing joint committees, which were often held in remote areas of a county. The control of these committees was much less effective than that of watch committees in the boroughs. By contrast with the weekly meetings of borough watch committees to hear a head constable's reports, and the responsibility of the former to the town councils, county standing joint committees usually met on a quarterly basis, to hear the chief constable's report and discuss police administration. They had the statutory right to determine police expenditure, while police matters were treated as lying outside county council interference. In practice, the influence of the justices predominated because of their historical and social links with the police.

Throughout the police system, then, different principles operated. In theory, the police of the metropolis were the only

[2] *Report from the Select Committee on the Police Forces (Weekly Rest Day), with Proceedings and Minutes of Evidence*, PP 1908 (353), ix. 679, Appendix XXII, 885; evidence given by John Kempster, editor of the *Police Review*; see also *Police Review*, 19 June 1908; J. Hart, 'The County and Borough Police Act, 1856', *Public Administration*, 34 (Winter 1956), 405–17.

force not subject to some form of democratic control. Even here, however, the commissioner or his subordinates could be brought under parliamentary scrutiny. When the question of the relationship between the Commissioner of the Metropolitan Police and the Home Secretary arose in the latter part of the nineteenth century, the Home Secretary, Henry Matthews, declared in the House of Commons that he was responsible for the general policy of the Metropolitan Police in the discharge of their duty. It would be

> intolerable that in such a town as London or in any large town, the Commander of the Police Force, or of any other Force should hold irresponsible authority, and be able to disregard the instructions of the persons who had to answer in Parliament for the conduct of the men under their command.[3]

At this period, therefore, a broad power of supervising police policy, loosely defined, was claimed by the Home Office for the Metropolitan Police and for the police authorities in the provinces. Troup was later to define 'policy' as 'the means and methods of carrying out these duties [the suppression of crime and maintenance of order] and to the preparations to be made for doing this effectively',[4] and this appears to be what Matthews had in mind in 1888. No one supposed that any conflict arose between lawful instructions relating to law enforcement or prosecution policy and the original independent common-law status of the constable.

The Home Secretary, as the central police authority, could be challenged in parliament over any other police force in England and Wales, but he was not answerable to the Commons for their administration and conduct. Over the provincial police as a whole, his role was a remote and indirect one. He had a general concern with the maintenance of the peace, and in seeing that the provincial police were efficient. Financial control by the central government increased as the exchequer grant principle developed: the Police (Counties and Boroughs) Act 1856 provided for the payment of a grant from the Exchequer if Her Majesty's inspectors declared that a local force was efficient in numbers and discipline. By the end of the century this amounted to half the cost of pay and clothing. Beyond this, the Home Secretary took no responsibility

3 *Parl. Deb.*, 3rd ser., 330, 1173–4 (14 Nov. 1888).

4 Troup, 'Police Administration', p. 15.

for the administration or actions of the provincial police. Local autonomy and diversity remained the norm.

This complex, cumbersome system was profoundly disturbed by the course of industrial unrest and disorder from the late nineteenth century onwards. In the past magistrates had always exercised control over the forces of order in cases of riot and disturbance. Troops had been frequently used. Although, in theory, the 'new' police had been formed to take over the role previously adopted by the army, old habits died hard. The police were at this time barely established and in no position to attract public confidence. Of the two types of provincial forces previously described, the county police had always been more effective at riot control than those of the boroughs. The county as a unit of administration was military, and its forces were trained and divided on military lines, with divisions, detachments, guards, and beats. County forces often came to the rescue of the small boroughs in times of civil disorder. Troops, however, were generally preferred, partly because the cost of these was borne by the central government, whereas borrowed police had to be paid for locally.

However, the disadvantage of using troops in civil disturbance was pointed out in 1839 at the time of the first Chartist troubles. The military were armed, so any action they took to disperse riots or crowds could be fatal. The soldier could not exercise individual discretion whereas the constable was vested with very wide discretionary authority. The presence of troops often exacerbated rather than subdued disturbances; nor was crowd control popular with the soldiers themselves.[5] Criminal liability for murder could arise in respect of lethal military activities against crowds. *The Times* commented in 1893 that a soldier called upon to assist the civil power in putting down a riot 'treads a path as narrow as the sword-edge that leads to Mahomet's paradise, without any better reward before him than a formidable purgatory'.[6]

As regards the procedure to be adopted when the army was

[5] *First Report of the Commissioners Appointed to inquire as to the Best Means of establishing an Efficient Constabulary Force in the Counties of England and Wales*, PP 1839 (169), xix. 89; J. Childs, *The Army of Charles II* (1976), 214–16; *Parl. Deb.*, 4th ser., 185, 925 (5 Mar. 1908).

[6] Quoted in D. Williams, *Keeping the Peace* (1967), 33.

requisitioned to aid the civil power, since the mid-eighteenth century the civil and military authorities had been empowered, respectively, to invoke and render assistance at the request of a magistrate. The way in which both should act was laid down in the *Manual of Military Law* and the *King's Regulations for the Army*. Troops arriving at the scene of disorder were met and accompanied by a magistrate, who was to be in possession of a copy of the Riot Act, the proclamation of which he should then read out if extreme disturbances took place. After this reading of the Riot Act, any rioters not dispersing within an hour were guilty of felony, and the magistrate could authorize the officer to order his men to fire. On the other hand, under the common law, it was not necessary for the Riot Act to be read out, or to wait for an hour to expire, to justify the use of military force to prevent outrage or damage. At any time the magistrate with the troops could request them to take action. It was also possible for troops, in extraordinary cases of danger, to take action without a magistrate being present at all. Perhaps understandably, the law of riot was frequently misunderstood by civil and military authorities alike, and the procedure took no account at all of the fact that a police force had now come into being.[7] The central point was, however, that both troops and magistrates had legal responsibility for their action. Troops, as noted above, were liable to the criminal law. Magistrates could be prosecuted by the Attorney-General for alleged breaches of their common-law powers in deploying or not deploying troops in the event of a riot.

In the earlier decades of the century the occasion for calling out the troops was usually working-class action on behalf of political objectives, as in the case of the Chartist troubles of the 1830s and 1840s. In the more tranquil decades that followed, troops were unnecessary. From the 1880s, however, it was generally industrial rather than political crises which brought troops out to cope with popular unrest. The liaison of the military with the police in

[7] The Riot Act of 1715 could make riot a felony punishable by death if twelve or more persons were assembled riotously, and failed to disperse within one hour of a reading by a peace officer of a proclamation ordering the crowd to disperse. At common law, riot (which could apply to any disturbance involving three or more people) was only a misdemeanour. For a fuller exposition see S. C. Greer, 'Military Intervention in Civil Disturbances: The Legal Basis Reconsidered', *Public Law* (1983), 580–99; Radzinowicz, *English Criminal Law*, p. 141; *Report of the Inter Departmental Committee on Riots* HMSO, (1895).

strikes, lock-outs, and other industrial troubles became the mainspring for the encroachment of central government over the entire disparate fabric of the police.

A violent episode at Featherstone in Yorkshire in 1893, when two men were shot down and killed by troops during a colliery dispute, brought home forcibly to the government the danger of using troops in this kind of situation, and the inadequacies of traditional methods of law enforcement. The Featherstone incident occurred during the miners' lock-out of 1893, the largest trade dispute in the history of the MFGB to date; between July and November 1893 many coalfields were paralysed. After a six-weeks stoppage there were disturbances in the West Riding of Yorkshire. On 7 September the manager of Ackton Hall Colliery at Featherstone asked for police protection as surface men were being prevented from working the colliery owing to intimidation. He was told by the chief constable, Captain Russell, that the police had no further manpower available as they were already policing the Doncaster race-meeting. He then contacted the nearby mill-owner and magistrate, Lord St Oswald, to use his authority as a justice to telegraph for the military. A small contingent of twenty-eight soldiers arrived, but there was no magistrate available to give them orders. Their very presence angered the crowd, and in the ensuing mêlée the colliery at Featherstone was set on fire. A magistrate came after some time to read the Riot Act, but, before the customary hour given by the proclamation had elapsed, troops tried to clear the colliery. Strikers threw stones and other missiles; the troops charged with fixed bayonets, and two people were shot dead, with another eleven to fourteen hit by bullets and injured.[8]

These alarming events caused a widespread popular outcry. The old bitterness of the Chartist era, in particular of the Newport march in 1839, was now revived. This was the first time for almost half a century that people had been wounded or killed through shots fired in the suppression of riots or disturbances. Although the first inquest held upon the deaths of the men who were unfortunately killed at Featherstone returned a verdict of justifiable homicide, in the second inquest the jury refused to return that verdict and 'apparently shrank from the only other logical conclu-

[8] *Report of the Committee Appointed to inquire into the Circumstances Connected with the Disturbances at Featherstone on 7 September 1893*, PP 1893–4 [C. 7234] xvii. 385.

sion open to them namely that of returning a verdict of wilful murder against the Magistrates and troops'. A committee of inquiry was set up to examine the incident at Featherstone; although it gave a clear and unequivocal vindication of the action of the troops, it criticized the absence of any magistrate to meet the troops and conduct them to the colliery. Indeed, the absence of any justice with local knowledge was, according to the committee, a prime cause of the tragedy.[9]

Asquith, the Liberal Home Secretary, now appointed a departmental committee to define the several and relative responsibilities of the civil and military authorities in cases of riot. This committee, reporting at the end of 1894, spelt out more fully than before the basic principles governing the use of troops in civil disturbances. Its recommendations formally recognized that the issue now was the circumstances in which the army should come to the aid of the police and what they should then both do. Troops should be used to aid the civil power only as a last resort, when the police were unable to cope. Every possible arrangement should be made beforehand to enable the authorities to deal with rioters by means of the constabulary alone. Mutual aid agreements—the lending of police by one force to another, as recommended by Section 25 of the Police Act of 1890—should be entered into by any counties and boroughs liable to become the scene of disturbances, as a precautionary measure. Therefore, in the event of unrest, the authorities would be able to act through the employment of civil force. If troops were needed as a last resort, requisitions by magistrates should now be made through the chief constable, who, it was felt, was best able to survey the situation as a whole and to decide 'whether by a fresh disposal of the constabulary it may not be possible to dispense with assistance from the military'. In boroughs, requisitions should go through the mayors, as the duties which in a county belonged to the chief constable and county magistrates were in boroughs discharged by mayor and watch committee.[10]

Nevertheless, the recommendations of this committee circulated by the Home Office to mayors and chief constables in 1895 had little immediate effect. Police borrowed under mutual aid agreements had to be paid for by the aided force. Magistrates,

[9] *Parl.Deb.*, 4th ser., 17, 1728 (20 Sept. 1893); PP 1893–4, [C. 7234], xvii. 395.
[10] *Report of the Inter Departmental Committee on Riots* HMSO (1895).

many of whom were owners of mines, factories, or other industrial concerns, still had power under the common law to requisition troops, who in turn were bound to obey. Chief constables themselves often preferred to use troops rather than police. The former were felt to be better adapted for riot control. In the six-month lock-out in the South Wales coalfield in 1898, for instance, Captain Lindsay, the chief constable of Glamorgan, in correspondence with the Home Office, reported that he had at his disposal 488 foot and 12 mounted constables. He had lent 70 foot police to Cardiff and Swansea. He added:

It has, however, been found that the presence of a military force gives a greater feeling of security to the law abiding part of the population and impresses the would-be lawbreakers with the futility of defying the lawful authority. An importation of police on a large scale has therefore been found to be less effective.[11]

The introduction of the military, he claimed, had been 'entirely the action of the Justices'; he ignored the fact that at least two of the latter were local coal-owners, with an obviously partisan perspective on the dispute.

During the Penrhyn Quarry strike in Caernarfonshire in November 1900, the chief constable, William Ruck, dismissed borrowed police but retained the use of soldiers, even though there was no disturbance. H. B. Simpson of the Home Office commended this response as

a good instance of the value of soldiery in preventing the outbreak of disorder. It would be a waste in circumstances such as are described . . . to keep police from other counties idle at Bangor on the chance of disturbance but the same objection does not apply to soldiers whose presence moreover has more effect.[12]

However, the Home Office itself became suspicious when it heard from Major-General Swaine, the officer commanding the North-Western District, who wrote in June 1901: 'I am inclined to think that matters are not being well managed there. . . . I believe in this case, a large force of police would do all that is required.'[13]

[11] Chief constable of Glamorgan to under secretary, Home Office, 18 June 1898, Con 11/234 (Glamorgan Police Records, County Hall, Cardiff).

[12] Minute by H. B. Simpson on action of chief constable in Penrhyn Quarry dispute, 10 Nov. 1900 (HO 45/10263/X80592/7).

[13] Major-General Swaine to Under-Secretary of State for War, 4 June 1901 (ibid., 22).

Questions were subsequently asked in the Commons on the use of the military in the Penrhyn dispute, both by Keir Hardie, and by Lloyd George, the member for Caernarfon Boroughs. The latter argued that Ruck had decided, against the wishes of his standing joint committee (of whom only Lord Penrhyn, the local quarry owner, was in agreement with him), that military force was needed. He had then called in a magistrate from another part of the county to make the necessary requisition.[14] The Home Office admitted privately that this was 'a curious state of things', but it had encouraged chief constables to take more responsibility in the area of requisitioning the military. Some local authorities were even more critical. The Caernarfonshire County Council, the Bethesda Urban District Council (UDC), the Bangor Borough Council, and others wrote to the Home Secretary to protest at Ruck's use of troops. They also questioned the decision-making process involved in calling troops:

> The Caernarvon County Council place on record an expression of its strong and unqualified disapproval of the action of the person or authority responsible for invoking military aid . . . and consider it an unwarrantable interference with the liberties of the people to import troops into the county without the sanction of the Standing Joint Committee, as the duly constituted authority appointed to deal with questions of Police administration and good government of the county.[15]

The very availability of troops here added considerably to the tension that arose.

In fact, troops were called out to assist the civil power on twenty-four occasions in the thirty-nine years up to 1908, while mutual aid agreements existed between only 30 counties and 27 boroughs out of the 186 police forces recorded for that year in England and Wales.[16] In 1908 a Labour MP, G. J. Wardle, moved a motion in parliament on behalf of his party, voicing concern about the continuing employment of troops in labour disputes, and also that magistrates who were interested parties had the power to call out troops in cases of alleged disturbance. In the debate which followed attention was called to the fact that the Territorial Army Act

[14] *Parl. Deb.*, 4th ser., 99, 50 (8 Aug. 1901); ibid., 1329–30 (17 Aug. 1901).

[15] Quoted in Jones, *Quarrymen*, p. 253.

[16] *Report of the Select Committee on Employment of Military in Cases of Disturbances*, PP 1908 (236), vii. 367.

of 1907 would now enable the Territorials to be used in connection with labour troubles. This could involve trade unionists who were members of the Territorial Army. Haldane, the Liberal Secretary of State for War, promptly repudiated this suggestion, but the Home Secretary, Herbert Gladstone, did agree to set up a committee of inquiry into the use of troops in disturbances.[17]

The Select Committee on Employment of Military in cases of disturbances reported in 1908. It endorsed the findings of the committee on riots in 1895. To encourage a civil response, it also recommended that further powers should be afforded to chief constables and mayors to enlist additional men into police forces for temporary purposes, and that inducements should be given to police authorities to make provision for a mounted force. The Home Office now circularized the provincial police on the recommendations of the 1908 committee. One major innovation sought to deter police or magistrates from requisitioning troops too freely; the circular recommended that, when the occasion for calling out troops seemed imminent, chief constables or mayors should send a telegram to the General Officer Commanding (GOC) of the command in which they were situated, inquiring to whom the application for military aid should be sent, and that this telegram should also be sent to the Secretary of State for War. This was clearly an attempt to prevent local police authorities from requisitioning military aid independently of the knowledge of the central government.[18] The circular represented a positive effort by the Home Office to devise a more efficient police response to disturbances, and ensure that troops were only called in as a last resort. With the advantage of hindsight, Edward Troup, now permanent under-secretary at the Home Office, later wrote that this circular was of major importance. There can be no doubt that he saw it as beginning the process of 'establishing the position in which county and borough forces, while remaining under local control, are now able to act to a great extent on uniform lines and almost as one organisation'.[19]

However, as has been noted, in the years before the First World War the Home Office still exerted little influence over the provincial police; circulars were couched in the form of 'advice' and there

[17] *Parl. Deb.*, 4th ser., 185, 914–26 (5 Mar. 1908).
[18] HO 158/14 (163,219/10), 15 Apr. 1909.
[19] Sir E. Troup, *The Home Office* (1925), 49; id., 'Police Administration', p. 12.

was much difficulty giving effect to them. As regards the recruitment of additional men for temporary purposes, the police authorities had the power of supplementing their forces in an emergency (under the Special Constables Act 1831, which provided for the appointment of special constables on any occasion when disturbances had taken place or were apprehended, reinforced by Section 196 of the Municipal Corporations Act 1882, which required that a sufficient number of men in the boroughs and cities should be nominated each year to serve as special constables if called upon). But there had grown up a tradition of leaving these powers in abeyance, in favour of calling for volunteers in times of disorder. In any case, there was no organization to instruct these special constables when they were called out and this rendered them largely ineffective in practice.[20] The whole system of mutual aid was cumbersome, while these written agreements in no way compelled one force to help another. Each authority remained free to refuse or accede to requests for help. This was, indeed, a fundamental weakness in progress towards anything resembling a national force. On the financial side, watch committees in the boroughs were notoriously parsimonious, and in any case were dependent for finance on town councils and so less free to carry out administrative instructions from the Home Office. It was much easier in the counties, because of the independent financial position of the standing joint committees in relation to the county council and the independent position of the chief constable. Yet even here, where Liberals or Labour dominated the elected council representatives, objections could be made over the use of local police resources for strike-breaking purposes.

The difficulties in the way of putting this Home Office circular into effect, particularly in the boroughs, are illustrated by some examples from South Wales. In Carmarthenshire, for instance, the chief constable rapidly formed mutual aid agreements with the forces of neighbouring Glamorgan, Pembrokeshire, and Cardiff along lines set out by the Home Office. He also asked his standing joint committee for permission to increase the mounted force.[21] In the borough of Neath, the watch committee declared that the

[20] For a fuller discussion see R. Seth, *The Specials* (1961).

[21] Chief constable's report to Carmarthenshire Standing Joint Committee, Oct. 1909, Jan. 1910, Apr. 1910 (County Hall, Carmarthen).

thirty-six special constables already appointed yearly met the requirements of the circular; they already had a mounted contingent and had mutual aid agreements with neighbouring police forces.[22] At Cardiff, the city also had mutual aid agreements with surrounding police forces. But the head constable dismissed the idea of the enlistment of temporary constables. Such men would be 'quite untrained and therefore useless for the discharge of police duty. . . . Moreover they would have to be paid a retaining fee.' Special constables sworn in under the act of 1831 would be quite sufficient.[23] In Swansea the town clerk was instructed by the watch committee to communicate with the police authorities of Glamorgan, Carmarthen, Monmouthshire, Somerset, Devon, Bristol, Cardiff, and Newport, with a view to entering into mutual aid agreements. The head constable was authorized to hire horses for twenty mounted men, and to make a list of suitable men to serve as special constables.[24] In the southern district (which included South Wales), however, the inspector of constabulary complained that many police authorities seemed

> to overlook the very considerable moral effect produced by the presence of well turned out, smart mounted police officers in the midst of a hostile or unruly crowd. The necessity of equipping and training mounted men . . . to answer an immediate call in case of disturbance or riot is not sufficiently understood. Borrowing from other forces may be of value when a disturbance is apprehended in advance . . . but such a system breaks down when a riot occurs without warning. . . . A police force which makes no satisfactory provision for dealing with such a contingency cannot be altogether efficient.[25]

The Home Office, then, had little influence over the provincial police authorities whether their police were efficient or not, especially those of the boroughs. Here the chairmen and members of watch committees often failed to turn up for the annual Home Office inspection of the force. Indeed, the existence of the smaller borough police forces was felt by the Home Office to be a major set-

[22] Neath Borough Watch Committee Minutes, 6 July 1909 (County Hall, Swansea).

[23] Head constable's report to Cardiff City Watch Committee, 13 Oct. 1909 (Cardiff Central Library).

[24] Swansea Borough Watch Committee Minutes, 6 July 1909 (Swansea Guildhall).

[25] *Annual Report of HM Inspector of Constabulary*, PP 1910 (106), lxxv. 592.

back to the formation of a co-ordinated police response to disorder.[26]

In the relationship between the provincial police and the Home Office, the years 1910–12 marked a crucial turning-point. The inadequacy of leaving the provincial police authorities to meet the challenge of serious labour unrest was now dramatically brought home to Troup and his colleagues. In the spring of 1910 the Home Office interfered in an unprecedented way in a strike at Newport Docks to prevent serious disorder and widespread use of troops. The loading of vessels owned by the Empire Transport Company and Houlder Brothers was undertaken by imported, so-called 'free labour'. As soon as the imported men began loading on 18 May, every worker in the docks was called out. The police, protecting the non-union imported labour, had to give way to mass pressure and the imported workers were forced to leave the town. The employers now appealed to Churchill, the Home Secretary, for protection. Troup advised the mayor to borrow Metropolitan Police, but was reconciled to the fact that, under the common law, if the mayor or magistrates requisitioned troops, 'they must be ready to go'.[27]

In fact, the dispute appeared to be settled on 22 May. Then, however, the employers refused to accept an arbitration award and on 26 May the watch committee, on the advice of Haldane (who was acting as Home Secretary in Churchill's absence) actually refused to allow local police to protect blacklegs or non-union labour wishing to unload Houlder's ships. They even threatened to use force to drive the 'free labour' men out of the town if they were brought in. They argued that to use police or troops to shield blacklegs would lead to further riot, bloodshed, and possibly a general strike in Newport. A stoppage in the neighbouring Monmouthshire collieries would almost inevitably follow. A Home Office memorandum noted: 'In these circumstances it appeared practically impossible to provide a police force sufficient in every way to deal with the situation.'[28] Churchill now consulted the Law Officers of the Crown as to whether the actions of the

[26] Minutes of evidence of C. E. Troup, PP 1908 (236), vii. 378; HO 158/15 (200,074), 14 Feb. 1911.

[27] R. S. Churchill, *Winston S. Churchill*, ii. (1967), 372.

[28] Home Office memo. on the Newport dock strike: Case for the Opinion of the Law Officers, 18 June 1910 (HO 45/10608/192905/31).

Home Office had been permissible, legally. They found that in an emergency it was right to forbid the exercise of a legal right if its exercise would be provocative. However, the lawyers added that this was 'a rare exception of grave emergency'.[29]

A heated debate later took place in the Commons over Haldane's actions in supporting the watch committee's refusal to give adequate protection to blacklegs. Churchill countered by declaring that it was 'a question of the sufficiency or insufficiency of police protection'. Five hundred additional police would have been needed to protect the 'free labour' if these imported men were allowed in to load ships, in addition to extra police to relieve those police. He added that the employers, Houlders, had not carried out their part of the agreement in any case. Haldane pronounced: 'I came to the conclusion that what would otherwise be legal action on the part of Messrs Houlder would be illegal if persisted in in the then circumstances.'[30] Although the actions of central government at Newport were carried out in exceptional circumstances, the principle of central government intervention in local affairs to prevent the use of troops in a labour dispute had been established.

When a major coal strike broke out in the Ely Colliery, Penygraig, in the Rhondda valley in November 1910 and spread throughout the Rhondda and Aberdare valleys, the Home Office again interfered dramatically with the principle that the preservation of law and order was the prerogative of the local police authorities. Over 30,000 men were on strike, and much disorder and damage to property resulted. The chief constable, Captain Lindsay, borrowed police from neighbouring forces, but after disturbances at Llwynypia on 7 November he also called for military aid, involving two companies of infantry and 200 cavalry. He had been pressed to do this by local colliery-owners, against the wishes of local police superintendents. Churchill was told of the requisiton when the troops were actually *en route* for Glamorgan; he now intervened decisively. After discussion of the crisis with Haldane and the Adjutant-General, he told Lindsay that police alone should be used to preserve order in the first instance. He issued instructions that the infantry requested should be held up at Swindon. Instead, he dispatched 300 Metropolitan Police, 100 of whom were mounted.

[29] Opinion of HM Solicitor-General and S.A.J. Rowlatt, 20 June 1910 (ibid.).
[30] *Parl. Deb.*, 5th ser., 18, 372–5, 403–4 (22 June 1910).

They were a picked force of constables experienced in the handling of turbulent crowds and were 'for every purpose better suited to the needs of the situation than an equivalent body of military'. As a precaution, however, 200 cavalry were to be sent to the district at the same time, for use as a last resort.[31]

The situation in the Tonypandy area deteriorated, and serious rioting occurred on 8 November before the Metropolitan Police had arrived. That evening Lindsay told General Macready, who was in charge of the troops at Cardiff, of the riotous situation in Aberaman.[32] Macready, with Churchill's authority, then moved the cavalry to Tonypandy and Aberaman; at 10.30 p.m. the Metropolitan Police arrived as well. A second and third contingent of Metropolitans were sent to the troubled areas on 9 November, bringing the total police in the area to 1,400, mostly employed in protecting colliery installations. Churchill was 'counting up on the action of police . . . to avert the necessity for using the military'.[33] In a highly significant move, rather than leave the direction of public order in the hands of local magistrates, Churchill placed constitutional power in the safe keeping of General Macready. The latter was told:

> If the emergency comes to the point where the police and civil authorities apply to you for the direct use of the military, you should then assume general control and act as you think best for the preservation of order and the prevention of bloodshed. . . . You will at the last moment consider whether the police forces can be used any further to quell riot without actually involving the military.[34]

This move by Churchill began what Macready later described as 'a hitherto untried policy for dealing with disturbances consequent upon labour disputes'. Unity of command of civil and military forces was being placed under a professional soldier, with Macready under the direct authority of the Home Office, as a

[31] Home Secretary to chief constable of Glamorgan (telegram sent 1.30 p.m.), 8 Nov. 1910, *Colliery Strike Disturbances in South Wales: Correspondence and Report*, Nov. 1910, PP 1911 [Cd. 5568], lxiv, 4, no. 10; R. S. Churchill, *Churchill*, ii. 373–5.

[32] Major-General Nevil Macready (1862–1946), Director of Personal Services at the War Office, 1910–14; later Commissioner of Metropolitan Police, 1918–20.

[33] Macready to Home Office, report for Tuesday, 8 Nov. 1910, PP 1911 [Cd. 5568], lxiv, 6, no. 19; Home Secretary to chief constable of Glamorgan (telegram sent 1.45 p.m.), 9 Nov. 1910, ibid., 7, no. 21.

[34] Home Secretary to Macready (telegram sent 6 p.m.), 9 Nov. 1910, ibid., 8, no. 23.

supposedly impartial force in the dispute. Churchill's démarche thus completely overturned the existing procedure for riot control. Industrial disorder of this kind was seen for the first time as a national emergency, one that required a co-ordinated response, civil and military, from the state.

Macready later made it clear in his memoirs that he deeply distrusted the views of the local officials. In Pontypridd, he wrote, they 'seemed to have lost all sense of proportion, and to be obsessed with but one idea: to flood the valleys with troops'.[35] On previous occasions when troops had been used in aid of the civil power, the numbers had usually been small, and the officer responsible had accepted without question the construction placed on the situation by employers and magistrates. Macready determined that this would not occur in South Wales in 1910. He believed that a soldier's role in such a crisis was 'solely to preserve order but in so doing he has the right to demand that neither side shall do anything which may aggravate and inflame the opposing party to commit acts of lawlessness'.[36] On 9 November Macready had at his disposal in South Wales:

2 Squadrons 18th Hussars at Pontypridd.
1 Company loyal North Lancashire Regiment at Pontypridd.
1 Company Lancashire Fusiliers at Llwynypia.
1 Company West Riding Regiment at Cardiff
1 Company Devonshire Regiment at Newport.
1 Company Royal Muster Fusiliers at Newport.

The very presence of all these troops, many of them patrolling the valleys, seemed enough to keep things tranquil. Macready laid down that 'in no case should soldiers come in direct contact with rioters unless and until action had been taken by the police'.[37]

To avoid alarmist reports resulting in the dispatch of troops, Macready instituted an intelligence system for the area. A civil servant, J. P. Moylan, was sent down to South Wales by the Home Office on 9 November to co-ordinate it. This system of industrial surveillance was indeed a considerable novelty. Captains Farquhar

[35] General the Rt Hon. Sir Nevil Macready, *Annals of an Active Life* (1924), i. 138.
[36] Ibid. i. 140.
[37] Memo. by Macready on certain points connected with the strike in South Wales, 5 Jan. 1911, PP 1911 [Cd. 5568], lxiv. 48.

and Childs and Major Horwood made up the intelligence committee, with their headquarters established at the New Inn, Pontypridd. There they defined a pattern for military and police action, both in coping with civil disorder and in maintaining a viable relationship with the local population.

By 12 November the strike was reported to be quiet. Churchill now felt that it was 'desirable that the infantry force in the valleys should be quietly strengthened under cover of the police in order to free these latter either for withdrawal to London or for movement elsewhere'.[38] Macready warned, however, that this would place great strain on such police as remained, and that if infantry were used 'to hold outlying collieries they may, of course, at any moment be brought in contact with the mob, but there will be no alternative to this if the police force is too weak to offer effective resistance . . .'.[39] Churchill decided to maintain the existing Metropolitan police strength, rather than risk premature intervention of the military. His position was assisted by the comparatively restrained way in which Macready handled matters, keeping the military in the background. Only when the police were overpowered at Tonypandy and Penygraig on 21 November did troops come briefly into physical contact with rioters. Significantly they were now used in an entirely different manner from the way in which they had been used prior to this time in aid of the civil power. Although requisitioned by the local magistrate, when the Lancashire Fusiliers and the West Riding Regiment arrived at Penygraig, they were now directed by Macready to assume a policing role. There was no reading of the Riot Act preliminary to their action.[40] Macready himself claimed that great care was taken that 'each body of military should be accompanied by at any rate a small body of police to emphasise the fact that the armed forces act merely as the support of the civil power and not as direct agents'.[41]

As the disturbances died down, there was a gradual withdrawal of additional forces. In January Macready left South Wales, and most of the Metropolitans had also departed by early February.

[38] Home Secretary to Adjutant-General, 12 Nov. 1910, ibid. 18, no. 44.

[39] Macready to Home Secretary, 13 Nov. 1910, ibid. 22, no. 55.

[40] Mr Moylan to Home Office, memo. sent 22 Nov. 1910, ibid. 38, no. 82; Macready, *Annals*, i. 152.

[41] Memo. by Macready on certain points connected with the strike in South Wales, 5 Jan. 1911, PP 1911 [Cd. 5568], lxiv. 48.

They were replaced by borrowed police from neighbouring counties and boroughs.[42] Thus the great confrontation for ever linked with the legendary name of Tonypandy came to its close, with many long-term implications for the reputation of Churchill himself. It left a legacy of bitter recriminations from Keir Hardie and other Labour leaders about police violence and brutality, and much local hatred towards the 'Glamorgans' and police borrowed from other areas. These executive aspects of the handling of the Cambrian strike, however, will be considered in context in Chapter 6.

The organizational features of the handling of the Cambrian collieries' disturbances generated much debate, especially over Churchill's decision to delay using troops until the local and borrowed police were clearly overpowered or unable to cope. The standing joint committee in Glamorgan criticized the chief constable for borrowing police without its authorization. He had been specifically authorized to enter into an agreement with the County of Somerset and the Borough of Swansea and with no other police authorities. They also criticized Churchill's decision in sending Metropolitans when the local authorities had requisitioned troops instead. Since they had not requested policemen from London, the standing joint committee in Glamorgan, with its Labour majority, now refused to pay the resulting account for their services.[43] When the Law Officers assured Churchill that the committee was within its rights in so doing, the Home Secretary responded by introducing an Expenses in Aid to Police Bill in early 1911. 'To make provision with respect to the payment of expenses incurred in aiding the police of any district by means of the employment of any part of His Majesty's Naval or Military Forces or of any members of the Police Forces of another district.'[44] By this measure, which was to apply retrospectively to the police alone from 1 November 1910, Churchill would be allowed to dispatch police, or military, or naval forces around the country in times of crisis, without their being requested by the local authorities—who would, nevertheless, have to pay the cost. Significantly, though, this bill received no support, least of all from the local authorities,

[42] South Wales coal strike reports, 1911 (HO 144/1554/199768/197a).

[43] *Glamorgan Coal Company Ltd* v. *Glamorganshire Standing Joint Committee and others; Powell Duffryn Steam Coal Co. Ltd* v. *same* [1916] 2 KB 206; Troup to Treasury Solicitor (draft letter), 25 Mar. 1911 (HO 144/1554/199768/308).

[44] *Parl. Deb.*, 5th ser., 23, 1534 (30 Mar. 1911).

and was withdrawn before coming up for a second reading. Reluctantly, the Home Office was forced to pay the full costs of the Metropolitans in South Wales.[45]

However, the standing joint committee was less successful in its refusal to pay for the borrowed provincial police. In a subsequent court action by one of the colliery companies to recover the cost of the borrowed police billeted there during the disturbances from the standing joint committee, it was decided that, although the police authority was not responsible for the expense of the Metropolitan Police, it was indeed liable for the expenses of the police borrowed by the chief constable from neighbouring counties without its ratification. An important feature of this decision, of course, was that it showed the independence of a county chief constable from his police authority with reference to borrowing police or incurring additional expenditure of this nature. The 'antecedent authority' of the police committee was shown not to be necessary.[46]

The events at Tonypandy, spectacular though they were, did not change departmental attitudes. The Home Office felt that the troubles in South Wales were quite exceptional and had been treated as such but they did not necessitate a change of policy in general. The general, long-established principle remained—that the responsibility for law and order lay with the local police authorities. When questioned on the point early in 1911, with reference to an inquiry from a local authority, Troup replied that the case of Tonypandy had been unique. The standard answer previously would have been that the preservation of law and order was an essentially local responsibility, 'and I see no reason why this reply should not be sent now'.[47]

The Home Office was put further to the test in 1911, which brought a wave of even greater labour unrest. The unusually hot summer of that year was probably the most disturbed that Britain had experienced since the days of the Chartists in the 1840s. It began with the national seamen's strike in June–July 1911, after which the London and other dockers came out on strike. By the

[45] Home Office minute, 17 Apr. 1911 (HO 144/1554/199768/333).
[46] [1916] 2 KB 364.
[47] Minute by Troup on the South Wales situation, 9 June 1911 (HO 144/1554/199768/359).

start of August Liverpool was caught up in almost total stoppages. Partial strikes of railwaymen, ostensibly in support of the dock workers in various parts of the country, began to break out, while the coal-mining industry remained deeply troubled. The combination of dock and railway strikes together resulted in threats of food shortages in London, Liverpool and Manchester, accompanied by considerable unrest and rioting. Churchill now regarded these associated labour troubles as a cause for national concern and action. 'The general strike "policy" is a factor which must be dealt with,' he wrote ominously.[48]

Troops were now dispatched around the country in consultation with the War Office. Several companies and battalions of infantry were based in the South Wales mining valleys, while 25,000 troops were held in readiness near the capital. Even so, Churchill's attitude to the use of troops remained much the same as in the previous year. The directive both to the police and military authorities was that troops were not to act until called upon by the civil authority, and only then if the officer in command was satisfied that all the resources of the police were exhausted.[49] The Metropolitan Police were dispatched instead of troops to Hull and Salford. They were also sent to Cardiff but were reinforced by troops here.

From the Home Office point of view, several of the organizational problems involved in allowing local authorities responsibility for the maintenance of law and order re-emerged during the seamen's strike. In the port of Cardiff there were disturbances on 18 July after the unloading and loading of ships by Chinese non-union labour. However, both the head constable and the mayor insisted that they had enough police on hand to cope with the crowds of pickets, since they had borrowed police under mutual aid agreements and also had 220 Metropolitans.[50] But the Home Office now received many letters of complaint from Cardiff employers that the police were insufficient to cope with the situation. Troup, in unwonted panic, wrote that the local authorities were 'not only doing nothing now but not even *preparing* to do

[48] R. S. Churchill, *Churchill*, ii. 379.

[49] Minute on the disposition of troops in South Wales, July 1911 (HO 45/210615/10649/81); R. S. Churchill, *Churchill*, ii. 379.

[50] Mayor of Cardiff to Home Office (telegram), 19 July 1911 (HO 45/10649/210615/69).

anything'.[51] The Home Office then telegraphed to the mayor to increase protection for ship workers willing to discharge cargoes. The mayor replied that 200 soldiers would be needed for this to be carried out, which would seriously imperil negotiations with the strikers. But, after Home Office pressure, on 21 July the head constable, with the agreement of the mayor, decided to call for military assistance, and two battalions of the Lancashire Fusiliers subsequently arrived.[52] However, they were split up into companies and placed to guard vulnerable points such as the docks and warehouses. The head constable insisted that they were being kept in readiness for an emergency, and were not being used actively to break the strike. Major Freeth, the officer in charge of troops in South Wales, reported that, so far as he was aware, the officer in charge of troops in Cardiff in 1911 'was never consulted by either of the above [i.e. the mayor or chief constable] as to the disposition of the military during the strike'.[53]

Events which took place at Liverpool contrasted sharply with those at Cardiff. By the end of the second week of August a general stoppage of work had occurred and disorders were mounting. Although the police had been reinforced by the arrival of 320 policemen borrowed from Leeds, Birmingham, Lancashire, and Bradford, on 11 August the mayor requisitioned the aid of troops at Seaforth Barracks with a second battalion held in readiness at Rhayader, and two squadrons of Scots Greys from York.[54] The battleship HMS *Antrim* was sent to Liverpool on 17 August to provide further protection and so that volunteer stokers could work the power station.[55]

Some wider implications emerged when the threat of a national railway strike loomed up in the second week of August. The Metropolitans were needed in London, while it would be difficult to borrow police under mutual aid agreements. Chief constables

[51] Minute by Troup on the situation at Cardiff, 20 July 1911 (HO 45/10649/210615/75).

[52] Head constable's report to Cardiff City Watch Committee on Cardiff strike 1911, 10 Aug. 1911.

[53] Minute by Major Freeth on Cardiff seamen's strike, 3 Aug. 1911 (HO 45/10649/210615/123).

[54] Head constable of Liverpool to Home Office, 15 Aug. 1911, PP 1911 (323), xlvii. 695; Home Office minute, n.d., ibid.

[55] Correspondence relating to the refusal to permit the employment of naval stokers at Liverpool Electric Power Station: Churchill to Lord Mayor of Liverpool, 17 Aug. 1911 (HO 45/10654/212470/120).

and police authorities were now urged to recruit special constables, and the government for the first time agreed that a limited number of these could be employed full time and paid 5*s*. a day, half of which cost would be borne by the Exchequer.[56] In London, Churchill told the Commissioner of the Metropolitan Police to employ up to 3,000 'trustworthy men' to do regular duty with the force. He felt it important that 'rioters should feel that the maintenance of order does not rest in the hands only of uniformed authority'.[57]

Much more significantly, on 16 August Macready was instructed by Haldane at the War Office to control the distribution and movement of all troops to be employed in protecting railways throughout the country. He met with railway directors and managers to work out his plans. A centrally organized system was created with a regional structure based on strike areas. Individual districts were under the command of a senior army officer with a headquarters usually at the principal railway junction of the area.[58] By 17 August, when the national railway strike began, 58,000 troops were employed throughout England and Wales in strategic locations. This was the largest number of troops to be used so far to combat an industrial dispute. It comprised practically the whole force of troops available in Britain, excluding Ireland. Indeed recruitment to the army actually went up 30 per cent during the railway strike compared with the six weeks preceding.[59]

Despite this throwing of troops around the country, there was uncertainty at times about what they would actually do. Some prominent magistrates were reluctant to requisition them and the military were always reluctant to act without civil sanction. A report to the Home Office about the situation in Nottingham, for example, describing the sending of a regiment of the Warwickshires to the city, stated: 'They would be extremely useful for assisting in the guarding of the railways in the neighbourhood; but there appears to be some doubt as to whether they are available for

[56] HO 158/15 (212,856), 17 Aug. 1911.

[57] Dixon, 'The Home Office', p. 197; Home Secretary to Mayor of Liverpool, 18 Aug. 1911 (HO 45/10654/212470/701, no. 19).

[58] Macready, *Annals*, i. 163.

[59] *Employment of Military during Railway Strike: Correspondence between Home Office and Local Authorities*, PP 1911 (323), xlvii. 698, no. 10; War Office memo. on army recruiting during strike (HO 45/10658/212470).

this purpose or should be left at the disposal of the city authorities.'[60] Sir Edward Henry, the Commissioner of the Metropolitan Police, now wrote to the Home Secretary asking what the police should do when they found themselves in need of military assistance:

> When a magistrate is present the procedure is known—but where no magistrate is present, the procedure does not appear to be clear.
>
> In London now, small numbers of military are holding Railway Stations, Power Stations and other important points. In the event of strikers endeavouring to rush these places, would military act without requisition by the police, or upon the requisition of any particular officer of police . . . who might call upon them to act?[61]

Indeed the elaborate command structure which divided operational control between local and central state acted as a severe inhibition upon the use of the military as an arm of the central state. With the concurrence of the War Office, Churchill now took drastic action. He suspended the Army Regulation which required the requisition of troops from a civil authority. He pressed general officers in the various military areas to use their common-law powers and to exercise their discretion as to whether troops were to be sent to a particular point.[62] The military forces were entrusted with the tasks of keeping the railways running, safeguarding the railways, and protecting those railwaymen who remained at work. Police authorities were circulated to this effect. The police and magistrates should co-operate in every possible way with the military, while it was essential that the police should give assistance in guarding the railways and 'supply effective protection to railwaymen outside the railway premises'.[63] The legal basis for the intervention of the military in the railway dispute was set out for the Home Office by the government Law Officers on 18 August. They re-emphasized the common law on this subject in a significant statement which still remains today the

[60] Report on strike situation from Nottingham to Home Office, 18 Aug. 1911 (HO 45/10654/212470/99).

[61] Sir Edward Henry to Home Secretary, 15 Aug. 1911 (HO 144/22936/257009/1).

[62] War Office circular on protection of railways by the military, 19 Aug. 1911; Railway strike, Aug. 1911, confidential memos. and reports (HO 45/10658/212470, no. 4).

[63] *Parl. Deb.*, 5th ser., 29, 2330 (22 Aug. 1911); Home Office to all police authorities (telegram), 19 Aug. 1911 (HO 45/10658/212470, no. 2).

legal basis of military intervention in aid of the civil power. They said:

> A soldier differs from the ordinary citizen in being armed and subject to discipline; but his rights and duties in dealing with crime are precisely the same as those of the ordinary citizen. If the aid of the military has been invoked by the Police and the soldiers find that a situation arises, in which prompt action is required, although neither Magistrates nor Police are present or available for consultation, they must act on their own responsibility. They are bound to use such force as is reasonably necessary to protect premises over which they are watching, and to prevent serious crime or riot. But they must not use lethal weapons to prevent or suppress minor disorder or offences of a less serious character and in no case should they do so if less extreme measures will suffice.[64]

The War Office now sent troops to many industrial areas, both with and without the requisition of the civil authorities; troops were dispatched to twenty-nine places on request, and to thirty-three without requisition.[65] The mayors of Manchester and Sheffield woke up to find that, despite the absence of disorder, their cities were under military occupation. Cromwell and his major-generals had come again. George Lansbury and the Poplar councillors in East London were incensed to find troops occupying the local power station. Troops were sent without requisition to Normanton, Doncaster, South Empsall, Nostell, Wakefield, and Ardsley, while detachments were stationed on railway lines between Doncaster and Leeds. It was reported that 'General Heath made this move after conferring with the chief constable of the West Riding and with his concurrence'.In some localities troops actually drove trains and served as guards.[66] The most alarming episode of all was the shooting of two men during disturbances at Llanelli in South Wales, as will be discussed in Chapter 6.

On 19 August the strike was declared to be at an end, partly because of pressures placed on the union by the international crisis over Agadir between the *entente* powers and Germany. By 25 August all troops had been withdrawn from rail centres. According

[64] Memo. by Law Officers, Rufus Isaacs and John Simon, regarding the duties and powers of soldiers so supplied if required to act when neither magistrate nor police are present with them, 18 Aug. 1911 (HO 144/22936/257009/1).

[65] War Office memo. on distribution of troops in railway strike 1911 (HO 45/10658/212470, no. 5).

[66] Ibid.; CAB 23/9 WC 522, 30 Jan. 1919.

to a ministerial colleague, C. F. G. Masterman, Churchill was actually disappointed at the rapid end to the strike: in belligerent mood now, he had been anxious to give the railwaymen 'a good thrashing'.[67]

The *post mortem* on the handling of this latest, most alarming, labour dispute now began. Churchill was openly criticized in the Commons in 1911 for sending troops around the country in advance of any disorder, and for suspending the Army Regulation which required the requisition of troops from a civil authority. He replied that military authorities had always enjoyed the power to move troops and also that

> the regulation which has hitherto restricted their employment in places where there was disorder until there had been a requisition from the local authority was only a regulation for the convenience of the War Office and generally of the Government and has in these circumstances necessarily been abrogated.[68]

He reminded his critics that he had earlier been attacked for initially refusing to send troops to Tonypandy: 'the feelings with which I acted then have never departed from my mind. But Tonypandy was a small affair and produced no great national reaction.' The Metropolitan Police had also been on hand in Tonypandy whereas in August 1911 they were needed to protect the capital.[69]

Churchill's defence failed to satisfy Labour members. Ramsay MacDonald denounced his 'new doctrine', while Keir Hardie contrasted the careful and theoretical discussion of the use of troops in aid of the civil power in 1894 and 1908 with their actual use in 1911.

> On this occasion, before a single man had gone on strike, troops were ordered out, ball cartridge was supplied to the troops, machine guns were lined up behind the regiments and the military authorities . . . were given an absolutely free hand to act where they pleased . . . in what they called the preservation of order. Talk about Revolution! The law of England has been broken in the interests of the railway companies of this country.[70]

67 L. Masterman, *C. F. G. Masterman*: *A Biography* (1939), 208
68 *Parl. Deb.*, 5th ser., 29, 2286 (22 Aug. 1911); CAB 23/9, WC 522, 30 Jan. 1919.
69 *Parl. Deb.*, 5th ser., 29, 2329 (22 Aug. 1911).
70 Ibid., cols. 2296, 2335.

A massive demonstration was held in Trafalgar Square on 26 August to protest 'against the unwarrantable extension of military authority and the unconstitutional imposition of martial law by the arbitrary ukase of the Home Secretary'.[71] The Labour Party Conference passed a resolution condemning the use of troops in trade disputes, and attacking the government for placing soldiers at the private disposal of the railway companies. The drafting of policemen and troops from outside into the troubled areas 'gravely increased the civil disturbance, as in Liverpool and Llanelly, and was actually the cause of the outbreak of rioting and the killing and wounding of a number of persons in these places . . .'. Their wholesale employment, together with prejudiced reports from the Home Office, 'must have served as warnings to even trade unionists as to where the sympathies of the government lay'.[72] The TUC passed a similar motion.[73] Blatchford's *Clarion* felt that the government had followed the example of 'Briand in France and the worst methods of American capitalism',[74] while the ILP *Labour Leader* declared that the government had determined to crush the strike by 'a policy of batons, bayonets and bullets'.[75] *The Syndicalist* published 'An Open Letter to British Soldiers' in which it appealed to members of the armed forces not to obey orders when called upon to shoot at strikers.[76] In fact five people were now prosecuted under the Incitement to Mutiny Act for attempting to undermine the loyalty and obedience of soldiers, including the editor Tom Mann.

This sense of outrage throughout the labour movement confirmed the feeling that the Home Office had initiated a new kind of anti-strike policy. Troup himself, however, blandly averred that

> The new departure taken in this case does not indicate any change in the future practice of dealing with disturbances, where the disturbances are confined to particular localities. But if at any future time a state of things should arise affecting the maintenance of order throughout the United Kingdom, it is clear that the assistance to be given to the magistrates and

[71] D. Williams, *Keeping the Peace*, p. 33.
[72] *Labour Party Annual Conference Report* (1912), 19.
[73] *Trade Union Congress Report* (1911), 155.
[74] *Clarion*, 1 Sept. 1911.
[75] *Labour Leader*, 25 Aug. 1911.
[76] D. Williams, *Keeping the Peace*, pp. 182–3.

the police must be organized under the direction and control of the central Government.[77]

When there was a prospect of disturbances extending over a wide area, as in the railway strike of 1911, 'the authority may be given once for all and the subsequent movements of troops be left to the military authorities who will then act in close co-ordination with the local civil authorities'.[78]

Whatever the justification by Churchill and his civil servants for the dispatch of troops around the country in 1911, the fact remained that their policy had caused widespread revulsion among the public. The Home Office now turned to encouraging local authorities to build up the provincial police forces and to enrol special constables so that mutual aid agreements would be easier to fulfil. The railway strike had shown that, while local police were often inadequate to deal with disorder, many citizens were willing to act as special constables. In Liverpool, for example, 4,142 special constables had enrolled for the duration of the railway strike and many employers pressed local police authorities for the further enrolment of these additional policemen.[79] In September 1911, therefore, the Home Office circularized the police authorities on the need to keep up the reserve of special constables, and to maintain a continuous registration of suitable men whose services would be available for the aid of the police if any serious future emergency should arise. The form their organization should take was spelt out. The First Police Reserve should be a virtually professional force composed of retired policemen and soldiers who would wear uniform on duty and be paid and be eligible for pensions in case of injury or retirement. The Second Reserve would be a non-professional force of special constables, generally unpaid and receiving only allowances for expenses or loss of wages but who might be paid if employed on regular turns of police duty.[80] Inspectors of constabulary were told

77 Memo. on the employment of soldiers without requisition from the civil authority, 21 Oct. 1911 (HO 45/10658/212470, no. 1).

78 Troup, *Home Office*, p. 51.

79 Liverpool City Watch Committee Minutes, 4 Sept. 1911 (Liverpool Central Library).

80 HO 158/15 (214,312), 15 Sept. 1911.

that the existence or not of a reserve, its members, and quality, should be taken into account when reporting on the efficiency of a local force.[81]

As so often in the past, however, this initiative by the Home Office came up against the obstacle of local autonomy, especially in the boroughs. At a conference of chairmen of watch committees and head constables of boroughs, held in London in October 1911, on the suggestion of the Manchester Watch Committee, it was emphatically insisted that local police watch committees would not wait passively while the Home Office encroached on their traditional territory.[82] A committee composed of the chairmen of twenty local watch committees concluded that 'the Home Office scheme was unworkable as far as the First Police Reserve was concerned'. Seventy members of the conference met Churchill on 10 November and were reminded by the Home Secretary of their duty of preserving order and of the willingness of the Treasury to pay for First Reserve special constables up to 50 per cent of the authorized strength of the police forces. But many doubts remained, especially about the concept of a First Reserve:

> It is not easy to see how a class of this description can be sustained in the manner indicated, which would in the slightest degree justify the annual expenditure which has to be borne by the Local Authority.
>
> This portion of the scheme bristles with difficulties, anomalies, and pitfalls, so far as the Local Authority is concerned, and, in the opinion of your deputation, after careful consideration, they cannot recommend your committee to adopt it.[83]

The members argued that the Second Police Reserve, the special constabulary, would be quite sufficient, while financial provision should be made for the employment of a certain number of training officers for these men. Eventually, the committee approved the formation of the special constabulary, with advertisements to be inserted in local newspapers 'inviting eligible Citizens between the ages of 25 and 50, to enrol as Special Constables to act in case of emergency'. Head constables would be asked to put this scheme into operation.[84]

The response however was patchy and dependent on local

81 *Police Review*, 5 Jan. 1912.
82 Cardiff City Watch Committee Minutes, 11 Oct. 1911.
83 Ibid., 8 Dec. 1911.
84 Ibid.

whim. Several boroughs in industrial areas now took initiatives of their own. In Cardiff the watch committee resolved at the start of 1912 to pay special constables a retaining fee of 1*s*. a week for up to a maximum of 200 men. By 20 February 100 had been enrolled, 83 of whom had been put through drill and given instruction. By April the head constable had 296, of whom 161 were unpaid and 135 paid a retaining fee.[85] In Liverpool, by contrast, the watch committee recommended that the two classes of police reserve be formed.[86] In Swansea advertisements were placed for special constables but by 27 February the total had reached only 45. Not all local authorities were so positive. In Manchester, although the watch committee approved the formation of a special constabulary, the scheme was referred back at a meeting of the city council; it was severely criticized on the grounds that it was 'a retrograde movement and too expensive'. In Durham also the proposal to form a special constabulary was rejected by the town council and referred back to the watch committee.[87]

In the counties, where the Home Secretary made regulations for the formation and payment of the First Reserve under Section 3 of the County Police Act 1839, efforts to fulfil the requirements of the Home Office circular over the forming of the special constabulary met with much more success, even though there was little enthusiasm for the special constabulary amongst working men in industrial areas. In Denbighshire, for example, over 300 men from different parts of the county had indicated their willingness to serve, and the standing joint committee decided that 100 of them should be enrolled at the rate of 3*s*. a day when on duty, with a retaining fee of £2 2*s*. per annum.[88] In Glamorgan, by contrast, where the pugnacious Chief Constable Lindsay felt that a force of 2,000–3,000 men should be raised (the standing joint committee had suggested only 60), he had managed to recruit only 100 by June 1912.[89] In Carmarthenshire the standing joint committee advertised for 40 men for the First Reserve, to be paid 5*s*. a day

[85] Head constable's report to Cardiff City Watch Committee, 20 Feb. 1912; 10 Apr. 1912.

[86] Liverpool City Watch Committee Minutes, 28 Sept. 1911.

[87] *Police Review*, 19 Jan., 23 Feb. 1912.

[88] Chief constable's report to Denbighshire Standing Joint Committee, 11 Apr. 1912 (County Record Office, Ruthin).

[89] Chief constable's report to Glamorgan Standing Joint Committee, June 1912 (County Hall, Cardiff).

when serving. By 1914 the clerk had enrolled 700 special constables in all.[90]

As regards mutual aid agreements, in 1912 the Home Office had circularized police authorities with model agreement forms and Home Office rhetoric now emphasized: 'The duty of one police authority to aid another in a time of emergency is but the extension of the duty of the individual citizen to do all that lies in his power for the preservation of peace.' The Select Committee on Employment of Military in Cases of Disturbances in 1908 had contemplated 'that police authorities would, in taking concerted measures of precaution, treat each other as parts of one organization with a common purpose towards which each should help the rest'.[91] The inspector of constabulary for the Southern District now reported that, despite much diversity between forces, the spirit of co-operation had improved. The following year he added that:

> Scales of charges to be paid for police lent to another have been fixed by most police authorities and this is as far as agreements for mutual aid can reasonably be carried; but there is no reason for fearing that any police authority will neglect its undoubted duty to lend men when circumstances at home permit of their doing so.[92]

However, as has been pointed out, the existence of these agreements in no way compelled one police force to help another. Each authority remained free to refuse or accede to requests for assistance. Labour members of police authorities often objected to their own police being lent, or police being borrowed, on the grounds that they would then be taking the side of the employer. Usually they objected on financial grounds as well.

The interests of the Home Office and the police authorities, then, did not necessarily coincide. The Home Secretary was concerned with the preservation of order nationally; the local authorities were, naturally, preoccupied with their own areas, expecially since they had to finance their forces largely from their own resources. Policing preparations in anticipation of disorder clearly depended on the inclination of the local police authorities concerned—and, no doubt, on their attitude towards the demands

[90] Chief constable's report to Carmarthenshire Standing Joint Committee, Mar. 1912 and July 1914.

[91] Home Office to chief constable of Bristol, 27 Sept. 1913 (HO 45/10710/242402/22).

[92] *Annual Report of HM Inspector of Constabulary*, PP 1914 (193) lxvii. 721.

and grievances of organized labour. In addition, the knowledge that the government would back them up with troops paid for by the Exchequer acted as a major deterrent to any concerted additional preparations to meet disorder.

Industrial unrest continued to be widespread in 1912. A national miners' strike on behalf of a national minimum wage began in late February, followed by a strike in the Port of London in April. A sympathetic stoppage by members of the TGWU in support of the miners was also feared. The new Home Secretary, Reginald McKenna, now proceeded more cautiously than Churchill had done. The policy of Churchill during the 1910 and 1911 strikes had been to give military officers on the spot 'support and abstention from interference' when they were aiding the civil pcwer during industrial unrest.[93] The more restrained policy being pursued by the Home Office over the use of troops in the strike now anticipated is illustrated in the response to requests by the South Wales justices. Before the coal strike broke out in late February 1912, the stipendiary magistrate of Pontypridd and Rhondda asked that the War Office send a strong military force to protect property because the chief constable of Glamorgan did not expect to be able to supplement the police force of the district to any appreciable extent owing to the anticipation of a general strike. It was not possible to raise a large force of special constables because of the purely industrial nature of the area. The chief constable of Glamorgan, Lindsay, characteristically suggested that the troops requested should consist of 3,500 infantry and 500 cavalry.[94] These should arrive some days before 29 February when the miners' notices were to be handed in because 'it is at least possible that the men in the Rhondda should precipitate matters by leaving off work two or three days before 29th and in the interval, if the military shall not have arrived, do something that would cripple the coal owners'.[95]

The Home Office files on this strike are of much interest. The question as to whether troops should be sent to South Wales in anticipation of disturbances or should be held at their stations until

[93] Macready, *Annals*, i. 157.

[94] Pontypridd and Rhondda Stipendiary Magistrate to War Office, 17 Feb. 1912 (HO 45/10675/218781, no. 1); *The Times*, 20 Feb. 1912.

[95] Pontypridd and Rhondda Stipendiary Magistrate to War Office, 17 Feb. 1912 (loc. cit.).

requested by magistrates on account of actual or imminent outbreaks of violence, was a delicate one, as Troup well knew. He consulted Macready at the War Office and then put both sides of the case.

The reasons for sending the troops at once are: (1) That any outbreak is likely to occur suddenly and the mischief might be done within two or three hours (2) That if the strikers mean mischief they may interfere with the railways, or induce the railwaymen not to work the troop trains.

But he realized that there were objections to taking this course in that 'it will cause the usual outburst of indignation from the Labour leaders and may possibly precipitate the strike. I do not believe it would *cause* disturbances, but, if disturbances occur, they will be attributed to the action of the Government in sending troops.' The alternative was to hold the troops ready to move at the shortest possible notice. However, it was almost impossible to do this without 'showing clearly to the public what is intended'. Whichever course was taken, it would not be possible to avoid for more than a few days longer showing that the government was prepared to reinforce the civil power in South Wales by the use of soldiers.[96]

McKenna now consulted the Prime Minister, Asquith. The Home Secretary had already been told by the magistrates at Llanelli that they did not want to be seen to be taking the owners' side in the dispute. From the experience of the previous August, it seemed probable that the introduction of troops into South Wales would create much bad feeling and, quite possibly, riot.[97] However, precautionary measures were in fact taken before the miners' strike. Additional troops were sent to barracks near places where there was a possibility of disturbance. Thus on 26 February arrangements were made for 5,000 troops to be concentrated at Darlington for use in the Durham coalfield, while Newport was to be the military nerve-centre in South Wales.[98] Local police authorities were circularized by the Home Office that these troops should be requisitioned as a last resort, and encouraged to enrol special constables. In future the Home Office should be given more complete information than it had hitherto received of actual or

[96] Memo. by Troup, 19 Feb. 1912 (HO 45/10675/218781, no. 3).

[97] Clerk to Llanelli Petty Sessional Division to Home Office, 23 Feb. 1912 (HO 45/10675/218781, no. 6).

[98] *The Times*, 27 Feb. 1912.

anticipated disturbance of the peace and the steps taken to reinforce the police. When any riot occurred, or when military aid was called for, chiefs of police should report at once to the Home Office and explain the circumstances which rendered aid necessary.[99]

In the event, the coal strike itself was a peaceful affair. When the gradual return to work began at the end of March, however, trouble was expected. Many requisitions for troops were now made by police authorities. The War Office Diary of Events during the strike throws an interesting light on the positions of the Home Office and the War Office with regard to the use of troops in aid of the civil power. Haldane, at the War Office, along with Isaacs, the Attorney-General, now wanted to return to the common-law principle that, if an officer received a request from a magistrate, the officer must, after communicating with the War Office, send troops, and that their actions on arrival at the scene of disorder rested with the commanding officer. Macready, for example, instructed the commander of the West Riding Regiment who was sent to Huntington Colliery in Staffordshire to 'ascertain the situation personally before actually introducing the troops into the colliery . . . collision between troops and population must be avoided to the utmost extent unless serious rioting takes place.'[100] Great care was now taken by the War Office that troops were sent in adequate numbers to deal with all emergencies, and that these troops came from distant areas to avoid fraternization with the locals.

At the Brynkinallt Colliery, Chirk, in North Wales on 27 March, there were reported to be 2,000 strikers at the pit, and trouble duly arose.[101] The forty police present were said to be physically exhausted. When a requisition for troops was made by Lord Trevor, the local magistrate (and, incidentally, the owner of the colliery), they were dispatched at once from Shrewsbury to the scene of the disorder on the authority of the War Office. They had instructions to keep well out of sight unless there were actual riots.[102] The officer in charge of the troops, which numbered 50, requested another battalion and 596 troops were sent from Alder-

[99] HO 158/15 (216,322/4), 19 Feb. 1912.

[100] Coal Strike 1912 War Office Diary of Events, 27 Mar. 1912 (HO 45/10675/218781/133).

[101] Ibid.

[102] Minute by Troup, 28 Mar. 1912, ibid. 129.

shot and arrived on 28 March. About 200 of these were placed on guard at the pit-head and in the yard, while a large body of police was stationed at the colliery gate. The men now returned to work and no trouble was reported. However, Troup at the Home Office was angry about War Office action here and reprimanded Macready for failure to consult about this movement of troops. From now on the War Office consulted with the Home Office with regard to requisitions from the civil authorities. These were strictly vetted and invariably the Home Office view prevailed. As Troup later noted in his memoirs: 'There was at one time a question whether the Home Secretary or the Secretary of State for War was responsible for the actual sending of troops but the Government decided in 1912 that the responsibility should remain with the Home Secretary.'[103]

These views contrast with Troup's pronouncements of the Home Office view in early 1910. When the mayor of Newport had given notice of his intention to requisition troops because of disturbances connected with the dock strike in the town, Troup had then stated, 'of course, if the Mayor or Magistrates requisition them they must be ready to go'.[104] A radical change from troops being requisitioned by local representatives, with their inherent accountability, to troops being used by the state with the resulting lack of local or national answerability had plainly taken place between 1910 and 1912.

The widespread use of troops, Metropolitans, and borrowed police in the years 1910–12 arroused bitter controversy. Fears were also expressed that in future strikes, perhaps by transport workers or post office employees, troops would be used to take their place. Despite Churchill's earlier denials, troops had, in fact, been used to maintain essential services during the 1911 railway strike. In 1912 the Attorney-General, Isaacs, while agreeing that blacklegging by soldiers was undesirable, added, 'I am not going to lay down the proposition that in no circumstances would it be desirable or necessary to employ soldiers to do some work which otherwise they would not be called upon to do'.[105] This was a portent for the future. In major strikes, troops, far from being used only in the last

[103] Troup, *Home Office*, pp. 50–1.
[104] Troup to Sir E. Ward, 21 May 1910, R. S. Churchill, *Churchill*, ii. p. 372.
[105] *Parl. Deb.*, 5th ser., 36, 1344 (10 Apr. 1912).

resort, could be used on a massive scale to assist or deputize for the police, to protect property and blackleg workers, and to uphold the official definition of the national interest.

In 1913–14 the main outbreaks of industrial militancy declined in number. A tense and precarious peace returned to the coalmines, railways, and docks. But the threat of large-scale industrial conflict remained a constant preoccupation of government and public. Indeed, the conclusion of the Triple Alliance between miners, railwaymen, and transport workers in the spring of 1914 raised to a new pitch alarm about a potential national confrontation between miners and the authorities.

During the First World War police chiefs became more accustomed to acting under governmental direction. The Defence of the Realm Regulations considerably reinforced the tendency to centralization and significantly increased police powers, while overriding many of those formerly exercised by the local authorities. Chief constables were brought into touch with the Home Office in new ways. The inspectors of constabulary were one valuable contact that the Home Office had with chiefs of police. A second one, however, to prove increasingly important, came through a branch of the Home Office, staffed by A. L. Dixon and C. D. Carew Robinson, which had been responsible before the war, under Troup's direction, for the Home Office 'war book'. On the outbreak of war this became the War Duties Division, with closer contact with borough and county police than the Home Office had ever had before. Another important link was to be the system of district conferences and the central conference of chief constables, inaugurated by the Home Office in 1918.[106]

In addition, a crucial arm of central government during the war was the Special Branch which was increasingly active in dealing with labour unrest. In June 1913 the formidable Basil Thomson had become head of the Criminal Investigation Department (CID) and of the Special Branch also. In the spring of 1916 Lloyd George's Ministry of Munitions asked him to prepare a new 'intelligence service on labour matters for the whole country on behalf of the Ministry', and Thomson agreed to do so. He drafted twelve sergeants from the CID into the ministry. However, there was a broad proliferation of wartime departments: the new

[106] Dixon, 'The Home Office', p. 2.

Ministry of Labour and National Service, the Board of Trade, the Admiralty Shipyard Labour Department, the Army Contracts departments were all concerned with various aspects of labour intelligence, as also were General Headquarters (GHQ) Home Forces. In April 1917, therefore, the War Cabinet, of which Lloyd George was now the premier, told all government departments in receipt of intelligence on labour unrest to pass it on to the Ministry of Labour, where it was collated. Sir David Shackleton, himself an old trade unionist ironically enough, now prepared a weekly statement, to be presented to the War Cabinet, 'as to stoppages, disputes and settlements and labour propaganda . . . together with a general appreciation of the labour situation'.[107] Thomson continued to send in his own reports on subversion to the Home Office. All these reports became another powerful weapon for central government in facing up to labour during the war.

Thus, despite the existence of the Defence of the Realm Act (DORA) and the Treasury Agreement to abolish strikes, the fear of industrial unrest continued to be widespread during the war. The impact of the Russian revolution in 1917 greatly reinforced fears of a possible insurrection. Police forces had been depleted by as much as 30 per cent. The Special Constables Act of 1914 made it lawful to appoint special constables at any time during the war, at the requisition of the chief officer of police. Even so, there were too few police available.

There were also ominous signs of discontent within the ranks of the police force itself. This had long been recognized as a problem. In 1893 the radical, John Kempster, founded the *Police Review* as the organ of the rank and file. Its publication was to be of major importance in ending police isolation and providing a forum for the airing of views and ventilation of police grievances. The nationalizing tendencies coming from above were therefore paralleled in a different way from below. Kempster attempted to elevate the status of the ordinary policeman. In his first leader on 2 January 1893 he commented on 'a tendency all too prevalent . . . to treat a policeman with less regard for his own self-respect than should prevail amongst men towards their fellow men in all ranks of life'.[108] By 1910, despite all the *Review*'s efforts, not much had changed. Morale was low. The county police had no right of appeal

[107] C. M. Andrew, *Secret Service* (1985), 196.
[108] *Police Review*, 2 Jan. 1893.

against autocratic chief constables in whose hands alone the discipline of the force lay. Chief constables could form their own association and hold conferences, and look after their own personal interests. Indeed separate associations of both borough head constables and county chief constables had been in existence since the 1890s.[109] By contrast, pay and conditions of service in the rank and file of the force generally had fallen behind the national average since 1900. Pay and status were commonly compared with those of artisans and miners. Promotion was at a standstill. Although the police weekly rest day had been approved in principle, it was slow to be implemented and many new duties had been imposed.

There were frequent demands in the pre-war years, especially from county councils, that the autocratic powers of county chief constables be curbed, and that standing joint committees be abolished and their powers transferred to the county councils. When standing joint committees had been formed in 1888 under the Local Government Act, the reason for their formation had been that the county councils were not considered to be 'educated in the science of government' and, therefore, not fit to undertake the duties carried out by the watch committees in the cities and boroughs in the management of the police. There were now demands from county councils that the standing joint committees, which had little power and were responsible to no one, should be reformed. In 1908 the West Riding County Council, for example, promoted a private bill, the Local Government (Transfer of Powers of Standing Joint Committees) Bill, to abolish the county police authority and transfer all its functions to the county council.[110] Another bill, the Police (County Authorities) Bill—the object of which was to assimilate the powers of the county police authorities with those of the cities and boroughs, and thus to confer upon the standing joint committees the same measure of control over police administration as was possessed by the watch committees—was introduced in the House of Commons in the same year by a private member, Sir Charles Schwann. In 1914 the main points included in this bill were reproduced in a bill introduced by Labour and Liberal members—the County Police (England and Wales) Bill.[111]

[109] Ibid., 29 May 1908, and HO 45/11034/A56752.

[110] *Police Review*, 28 Feb. 1908.

[111] Ibid., 17 Jan. 1908; PP 1914, 1 [Bill 199] 5 and 6 Geo. V.

Whilst popularizing and publicizing these attempts at reform, the *Police Review* conducted its own campaign on behalf of the county police to repeal the County Police Act of 1839 which conferred absolute powers on chief constables in counties.

> So many statutes replacing feudalism by local self government have been enacted . . . that it is somewhat surprising that the provisions of the County Police Act 1839 conferring absolute power on the County Chief constables has never been repealed. It is high time however that a determined effort was made in this direction.[112]

It voiced the view that there were some county chiefs of police who would be better employed 'in Eastern Europe where their ideas of justice would appeal to a despotic government'.[113]

These demands for reform of the county police came to nothing. Nor did pressure by London boroughs to gain control of the Metropolitan force achieve results. Discontent in the rank and file of the force generally led, in 1913, to a secret union of police officers being formed in London—the Metropolitan Police Union, the creation of a dissident young inspector named Syme. Shortly afterwards, the new police union gained provincial support and was re-christened the National Union of Police and Prison Officers (NUPPO). Its main object was to secure the right of conference and collective representation on matters affecting the pay, service, and pensions of the police. The Home Office viewed this development with much alarm. All union members, it declared, would be liable to dismissal from the force. On the other hand, it believed that the union would win little support and that the police would never achieve the power to strike effectively.[114]

Nevertheless, NUPPO made much headway. The *Police Review* commented in August 1918 on how NUPPO's quarterly report 'shows in a remarkable way the growing feeling of sympathy and the spirit of co-operation which now exists on the part of the workers of the land towards the police.'[115] The London Trades Council, with membership of 100,000 workers, had demonstrated eagerness to support the police in any claim they made to be recognized as a corporate body. Indeed, NUPPO was affiliated to

[112] *Police Review*, 22 Nov. 1907.

[113] Ibid., 8 Apr. 1909.

[114] V. L. Allen, 'The National Union of Police and Prison Officers', *Economic History Review*, 2nd ser., 11 (1958–9), 133–43.

[115] *Police Review*, 23 Aug. 1918; *TUC Annual Conference Report* (1918).

various labour bodies in the country, and this led to immense alarm in government circles. Discontent came to a head in London in August 1918 when, in the words of Leonard Dunning, one of the inspectors of constabulary, 'an organised attempt to seduce the police from their duty met with a regrettable amount of success'.[116]

On 25 August Thomas Theil, the provincial organizer of NUPPO, was dismissed from the police for being involved in union activities. On 27 August the executive met and drew up an ultimatum which was then dispatched to the Commissioner of the Metropolitan Police. It demanded an increase in pay, union recognition, and the reinstatement of Theil. Its demands were accompanied by an ultimatum that if they were not met by midnight on 29 August the rules relating to the prohibition of strike action would be suspended. The ultimatum was ignored and the strike began on the 30th. The whole of the Metropolitan Police now came out on strike—approximately 12,000 men; later that evening virtually the whole of the City of London police followed.[117] The government, with the Russian revolution fresh in its memory, was afraid of a mutiny of the entire Metropolitan Police; it also feared that this strike might even influence the army. Worse still, the strike was taking place when many industrial workers were taking action, and there was also a danger that the TUC might authorize sympathetic strikes. The Prime Minister, Lloyd George, declared that the country was nearer to Bolshevism than at any previous time.[118]

Ironically, it was now industrial action by the police themselves which prompted the first use of troops to combat civil disorder in the war. Indeed, government planning inevitably included a major role for the troops should civil disorder occur during the war. Schemes had already been worked out between 1910 and 1913, between the War Office and the Home Office, for meeting possible trouble in the metropolis during time of war. London had been divided into areas for the purpose of military aid; vulnerable points were to be specified by the Commissioner of the Metropolitan Police and arrangements were made whereby troops might be

[116] *Annual Report of HM Inspector of Constabulary*, PP 1920 (91), xxii. 465.

[117] G. W. Reynolds and A. Judge, *The Night the Police went on Strike* (1968), 40–5; Allen, 'The National Union', p. 136.

[118] Reynolds and Judge, *The Night*, p. 70.

posted and quartered so as to be ready where needed, on the home front.[119] However, the situation with regard to the use of troops in aid of the civil power had changed from that of pre-war years. The loyalty or self-discipline of troops, most of whom were conscripts, could not necessarily be relied upon. Macready, now Director of Personal Services of the War Office, commented that the officer class 'are not what they were in the days when we used to have strikes before the war. . . . The same applies almost equally to the men—[they] will not put up with what the troops I used to handle in strikes formerly used to put up with at the hands of the strikers.' Macready himself was terrified at the prospect of raw troops being used in civil disturbances during the war.[120]

However, in the crisis situation which had developed in the metropolis in August 1918, the use of troops to keep order was inevitable. While 20,000 special constables were enrolled on 30 August, Generals Smuts and Macready arranged with the GOC of the London district for 600 men to guard all government buildings in place of the usual policemen. Marines took up duty at the Admiralty and outside other naval establishments in London, and troops were posted all over the London area. The military commanders had a natural distaste for exercising martial law in London and the Cabinet was very hostile to the idea of an open show of force, but on the night of 30 August 1918 every London barracks was standing by, ready to go to the scene of any disorder.[121]

The same day Smuts told the War Cabinet that he had met the superintendents of the various police districts of the metropolis that morning. They felt that the men's demands over pay should be met and that, unless this was agreed *in toto*, there was no chance of a settlement. Should the pay rise be conceded, the superintendents believed that the men would then return to work and 'the demand for recognition of the Union would be dropped'. Smuts felt that the situation was very serious 'as the Union was affiliated to other trade unions and there was a possibility of the strike extending to other trades'. This view was endorsed by Major-General Sir Frederick Wodehouse, the Assistant Commis-

[119] Civil Trouble in the Metropolis in Case of War (HO 144/1650/179987).
[120] Macready to Troup, 30 Jan. 1918 (HO 144/22936/257009/5).
[121] Reynolds and Judge, *The Night*, p. 60; CAB 23/7 WC 467, memo. on police strike, 30 Aug. 1918.

sioner of the Metropolitan Police. He declared that he did not expect there to be any police on duty that night. Even *The Times* in a leading article stated that, 'To anyone who knows anything about the London Police it is at once evident that in taking the action they have the men are conscious of a strong case and firmly convinced of the justice of their cause'.[122]

On the morning of 31 August many strikers marched to the centre of London to meet the Prime Minister at Whitehall. The whole of Whitehall was under military protection, but in fact the military were well received by the striking policemen. Reynolds and Judge point out that

> Such a show of military force might have had an unfortunate effect at many strike demonstrations but this crowd was in far too good a humour to be worried by the appearance of a few rifles. . . . Several strikers reported that the soldiers had told them they were in sympathy with the strike and would not obey any orders to break it.[123]

Lloyd George met the executive of NUPPO at noon and agreed that Metropolitan Police pay would be substantially raised and that pensions and conditions would be improved. Theil and other dismissed officers were reinstated, but on the question of union recognition Lloyd George characteristically appeared to compromise. While he could not sanction the recognition of the police union in wartime, he felt there should be some machinery by which the police force could bring before the police authorities any grievances as to their conditions of service. Thus the main objectives of NUPPO were to be met, and the union executive left the meeting with the clear impression that their union would indeed be recognized at the end of the war. The terms of the pay settlement achieved in London were granted in many provincial forces also.[124]

Although the rank and file of the force were pacified, the strike in the metropolis in 1918 had shown that their loyalty could be suspect. This action by the police themselves now reinforced the government's determination to use troops to combat any threatened industrial unrest during the war. Indeed, with fear of Bolshevism spreading, in the threatened rail strike of September

[122] *The Times*, 31 Aug. 1918.
[123] Reynolds and Judge, *The Night*, p. 67; CAB 23/7 WC 467, 30 Aug. 1918.
[124] Allen, 'The National Union', p. 136.

1918 there is evidence that the government was prepared to use troops to maintain essential services, and to protect buildings, material, and personnel who remained at work. Chief constables were told in September 1918 that the government was determined that the attempt to cause a strike of railway workers should not be allowed to interfere with the successful prosecution of the war. Although chiefs of police were urged to make use of special constables, the Home Secretary had requested the military to help them to preserve law and order. Troops were now to be dispatched around the country to areas where disturbances were expected, as they had been in anticipation of a national railway strike in 1911. Police authorities were informed:

> If troops should arrive in your area before any requisition is made, you will understand that in the opinion of the authorities their presence is necessary to protect the working of the railways for the purposes of the war, and you should at once put yourself into communication with the Officer in Command and act in co-operation with him.[125]

In all, there were 50,000 infantry available. However, in the event there was little disorder, and the press and public were hostile to the strike which soon collapsed.[126]

During a total war, therefore, even with universal male conscription imposed from early 1916 onwards, thus enormously diversifying the composition of the armed forces, the use of the military in industrial troubles remained a possibility. It was held to be a clear option by the government in terms of both maintaining social order and running essential services.

By the end of the First World War no great progress had been achieved in gaining a unified police response to the perceived nation-wide challenge of labour. The Home Office had put pressure on local authorities to enter into mutual-aid agreements, and build up their reserves. New centralizing links between the Home Office and the police had been developed during the war. Nevertheless, as a leading Home Office official put it in 1919, the power of his department over the provincial police was 'the same as it was at the beginning'. Local autonomy remained an abiding obstacle,

[125] HO 158/21 (346, 578/9), 24 Sept. 1918.

[126] CAB 23/7 WC 477, 25 Sept. 1918. In fact the only troops to be moved were a battalion to Newport, South Wales.

while police loyalty itself was suspect. This helped give the armed forces a continued, prominent role in law enforcement.

During the nineteenth century the police had been under local control, and this was a situation encouraged by the government. With the onset of national labour disputes it urged local police authorities to collaborate in putting down disorder. But the Home Office had limited leverage over the local police. The police grant amounted to half the cost of police pay and clothing, and that was all. The Home Secretary could circularize the police advising them about the wishes of the government.

In 1912 it was acknowledged in parliament that the Home Secretary had 'an authority which has gradually grown up . . . of giving advice to the local authorities of the country'. But it was exceedingly difficult to ensure that this 'advice' was heeded over such questions as the formation of police reserves or mutual aid agreements. In addition, when chiefs of police in counties, with their greater freedom of manoeuvre, took their own initiative in summoning police for mutual aid, in the new climate of industrial tension questions arose about the borderline between the enforcement of law and order and the logistical issues involved in the management of police resources. The latter were certainly felt to be matters of local political concern and financial control.

Throughout the period the *Police Review* waged a campaign on behalf of the police rank and file for the repeal of the County Police Act of 1839 which conferred autocratic powers on county chief constables. In addition, there were demands from the county council members for standing joint committees in counties to be placed on the same footing as watch committees in boroughs, and to be made accountable to the county council for their actions in police management. Political pressures were being brought to bear on police organization.

In these changed circumstances the prerogative of the government to control the armed forces had been revived. This meant that troops became the major arm of the state in reinforcing the police with the resulting lack of democratic control this brought. The scale and frequency of the use of troops, with violent incidents as in the 1911 rail stoppage, deeply permeated public discussion of the labour unrest of the time. It became a focus of bitter controversy by the TUC and the Labour Party which spoke of 'Prussianism'. By 1918, indeed, the use of troops to combat strikers was no longer exceptional. Fears raised about the supposed infiltration of Bolshevism made the use of troops all the more probable as the standard response to aggressive action by the unions. The fundamental questions, about the relationships both of the army to the police and of local police forces to the central government, still remained to be explored and answered in the turbulent atmosphere of labour troubles after the war ended in 1918.

4

Police Organization and the Anti-strike Machinery, 1919–1922

AN explosive situation faced the Lloyd George government after the war, with a fear of widespread strikes in many industries. The threat of the Triple Alliance loomed ominously. The imminence of revolution was ever-present in the minds of the government and civil service. Furthermore, since the growth of wartime collectivism, the government itself rather than individual capitalists was largely in control of industry. Pressure from labour, therefore, could easily resolve itself into direct confrontation between unions and government. The police force was much depleted and, as has been seen, its morale was somewhat uncertain. The number of available troops was diminished by overseas commitments, while the loyalty of conscript soldiers could also not be taken for granted. Thus in 1919 the government, faced with the prospect of major national strikes, was confronted with the dilemma of precisely how the forces of law and order would be brought to bear effectively to cope with threatening industrial unrest.

Most military chiefs now hoped that troops would not be used on a massive scale in policing duties as they had been before 1914. They believed that the use of troops in aid of the civil power had got quite out of hand in the pre-war years and had strained constitutional conventions. At the same time, heated debates were taking place within the House of Commons and even in the Lloyd George Cabinet itself about the propriety of using troops to deal with industrial disturbances, even assuming that there were enough troops to go round given Britain's many international commitments and obligations at the time. The government always insisted publicly that it was the police and local authorities who were responsible for the maintenance of law and order. The armed forces should be called upon only as a final resort when all other means had failed. The war was over and the vaunted 'land fit for heroes' was to be policed by a civilian force alone. However, the reality as far as industrial unrest was concerned was radically different. The police often acted with a large military force to back them up. The tension of post-war industrial disputes was heightened by renewed military intervention, as events were to demonstrate.

The first example came in Glasgow. In January 1919 the Clydeside Shop Stewards Committee joined forces with the trade-union leaders to demand a forty-hour week to absorb the potentially unemployed after demobilization.[1] The government became deeply alarmed at the prospect of widespread disorder. The Commander-in-Chief of the Armed Forces in Britain, General Sir William Robertson, was ordered by the Cabinet to prepare his troops to assist the civil power in the event of a national strike of revolutionary character.[2] While volunteers could be found to run the essential municipal services, they had to be protected from the possibility of attack from supporters of the strike. The police forces, although depleted, were all said to be loyal, while the Secretary of State for Scotland, Munro, suggested that 2,000 special constables should be brought in to assist.[3] A mass meeting of some 30,000 strikers took place in George Square, Glasgow, on 31 January. Here a confrontation took place between them and the police, following the stoppage of the tramcar service on the south side of the square. The police drew their batons and made several charges; about forty people were injured in the mêlée.[4] The War Cabinet met that afternoon and Munro declared that the situation in Glasgow was more in the nature of 'a Bolshevist rising' than an ordinary strike. The following morning nineteen infantry battalions arrived in the city and six tanks were stationed in the cattle market. Soldiers with fixed bayonets guarded the railway station and patrolled the streets. The strike now quickly collapsed.[5]

Even so the situation which developed in Glasgow highlighted the weakness of the regular forces of law and order should a major riot have occurred. The police force was strained to the limit. The troops available were mainly second- and third-line units, many of them physically unfit; most of them were untrained in the discipline required should they encounter resistance from strikers. In addition, this strike seemed likely to attract support from other

[1] For a full account see McLean, *Legend*, pp. 121–38.
[2] CAB 23/9 WC 522, 30 Jan. 1919.
[3] Ibid.
[4] McLean, *Legend*, pp. 125–7.
[5] CAB 23/9 WC 523, 31 Jan. 1919; McLean, *Legend*, p. 126.

trade unions and the fear of a general stoppage was omnipresent. Alarm spread throughout the government. Ministers were now determined that, when the expected big strike came, it would be on ground chosen by the government,[6] and to prepare anti-strike machinery with this eventuality in mind. Churchill, recently appointed Secretary of State for War, instructed General Headquarters Great Britain (GHQGB) to 'prepare a complete scheme and organization of Military Forces throughout the United Kingdom to act in aid of the Civil Power, in the event of a national strike of revolutionary character'.[7]

On 4 February, therefore, the Cabinet appointed an Industrial Unrest Committee 'to make the necessary arrangements for dealing with any situation that might arise from industrial unrest both at the present moment and in the future'.[8] This committee was chaired by Edward Shortt, the Coalition Liberal Home Secretary. It consisted also of Stanley, the President of the Board of Trade, Horne, the Minister of Labour, Munro, the Secretary of State for Scotland, and representatives of the War Office and the Admiralty: law and order was one of its central priorities. It appointed five sub-committees to deal with the public utility services, transport, protection, communications, and electrical works. Inter-departmental arrangements were made with the Ministry of Food and the Coal Control Department to ensure the maintenance of essential services.[9] It was agreed in the Cabinet that the army and navy should play a major role in the maintenance of essential services.[10] The contingency plans involved the co-ordination of the police, the military, and civil administration at both regional and national levels to cope with the threat of future industrial unrest.[11] Sub-committee C, which was responsible for protection and the maintenance of order, was the one which specifically involved police and troops. Its membership varied according to the subject under discussion, but included the Commissioner of the Metropolitan

[6] CAB 23/9 WC 524, 3 Feb. 1919.

[7] Churchill to Lloyd George, 25 Sept. 1919; M. Gilbert, *Winston S. Churchill: Companion Volume IV* (1977), part 2, p. 881. Also CAB 23/9 WC 511 GT 6997, 'Use of Troops during the Threatened Strike', memo by Home Secretary, 18 Mar. 1919.

[8] CAB 23/9 WC 525, 4 Feb. 1919; CAB 27/59, explanatory note on Industrial Unrest Committee.

[9] CAB 27/59, ibid.

[10] CAB 23/9 WC 526, 4 Feb. 1919

[11] K. Jeffery and P. Hennessy, *States of Emergency: British Governments and Strike Breaking since 1919* (1983), 11.

Police and representatives of the War Office, the Railway Executive Committee, and the Scottish Office. The terms of reference were: 'To consider the arrangements for protecting during a strike 1) workmen who do not join the strike, 2) substituted labour employed at essential works or in transport, 3) stores of food and fuel and other vulnerable points, and, generally, the measures for the maintenance of public order.' During the first half of March 1919 the committee discussed such matters as the availability of naval and military personnel for protection duty, the ports and essential rail and road routes for the unloading and transporting of bulk food supplies, and the protection of large food stores and convoys of vehicles.[12]

The reconstitution of the Triple Alliance in February 1919 was a formidable challenge, and a further powerful reason for stepping up contingency planning for a general strike. On 18 February and 7 March a number of chief officers of police were called to a conference at the Home Office at which the government's general plans were explained and the local arrangements which might be made in the event of a strike by the Alliance were discussed.[13] When a general transport strike threatened soon after, the Home Office now circularized chiefs of police about such matters as the protection of convoys and the necessity for keeping open main routes of supply. They were instructed to issue daily reports to the Home Office about the strike situation in their areas. Military aid should only be requisitioned as a last resort.[14] This was mere window-dressing. On 25 March the Cabinet agreed that, in the event of large-scale strike action, the military authorities could decide where, and when, the troops should be used, and without having a requisition from a magistrate; the 1911 railway strike was cited as a precedent.[15]

Indeed, a key role was prepared for the military in the major post-war strikes. Their loyalty in industrial disputes had been confirmed at the end of January, when a secret circular had been issued by the military authorities asking commanding officers whether their men would assist in strike-breaking, where they stood in relation to trade unionism, and how they would respond

[12] Dixon, 'The Home Office', p. 237.
[13] Ibid.
[14] HO 158/20 (377, 100/56), 21 Mar. 1919.
[15] CAB 23/9 WC 551, 25 Mar. 1919.

to orders for assistance to preserve the peace. It was found that, although most were hostile to the idea of strike-breaking, the answer to the last question was affirmative and that troops would protect property and persons.[16]

The expected strike by the Triple Alliance, in the spring of 1919, did not, in fact, take place, much to the relief of the government. The Industrial Unrest Committee continued to rely on the army to provide adequate protection. By July 1919 it had worked out a scheme, in conjunction with Field Marshal Haig, the Commander-in-Chief of the Armed Forces, for the priority of services to be protected by the military in the event of a Triple Alliance strike.[17] The principal requirement was a sufficiently mobile armed force distributed so as to be available in any place where revolution or riot might arise. Assuming that such a reserve was provided, the second requirement was that docks where food was to be loaded and unloaded and the main lines of food supply were to be protected. The third was that road convoys be protected and the fourth that mines be preserved.[18] The navy too was ready to assist the civil power in the maintenance of order and the protection of vulnerable points. It was said to have 1,200 marines at Portsmouth who could be moved by sea to any point to be drawn on by the military authorities. The Royal Air Force had undertaken to co-operate with the military and was available for reconnaissance and communication purposes.[19] If these resources proved insufficient, forces would even be brought back from the Expeditionary Force in continental Europe.

There were many objections to this dependence on the military. Soldiers disliked acting in aid of the civil power, and the government feared their use would arouse much opposition. However, there seemed to be no alternative as the government had little influence over the provincial police to ensure an effective response to an emergency. Police numbers were much depleted after the war, but, even if there had been an adequate police force to meet threatened industrial unrest, another vital problem that now

[16] *Parl. Deb.*, 5th ser., 116, 1469–514 (29 May 1919).

[17] CAB 27/59, explanatory note on Industrial Unrest Committee.

[18] Protection Sub-committee memo. drawn up to show the present position of the country in relation to the emergency which would arise in the event of a national strike, 20 July 1919: Thomas Jones Papers, Class C, Vol. 5 (National Library of Wales, Aberystwyth).

[19] Ibid.

emerged was recurring trouble within the ranks of the police force itself. The government anticipated a general police strike by the spring of 1919 as part of the industrial turbulence of the time.

Despite the settlement with the Metropolitan Police in September 1918, Lloyd George had refused to recognize NUPPO during wartime. The Metropolitan Police, however, did gain a Representative Board set up to represent members of the force in matters connected with conditions of service and general welfare other than discipline. It was to be elected annually among all officers and men below the rank of chief inspector, and an executive committee was also to be elected. Members of the police were not prevented from being members of NUPPO so long as such a Union did not attempt to interfere with the regulations and discipline of the Service or to induce members of the force to withhold their services. If such an event should occur, the members of the force would be called upon to sever their connections with it.[20] As a result, union membership was boosted from 10,000 in August to 50,000 in November 1918, representing perhaps five-sixths of the police forces of the country.[21] Officials of NUPPO then proceeded to take over the executive committee to the newly established Representative Board. This aroused much apprehension. General Macready, who had succeeded Sir Edward Henry as Commissioner of the Metropolitan Police after the strike of August 1918, told Lloyd George that the formal recognition of NUPPO was impossible 'if the country is to have an efficient body of police on whom the authorities can absolutely rely'.[22]

Meanwhile, in January, members of the executive of the Representative Board put forward demands for union recognition and increases in pay. Another strike was feared; Macready took the precautionary step of arranging for troops to occupy ninety key police stations in London should any strike occur.[23] The Labour *Daily Herald* commented:

> There is only one thing which really worries our rulers. . . . That is the fact that the police are no longer to be depended upon as a weapon of capitalism. The police are now enrolled with their fellow workers in the Trade Union movement. Their Union has just put forward a programme of

[20] *Police Review*, 20 Sept. 1918
[21] *Prison Officers' Magazine*, Nov. 1918
[22] Macready, *Annals*, ii. 348.
[23] Ibid. ii. 333.

which the most important item is the demand for recognition. So important is it that the press are busily engaged in proving that it is impossible. . . . They say that the police are a semi-military body and that it is unthinkable that such a body should have its union recognized.[24]

Confronted with this crisis in the law-enforcement system, Shortt urged the Cabinet at the end of January that there should be an impartial inquiry into the whole question of police pay and conditions.[25] In March 1919, therefore, a committee was set up under Lord Desborough to inquire into methods of recruitment, conditions of service, rates of pay, pensions, and allowances for the police forces in England, Wales, and Scotland. Its findings were to have very considerable significance for the future.

In the interim the Cabinet decided in March that NUPPO should not be given formal recognition, and this was now announced in the press.[26] At the same time new Representative Boards were created for the four main grades of Metropolitan Police—constables, sergeants, inspectors and superintendents, and chief inspectors. As the NUPPO executive mainly consisted of constables, its power was reduced at a stroke.[27] However, NUPPO itself seemed even more menacing now. At the end of March it altered its constitution. The rule which forbade strike action was reformulated, and a strike was now made permissible if a two-thirds majority in favour was obtained.[28] NUPPO had become affiliated both to the London Trades Council and to the TUC, while Marston, one of its leading executive members, was appointed to the joint committee of unions and management at the National Industrial Conference.[29] In April one of the union's officials. Constable Spackman, was dismissed from the Metropolitan Police for advising policemen to boycott the new Representative Board, and strike action now seemed likely.[30] The *Daily Herald* reported on 28 May that the large majority of police had voted for a strike.

The Cabinet's reaction, of course, was one of intense anxiety. Shortt warned his colleagues of the 'firebrands in the Force who

[24] *Daily Herald*, 1 Feb. 1919. The membership of NUPPO was said to have been organized in 200 branches in Jan. 1919 (*The Times*, 25 Jan. 1919).

[25] CAB 23/9 WC 524, meeting of 3 Feb. 1919.

[26] CAB 23/9 WC 544, meeting of 13 Mar. 1919; *Daily Herald*, 22 Mar. 1919.

[27] Macready, *Annals*, ii. 352–4.

[28] Allen, *Trade Unions*, p. 139.

[29] *Daily Herald*, 9 Aug. 1919.

[30] Allen, 'The National Union', p. 139.

were working with confessed Bolsheviks' and bringing pressure to bear on the union's policy. Special Branch men were therefore detailed to spy and report on their police colleagues.[31] Before the result of the strike ballot was known, the Home Secretary announced in the House of Commons that the police would be given substantial pay increases retrospective from 1 April.[32] On 29 May, Macready's May Order spelt out for every officer in the force the consequences of industrial action—instant dismissal and loss of pension rights. The policemen were reminded that, as they were not workmen in the terms of the Trade Disputes Act 1906, they could not claim legal protection and had no right to picket. NUPPO officials remained defiant, but they did admit that a government announcement about pay increases took much of the steam out of the demand for a strike. There was also the certainty of military intervention. Finally, it was agreed that a strike be postponed.[33] On 6 June, with the endorsement of the Labour Party, Shortt announced in the Commons that proposals had been worked out for an organization of the police to be managed by themselves to safeguard their own interests. When this organization was completed, all serving police officers would be called upon either to leave NUPPO or else face dismissal.[34] The Police Bill, based on the recommendations of the Desborough Committee and incorporating Shortt's proposed pay concessions, was introduced on 8 July. The government's position now seemed to be unassailable.

Nevertheless, there continued to be immense alarm in government circles, especially when the NUPPO executive now called for a police strike on 31 July. Work would not be resumed until the clause in the Police bill prohibiting the union was withdrawn. The strike this time proved to be more nation-wide than the previous August, with the key centre of unrest on Merseyside. The government now put its anti-strike measures into operation. The navy was requisitioned and on 2 August the battleship *Valiant*, together with the destroyers *Venomous* and *Whitley*, left Scapa Flow and sailed for the Mersey. Nine hundred troops were drafted into the

[31] CAB 23/15 WC 571 A, minutes of meeting held 27 May 1919; Critchley, *History*, p. 188.

[32] *Parl. Deb.*, 5th ser., 116, 1225 (28 May 1919).

[33] Allen, 'The National Union', p. 140.

[34] CAB 23/10 WC 577, 6 June 1919; *Parl. Deb.*, 5th ser., 116, 2487–99 (6 June 1919).

city and 730 special constables were enrolled.[35] Sacking and violence took place in Liverpool in the absence of police. Troops and those remaining police who had ignored the strike call, CID men, and special constables worked together to suppress disorder. A general strike was called for the city of Liverpool; but it proved difficult to persuade trade unionists that they had anything in common with the police, who had been so closely identified with the owners in previous industrial trouble. In addition, many were not in favour of a trade union for the police. Pitched battles ensued between police and troops and rioters, and on 3 August the last man to be shot dead by a soldier acting in support of the civil power in England and Wales was killed, and the Riot Act read for the last time. Although a band of looters and plunderers went wild over the Bank Holiday weekend, the few remaining police and troops were able to quell the disturbance by Monday, 4 August.

Sympathetic strikes now took place by drivers and foremen in London and Liverpool.[36] The strike in the country reached its peak on 4 August—1,156 strikers from a force of 18,200 Metropolitan policemen, 58 from 970 in the City of London, 119 from 1,320 in Birmingham, 954 from a force of 1,874 in Liverpool, 114 from 180 in Birkenhead, and 63 from Bootle.[37] The strikers, however, were isolated by the proposals of the Desborough Committee which had been incorporated with the Police Bill now before parliament. A total of 2,365 police strikers were dismissed immediately and never reinstated.[38] NUPPO now disintegrated both financially and organizationally within a number of days.

The Police Bill, incorporating most of the recommendations of Part 1 of the Report of the Desborough Committee on Police Pay and Conditions of Service, received the Royal Assent on 15 August. It radically reshaped the degree of control exercised by central over local government. The Desborough Committee had been a powerful body. It included Desborough himself, Lord Gorell, deputy director of the War Office, F. D. Blake, a Liberal baronet, Henry Craik, a civil servant, James Remnant, a future Tory peer, and two Labour MPs, James Sexton and James O'Grady. Its findings, contained in the first report on 1 July 1919

[35] Reynolds and Judge, *The Night*, pp. 160–2.
[36] *The Times*, 6 Aug. 1919.
[37] Allen, 'The National Union', pp. 142–3.
[38] Ibid.

and a second on 1 January 1920, commanded a good deal of respect and helped defuse a tense and dangerous situation.[39]

The committee claimed that its recommendations were justified because

> The natural development by which police administration has come more and more to be a matter of national rather than purely local concern, makes it . . . desirable that there should be more uniformity in the conditions of service of the Police, and consequently increased supervision and control by the Central Government.[40]

Its first report recommended that the pay and conditions of service of all ranks of the police force should be improved and standardized and placed under the control of the Home Secretary; and that representatives of police authorities, and all ranks of the police service, should be given an opportunity to offer their collective advice before changes were made. A national representative body for the police was to be formed and the

> direct supplementary grant from Imperial Funds which was instituted last year to be increased as from and including the financial year 1918–19 so as to cover at least one half of the cost of the Police, . . . this direct grant to be calculated in each year on the expenditure of that year instead of on the expenditure of the previous year.[41]

In its second report, issued in 1920, the Desborough Committee variously recommended that a police department in the Home Office be created to cope with its new responsibilities, and that the number of constabulary inspectors be increased from two to three. The Home Secretary should have the power to approve the appointment and dismissal of all chief constables, and to prescribe standard terms and conditions on which police should be lent from one force to another. Constables should have power to act in other areas without being sworn in; all ranks should have the right of appeal against an order of dismissal; all separate police forces in non-county boroughs in England and Wales with under 50,000 population should be merged in the county forces; standard

39 *Report of the Committee on the Police Service, England, Wales and Scotland*, Part I, PP 1919 [Cmd. 253], xxvii, 709; *Report of the Committee on the Police Service*, Part II, PP 1920 [Cmd. 574], xxii, 539; *Parl. Deb.*, 5th ser., 117, 1621 (8 July 1919); ibid. 119, 1836 (15 Aug. 1919).

40 PP 1920 [Cmd. 574], xxii, 563.

41 PP 1919 [Cmd. 253], xxvii, 727. On these financial aspects, see Appendix Table 4 below.

conditions of service for all forces should be prescribed by the Home Office; while powers of appointment, promotion, and discipline should be placed in the hands of chief constables in boroughs as well as in counties. Uniform should be standardized by the Home Office, and no chief constable should be appointed without previous police experience save in exceptional circumstances. Its recommendations, therefore, covered all the major aspects of the organization of the force.

The Police Act 1919 empowered the Home Secretary to make 'regulations as to the government, mutual aid, pay, allowances, pensions, clothing, expenses and conditions of service of the members of all police forces within England and Wales'. The Act also contained the important reservation that such regulations should only be made after consultation with a council of representatives of local authorities and various ranks of the service (the Police Council). The Exchequer grant, which until 1918 had only covered half the cost of pay and clothing, was put permanently on a new footing: the Exchequer now was to pay for half of the whole cost of the police. The Act made industrial relations history when it provided for the organization of a national representative body for the lower ranks of the service to be called the Police Federation. It went on not only to prohibit policemen from joining a trade union, but to make it a criminal offence to induce a policeman to strike. Thus, while inaugurating the Police Federation, it killed the embryo police union stone dead.

Indeed, the recommendations of the Desborough Committee, the Police Act, and the regulations made by the Home Secretary which followed it, attempted to end the isolation and separatism which were the major features of the nineteenth-century police force. There now followed successively the foundation of the Police Council, the Police Federation, the introduction of standardized and greatly increased rates of pay, and the establishment of F Division as a branch of the Home Office (under A. L. Dixon) to deal with the whole range of police administration and problems. Inspection now became more searching, and began to penetrate systematically into all aspects of county and borough police work. Borough head constables were now designated 'chief constable' and no person without previous experience or qualification was to be appointed to this post in either boroughs or counties; these appointments had to be approved by the Home

Secretary. In effect, all these provisions, together with the new police grant and the constant flow of circulars, dramatically increased Home Office control over the administration and conditions of service of the provincial police and opened up a new era for the police service as a whole.

The links between the Home Office and the provincial police were now reinforced in a positive fashion. After Desborough, the Police Federation was set up to enable members of the police rank and file to bring before the authorities, local and national, 'all matters affecting their welfare and efficiency other than questions of promotion affecting individuals'. Branch boards were established in each force for the three ranks of constable, sergeant, and inspector, and they were permitted to combine into joint branch boards, with central committees of each rank elected annually. The three central committees could meet as one and submit representations direct to the Home Secretary.[42] At least the rudiments of consultative democracy now existed.

Far more important were the new links established between the Home Office and chief constables. District conferences of county and borough chief constables had already been instituted during the war in 1918, with a central conference to which each sent delegates, sitting under the chairmanship of the Home Secretary. At its fourth meeting in December 1920 these central conferences of chief constables attained permanent form. Shortt proposed 'that in future these conferences should be the recognised channel through which collective representations may be made to him by chief constables, not only on matters of their executive duties, but on pay, pensions, allowances . . . and the police service generally'.[43] These conferences were to meet twice yearly, and became an important medium by which chief constables gained a voice in policy-making. Another factor was the role of the inspectors of constabulary. The inspectors were invariably drawn from the ranks of chief constables, and this became an important element in ensuring that the views of the latter prevailed at the Home Office. Inspectors of constabulary were creatures of the system, protective of the administration, and never publishing detailed critical reports of individual chief constables. A typical

[42] Critchley, *History*, pp. 194–5.

[43] Copy of Minutes of Fourth Meeting of the Central Conference of Chief Constables, June 1920 (HO 45/17913/400508).

case was Sir Leonard Dunning, former head constable of Liverpool, who became a highly influential inspector in 1912 and served for much of the inter-war period. Major General Sir Llewelyn Atcherley was another. He had been chief constable of Shropshire, then chief constable of the West Riding of Yorkshire, and he served as inspector of constabulary between 1919 and 1936.

Far from curbing the autocratic powers of the county chiefs of police—which many of the rank and file of the police force themselves had pressed for in the pre-war years—the militaristic character of county policing was left untouched, as was the historic association of the county chief constables with the magistrates. There was no mention of reforming the composition or status of the standing joint committee, which continued in its position of independence from the county council, and answerable to no body for the few powers it exercised. In fact, a Home Office witness before the Desborough Committee went so far as to urge that 'if boroughs are now going to be put very much on the same footing as counties with regard to finance . . . it would be a very good thing to have the Watch Committee a Joint Committee of half Town Councillors and half magistrates'.[44] This suggestion was not taken up. In fact a major blow to Home Office plans seemed to have occurred when the Desborough Committee's recommendations that chiefs of police in boroughs be endowed with the same powers of appointment, promotion, and discipline as their county counterparts failed because of opposition from local municipal authorities.[45] Nevertheless, the position of the borough chief constables was significantly strengthened against their police authorities in the coming years.

Legal theory was now brought in to build up the government's claims. From this time on the Home Office began to popularize the theme that the keeping of the King's Peace was 'a Royal prerogative as old as the monarchy itself'. It was a doctrine that further helped to erode police accountability. Ultimate responsibility for the police fell on the Home Secretary, who exercised 'a general controlling and coordinating authority over the whole country'. Constables were associated specifically with the enforcement and

[44] *Report of the Committee on the Police Service, England, Wales and Scotland, Minutes of Evidence*, PP 1920 [Cmd. 874], xxii. 1056, evidence of H. B. Simpson.
[45] Critchley, *History*, pp. 197–8.

interpretation of the law rather than with political control. Dunning had told the Desborough Committee in 1919 of the 'popular misconceptions' existing about the duties, powers, and legal status of the constable.

He is not . . . an agent of the government, exercising powers derived from that fact, but is a citizen, appointed from, among and by his fellow citizens, and he exercises powers which are possessed . . . by his fellow citizens, . . . not given by the Common Law to him as a constable, but are given to the citizen. . . . The citizen is still bound, at the direction of the magistrate, or on the appeal of the constable, to take his part in the preservation of the peace.[46]

While the Home Secretary at first proceeded cautiously, it soon became clear that the provisions of the Police Act were a direct blow to city and borough police authorities, many of whom had in 1919 a Labour majority among their membership for the first time. They sensed that the new Home Office Regulations would transfer powers previously exercised by them to the chief constables in some respects, and to the Home Secretary in others.[47] In addition, and just as important as the Regulations, Home Office circulars sent to police authorities and chief constables carried much more weight than they had done before 1914, simply because of the increased power of central government. They proved to be one of the chief ways in which the process of the co-ordination of police activity was ensured. As well as securing co-operation between forces, vital at times of industrial emergency, they were also used to give details about new duties, or to remind forces about existing duties frequently imposed upon the police by statute. They were aimed at establishing a common policy with regard to the enforcement of the law of the land. These circulars were couched in terms of 'advice'. But they were always regarded as 'instructions' and rarely disobeyed. As Sir Leonard Dunning, now one of the inspectors of constabulary, pointed out in 1929:

The fact that the Home Office has apparently no definite power to make such regulations is immaterial because anything, call it regulation, instruction, advice or what you will, circulated by the Home Office would be accepted without question and when adopted by the local Police

[46] PP 1920 [Cmd. 874], xxii. 665, evidence of L. Dunning. An important case taking the principle of the independent status of the policeman still further was that of *Fisher* v. *Oldham Corporation* 1930, discussed below, p. 143.

[47] *Police Review*, 1 Oct. 1920.

Authority would become an order, disobedience of which would be punishable under the disciplinary code.[48]

Police authorities were said to attach great importance to these circulars and effect was 'invariably given to the views therein expressed'.[49]

The government's acceptance of such far-reaching proposals as those of the Desborough Committee did significantly affect the position of the provincial police forces in relation to the central government. After the Police Act of 1919, outside the metropolis the position remained that the local authority was responsible for the efficiency of the police, while the responsibility for police action was shared by chief constables and magistrates. But this was subject to three important factors: (1) the Home Secretary's Police Regulations, which aimed to secure a high degree of uniformity in conditions of service and in duties; (2) a supervision of administration by the Home Office exercised through its inspectors; (3) a constant flow of Home Office advice as to duties, based on the collective wisdom of police authorities and officers, the inspectors, and the administrative officers of the department. All these implied a growing central direction from Whitehall.

The supreme test of these enhanced powers of the Home Office and the police had yet to come in the post-war period. In 1919 the industrial situation continued to deteriorate, and the threat of major national strikes harrassed the government.

In the autumn of 1919 a serious industrial crisis broke out with very little warning—'as a thief in the night', as Lloyd George wrote to his wife. This was the national railway strike which began on 27 September and was rightly regarded by the government as a crisis of unprecedented magnitude which would paralyze the economy. The Cabinet declared it was 'going to be fought with the full resources of the community'.[50] Just before the strike chief constables had been circularized by the Home Office that requisitions for troops should, as usual, only be made in the last resort. They were instructed to keep the Home Office informed of the strike in

[48] *Report of the Royal Commission on Police Powers and Procedure*, ii. *Minutes of Evidence, Part I* (HMSO 1929), p. 61.

[49] Inspector W. Jones, 'The Scope and Functions of Local and Central Control in Police Administration', *Police Journal*, 5 (1932), 525.

[50] Lloyd George to Mrs Lloyd George, 26 Sept. 1919 (printed in *Lloyd George Family Letters, 1885–1936* ed. K. O. Morgan (1973), 190); *The Times*, 29 Sept. 1919.

their areas, especially with regard to outbreaks of disorder, the arrival or departure of requisitioned troops, and any change in the general situation. These intelligence reports were to be communicated to the Home Office by telegraph or telephone.[51] Special constables should be enrolled and an official appeal in the press was now made, inviting volunteers for this force. However, as soon as the strike broke out, Haig's emergency plan for the use of troops was at once initiated. Thirteen battalions and three cavalry regiments were moved to key rail centres. In all 23,000 troops were called out, mostly for furnishing small guards and detachments for the protection of convoys, while a further 16,000 were held back in barracks as a mobile reserve, and seventy-three battalions and three cavalry regiments were held in reserve by Commands and at GHQ.[52] Little disorder of any kind had yet occurred.

The military commanders were very reluctant to use their forces in a policing role, and the politicians feared that the widespread use of troops might inflame passions. On 30 September chiefs of police were now telegraphed by the Home Office to report at once on the strike situation with regard to the state of feeling among the strikers, the state of feeling among the workers, particularly as to the prospect of sympathetic action, and the state of public feeling as to the strike. The replies to this circular indicated that there was less and less support for the strike among the railwaymen. On 2 October, after a meeting at the Home Office of Churchill, the Secretary of State for War, Shortt, the Home Secretary, and Haig, the Commander-in-Chief of the Armed Forces, the attention of the Strike Committee (which had replaced the Industrial Unrest Committee before the strike began) was called to the need to build up the special constables 'so as to relieve the military as far as possible from furnishing detached guards'.[53] However, so far the response to the call for special constables had been disappointing and a new development in the history of law enforcement now took place. The Cabinet Strike Committee decided that it was essential to set up a new organization to be called the 'Citizen

[51] Civil Disturbances and the Employment of the Military in Aid of the Police (notes for the use of chief constables), Aug. 1919 (HO 158/21 (257,009/13), 9 Sept. 1919).

[52] Haig to Secretary of State for War, 17 Oct. 1919 (WO 32/5467); Dixon, 'The Home Office', p. 240.

[53] CAB 27/61 SC 79, 2 Oct. 1919.

Guard'. Its purpose was to 'meet all contingencies and to relieve the military force as far as possible'. This force was to be recruited locally by military and naval personnel but would be sworn in as special constables and placed under the control of chief constables.[54] An appeal to enrol was made to all citizens on 4 October. However, no particular thought had been given to what the difference might be between these Citizen Guards and the special constabulary. The new title seems to have been chosen because it was 'believed that this name would prove a stimulus to recruiting'.[55] Although 70,000 were said to have enrolled by 5 October, the railway dispute was settled the same day, and the force then disbanded almost as soon as it had come into existence.

After the railway strike Lloyd George and the Cabinet were briefly in a mood of euphoric self-congratulation. The rapid settlement of the strike was seen as a powerful tribute to their anti-strike organization, and to the role of both police and troops within it.[56] It should be noted, however, that the strike had taken place at a relatively favourable time for the government. Protection of key centres was much facilitated by circumstances; more troops were available in Britain than for many months past (or than would be in the future after demobilization).

In the autumn of 1919 emergency planning procedures were kept actively in being. The Cabinet's Strike Committee was replaced on 20 October by Eric Geddes's Supply and Transport Committee (STC) which continued in existence until 1921. It would concentrate on the enrolment of volunteers to maintain essential services in an emergency, and on building up an emergency infrastructure. Without doubt, the industrial crisis was very far from over after the railway strike. Above all, in the angry aftermath of the Sankey Commission on the mining industry and the government's refusal to nationalize the mines, there remained the supreme problem of living with the MFGB. Until the threat of strikes or major stoppages in the mining industry had been met, the government's plans would remain uncertain as to their effectiveness.

[54] CAB 27/77 TSC 22, Appendix B, proposed formation of Citizen Guard to assist Police.

[55] Jeffery and Hennessy, *States of Emergency*, p. 19.

[56] CAB 27/77 TSC 22, Special report by the chairman of the Protection Subcommittee submitted in accordance with the decision of the War Cabinet of 14 Oct. 1919.

A major setback to governmental planning followed. The Army High Command now wanted troops to be used to aid the civil power only as a last resort under the common law, not in a policing role as they had been during the major post-war strikes: the police strike, and the railway strike. To Haig and other senior military officials at GHQGB and the War Office, one moral to be drawn from the rail strike was that it had afforded clear proof of the inadequacy of the police. In a succession of post-war strikes, 'with the exception of London the police forces throughout the country were insufficient to cope with a new condition of things'.[57] As a result, military and naval personnel had been employed on duties that were quite inappropriate for them—for instance, the use of naval ratings to pump out mines in South Yorkshire during a strike there in July 1919, and the guarding of railway lines and installations during the railway strike. The Citizen Guards should thus be built up to relieve the armed forces of these unsuitable duties.[58]

The War Office now firmly believed in the value of a part-time—and largely civilian—body to reinforce the police at times of unrest. A Citizen Guard would reduce the likelihood of small bodies of troops being scattered throughout the country, and often being used in a policing role. Shortly after the end of the railway strike, the Quartermaster-General, Sir Travers Clarke, recirculated a memorandum on the distribution of troops, the paper going first to Sir George Macdonagh, the Adjutant-General, who was formally responsible for duties in aid of the civil power. This paper laid down:

> We have not merely greatly strained the military machine but the British Constitution as well. We should insist on the Home Office doing its own work. . . . It is only when the civil power has been proved powerless to carry out this work that the military should be called in. Nothing could be worse both for the Army & for the State than than it should be supposed that the former is being maintained for the purpose of coercing the latter. I am of opinion that we ought not to keep up large forces in the UK for the purpose of dealing with civil disturbance. . . . If in any district the civil forces should prove insufficient, such troops as are available should reinforce them, but it will be a bad day for the Empire if the Government of this country has to look to the bayonets of its troops for its support.[59]

57 Haig to Secretary of State for War, 17 Oct. 1919 (WO 32/5467/1A).
58 Ibid.
59 Macdonagh to DCIGS, 13 Oct. 1919 (WO 32/5611).

Soon after this, the Secretary of State for War agreed in principle to the return of all troops in Britain to their peacetime stations and to break up the civil disturbance staff at GHQGB.[60] Thus the War Office was attempting to limit its liabilities to the civil power.

A vital aid for the successful breaking of the railway strike by the government had been the intelligence reports received from various sources. The Strike Committee received such reports throughout the country both about the way in which the machinery for the distribution of essential supplies was functioning, and also on the mood of labour.[61] The Special Branch, under the direction of Sir Basil Thomson, from the newly established Home Office Directorate of Intelligence, sent in somewhat lurid weekly reports on revolutionary organizations throughout the length and breadth of the United Kingdom. In May 1919 the Special Branch had been given a co-ordinating role over intelligence collection and made independent of the CID. Thomson himself was given the title of 'Director of Intelligence'.[62] The most important body to date uncovering information about labour unrest was the Intelligence Organization at GHQGB, intended to inform the army about the situation in the industrial world. Haig and the Army High Command, however, were deeply hostile to soldiers being used as 'spies'.[63] The army now began to dismantle its intelligence machinery, and in December 1919 the Special Branch took over all the intelligence work conducted by the army into the mood of labour since the start of the year. Troup told the Army Council that intelligence work would now be carried out by Thomson's police organization, and also by chief constables of counties and boroughs. The latter would communicate their information to military officers appointed to receive it, and act as liaison officers with the civil authorities.[64] The intelligence organization at GHQGB would disappear. However, in February 1920 the police themselves were circulated by the Home Office that they should discontinue such inquiries as too much public

[60] Copy of Military Members Meeting Decision, 23 Oct. 1919 (ibid. 17A).

[61] CAB 27/74, STC 23 Oct. 1919–31 July 1920.

[62] For the Special Branch, see R. Deacon, *The History of the Secret Service* (1969); B. Thomson, *Queer People* (1922), and id., *The Scene Changes* (1939); Andrew, *Secret Service*, pp. 224 ff.

[63] Memo. on the Intelligence Organization at GHQGB for dealing with industrial and revolutionary unrest in the United Kingdom, 15 Oct. 1919; cover note by DMI and CIGS, 12 and 18 Nov. 1919 (WO 32/5553).

[64] Troup to War Office, 6 Jan. 1920 (WO 32/5553).

suspicion was aroused. Thomson and the Special Branch were, therefore, left on their own, and Thomson's staff was duly increased to deal with this work.[65] Over the next one-and-a-half years he figured prominently—though often ineffectively—in the governmental response to labour unrest.

Renewed efforts were now made by the Home Office to try to build up the Police Reserve. Chief constables were circularized as to their views about the formation of a Citizen Guard for use in industrial emergencies. On the whole the replies were in the negative. Chiefs of police felt that the formation of such a 'third force' could well be provocative, trade unionists would not join, it would discourage the formation of the special constabulary, and might look like class war.[66] The idea of the Citizen Guards was therefore dropped in favour of strengthening the special constabulary. In December 1919 chief constables were circulated to this effect by the Home Office. They should appoint or retain a sufficient number of able-bodied special constables to serve as the nucleus of an expanded police force. It should be impressed on the public that this was a wholly civil organization, run by the chief constables. Troup reiterated the Home Office and Cabinet view in a letter to Macready in December 1919:

> The government have decided that on the occasion of the next strike the military are not to be used for protection purposes but are to be kept in hand until it is necessary to use them to suppress riot or revolution. The WO are apparently under the impression that we can and should provide half a million trained special constables for protection purposes. . . . The one thing to avoid is the appearance of setting labour and the middle classes against one another.[67]

The left viewed proposals to integrate special constables with the regular police system as highly alarming. The *Merthyr Pioneer*, for example, felt 'These recommendations take away popular control of the police and leave the citizen without appeal save to Whitehall, thus directly menacing the organized labour movement.' The *New Statesman* believed they would 'become a class force intended almost solely for use in labour troubles'. In fact, as before the war,

[65] HO 158/21 (393, 237/8), 27 Feb. 1920; *Parl. Deb.*, 5th Ser., 127, 238 (23 Mar. 1920).

[66] Home Office correspondence with chief constables about Citizen Guard, Oct.–Dec. 1919 (HO 144/1603/390739/1).

[67] Troup to Macready, 21 Dec. 1919 (MEPO 2/1828).

many local authorities, not necessarily Labour-dominated at all but conscious of the cost element, were reluctant to set up either a special constabulary or a mounted police force. This especially applied to borough watch committees. The position had however changed significantly since the passing of the Police Act and the Home Office was now able to apply pressure to get reluctant watch committees to take a more positive view.[68] At the end of 1919 there were said to be 90,000 special constables immediately available; in a serious emergency, about 60,000 more might join. However, as before the war, the special constables were unevenly distributed and their numbers were smallest where they would be needed most.[69] Little confidence was felt in their numbers. Macready himself had warned of the uselessness of special constables. They would in part be drawn from trade unionists and were unlikely to 'risk their whole future by taking part in measures which—to put it baldly—are meant to counteract trade union action.'[70]

In January 1920, with troubles in the mines, docks and elsewhere imminent, the government was in a state of near-panic. The mood of alarm spread and the Cabinet took up the question of protection, and the capability of the army to assist the police in this vital respect. Sir Robert Horne, the Minister of Labour, declared that Bolshevist forces were likely to take action in the event of a miners' strike, 'especially if they were joined by the transport workers'. The railway strike had taken the revolutionaries by surprise; next time they would be geared for action.[71] Sir Henry Wilson recorded that the Cabinet believed 'the police were powerless, that the Citizen Guard had been forbidden by the Unions, & that now the Unions would not allow Special Constables to be sworn & treated them as blacklegs'.[72]

The government, therefore, turned its mind to other, more original, possibilities. A conference of ministers on 16 January 1920 proposed that the 20,000 ex-army officers known to be out of

[68] *Merthyr Pioneer*, 15 May 1920; *Police Review*, 15 Mar. 1920; *New Statesman*, 3 Apr. 1920.

[69] CAB 27/74, STC 23 Oct. 1919–31 July 1921, Home Office memo. TC 33 (measures for protection to be taken in the event of a strike), 24 Dec. 1919.

[70] Macready to Troup, 22 Dec. 1919 (MEPO 2/1828).

[71] CAB 23/35, Conference of Ministers, 18 Jan. 1920.

[72] Wilson's Diary, 15 Jan. 1920, quoted in Jeffery and Hennessy, *States of Emergency*, p. 34.

employment should be mobilized to assist the police.[73] Troup suggested to the STC that a force of temporary volunteers of not less than 10,000 in number should be obtained for a period of six to eight months. It should be armed and available for dispatch anywhere throughout the United Kingdom. It would be organized and controlled as a military force, but not recruited, as the Citizen Guards had been during the railway strike, exclusively from the middle classes.

In the event, however, these new proposals fell flat. Senior army commanders felt there would be numerous difficulties. The ex-officers available would not be of the type required, 'since the best of them have already gone back to their civil occupation and want to stay there'.[74] The Black and Tans in Ireland were to prove a more practicable and immediate use for men in this category. An impasse seemed to have been reached over the forces to provide protection should a major strike occur. The Home Office view was now voiced by Troup. He wrote:

> The weakness arises not from any failure on the part of the civil authorities—the police are stronger and the special constabulary better organized and more capable of expansion than before—but because the Army is so reduced that it cannot give the support which it has given in every big strike since 1911.[75]

Faced with the weakness of the civil forces and their obvious inability to meet the expected revolution, the Chief of Imperial General Staff (CIGS), Sir Henry Wilson, now secretly began to make counter-revolutionary plans. These included a much larger share in internal protection for the army than he had hitherto visualized. He revived Haig's civil emergency plans and worked out a strategy to meet potential revolution. The War Office, however, was prepared for the worst since there were very few troops available in Britain to meet industrial trouble.[76]

Much to the relief of the Home Office and the CIGS, the expected strike by the Triple Alliance in the spring of 1920 did not materialize. But it was felt that it would not be long delayed. On 17

[73] CAB 23/35, Conference of Ministers, 16 Jan. 1920.

[74] Cover note by DMO to DCIGS, 28 Jan. 1920 (WO 32/5467).

[75] CAB 24/96 CP 490, memo. by Troup, 19 Jan. 1920. By March 1920 there were 54,000 police in England and Wales apart from 91,000 special constables; CAB 27/74, report to the Protection Sub-committee by the Home Secretary, 26 Mar. 1920.

[76] Jeffery and Hennessy, *States of Emergency*, pp. 34–5.

August the Cabinet gave its view that the next strike 'might turn out to be the crucial contest with labour', even similar to a state of civil war.[77] The STC reported that there were now only 38 infantry battalions in Britain, as contrasted with 128 during the railway strike in September 1919. It had to be accepted, therefore, that the police, assisted only by special constables, would be primarily responsible for the maintenance of law and order, and for protection purposes.[78] By July 1920 police regulations were in force which made lawful the carrying of guns by policemen under certain conditions, for self-defence. The Firearms Act, which received the Royal Assent on 16 August, enabled weapons to be used by police and civilians in emergencies. In addition, the CIGS and War Office stockpiled rifles and machine guns throughout the land to arm the police and loyalist supporters.[79]

However, when negotiations between the coalowners and the MFGB broke down in August and September, the Supply and Transport Organization was actively prepared. Contrary to the government's previous position, the military were at once brought into the scheme. All drafts of troops were suspended and fourteen infantry battalions brought back from the Rhineland, and from Ireland. Eight hundred officers and men were earmarked to protect power stations and railway installations, while the navy should also be used to protect vulnerable points and maintain essential services.[80] However the wide powers conferred on the government under the Defence of the Realm Regulations to take measures of this nature had now lapsed. The Judge Advocate, General Sir Felix Cassel, had confirmed in the spring of 1920 that 'blacklegging' orders to troops were now illegal, and the Law Officers of the Crown agreed with this opinion.[81] Had these findings become public, the political implications would have been explosive. There was now a need to pass a law replacing DORA's provisions and expressly allowing the government to use troops as blacklegs. Between the spring and autumn of 1920 the

[77] CAB 23/22, 45 (20) Cabinet conclusions, 17 Aug. 1920.

[78] CAB 27/73, TC 13, STC, 2 Sept. 1920.

[79] *Parl. Deb.*, 5th ser., 130, 1790 (21 July 1920); Jeffery and Hennessy, *States of Emergency*, p. 49.

[80] CAB 24/111 CP 1853, memo. by the CIGS, the Internal Situation and Military Precautions, 13 Sept. 1920; Jeffery and Hennessy, *States of Emergency*, p. 50.

[81] CAB 27/74 TC 59, CAB 27/75 TC 87, Neal to Churchill, 15 Mar. 16 Apr. 1920; CAB 24/105 CP 1253, memo. by Worthington-Evans, 11 May 1920; CAB 23/21, 37 (20) Appendix II, Conference of Ministers, 14 June 1920.

government applied itself to preparing a bill, the object of which was to 'give the government full powers to meet a potentially revolutionary situation'.

On 16 October 1920 the MFGB did indeed begin its long-awaited national strike. Two battalions of guards promptly moved from Aldershot to London, while armoured car companies were sent to Scotland, York, and Worcester.[82] On 21 October the railwaymen announced that they, too, would come out on strike in sympathy with the miners if negotiations with the latter were not resumed within three days. Two further battalions of infantry were moved to Liverpool, and tanks to the north of England. Naval ratings would be used to man power stations, and the Admiralty would dispatch a battleship to Liverpool immediately for the purposes of protection if required.[83] Finally, on 22 October an Emergency Powers Bill was presented to the House of Commons by Shortt. Despite criticism from many Labour members, it was rushed through and received the Royal Assent on 29 October. But the miners' strike proved to be generally peaceful. In fact, no public appeal was made for special constables, the regular police coping with such disorder as occurred. A railway strike did not take place. The miners returned to work on 3 November. There had been no need to declare a state of emergency or to use troops on this occasion.

The most important legacy of the strike was the Emergency Powers Act 1920, with its corollary, the Emergency Regulations. It gave the government confidence that it could outface any threatened Triple Alliance strike. It provided for the declaration of a state of emergency to last for one month at any time 'any action has been taken or is immediately threatened by any persons or body of persons of such a nature . . . as to be calculated . . . to deprive the community . . . of the essentials of life'. Under this, the executive was empowered to make any regulations necessary to secure the supply of essential services 'for the preservation of the peace' and 'for any other purposes essential to the public safety and the life of the community'. The government's organization now possessed a legal basis. During the next few months it was to be placed on a sound permanent footing, with both police and troops central to its operation. Another important development

[82] Jeffery and Hennessy, *States of Emergency*, p. 55.
[83] CAB 27/73 TC 20, STC, 22 Oct. 1920.

came on 22 October 1920 when chief constables were informed confidentially of the government's emergency plans, and were given the name of the chief civil commissioner in London and the names of eleven civil commissioners who were the regional officers in the eleven districts into which the country had been divided for the purposes of any emergency. The latter were to assist local authorities in organizing essential local services and to co-ordinate local resources, excluding matters relating to food and the maintenance of law and order.[84]

The major clash for which the government had been preparing came with the miners' strike on 1 April 1921. Even more alarming was the anticipated general strike by the Triple Alliance. The proposals of the coalowners for swingeing wage cuts, following decontrol of the mines, were rejected by the miners. A lock-out began and the MFGB asked the Triple Alliance to come out on strike in sympathy, which it appeared likely to do. On 31 March the STC authorized the Home Secretary to make an immediate proclamation under the Emergency Powers Act: on 1 April the government issued the first set of regulations promulgated under the Act. So far as protection was concerned, the Home Secretary's powers were supplemented in several directions under the Emergency Regulations; so were those of the police. The Home Secretary could now authorize chief constables to prohibit meetings and marches. The police were allowed to arrest without warrant dubious persons and also to search suspected premises. However, no one would be guilty of an offence by reason of his taking part in a strike. The most contentious regulation was one that laid down that the Home Secretary could order the armed forces to perform any service declared to be of vital importance to the community; it materially altered the position of the armed forces in relation to the central state. Although they generated a heated debate in the House of Commons on 5 and 6 April, with much opposition from Liberal and Labour MPs, the regulations passed with a comfortable majority.[85]

The miners' strike precipitated the situation the War Office had predicted for months. There were few troops available, while the position so far as special constables were concerned was little

[84] Dixon, 'The Home Office', p. 242.
[85] *Parl. Deb.*, 5th ser., 140, 129–236 (5 Apr. 1921); ibid., 297–372 (6 Apr. 1921).

better than it had been at the end of 1920 when 93,000 special constables were reported to be available if required in the provinces and 13,600 in the metropolis.[86] The government now prepared for the worst and the use of troops was central to its planning. On 31 March, at a meeting of the Home Secretary with representatives of the Air Ministry, the army, and the navy, the military and naval resources were discussed as were the areas to which the armed forces should be moved in an emergency. If the Triple Alliance initiated a strike, the War Office would move troops around the country for protection duties and the maintenance of essential services.[87] During the first week of the strike urgent measures were taken by the Cabinet with this in mind. Two battalions of troops were brought back by the War Office from Malta, and further troops from the Rhineland. While the Territorial Army was not immediately called up, the Secretary of State for War was instructed to draft legislation to call up the army reserve and consider all steps required to pass it through both Houses of Parliament in a single day, if necessary.[88] Troops, tanks, and armoured cars were concentrated in London, Liverpool, Glasgow, York, and Worcester, while three cavalry regiments and seventeen infantry battalions were moved to London for dispersal around the country.[89]

In spite of this planning for the use of troops on a large scale if a Triple Alliance strike occurred, in fact the 'Coal Only' plans were put into being at the beginning of the strike. The Home Office instructed chief constables as usual that troops were to be requisitioned as a last resort; they should concentrate on the enrolling of special constables. In fact police and special constables kept order; there was little trouble. Chief constables sent daily reports to the Home Office about the state of the strike and public order in their areas. After a week, however, there were numerous causes of local concern for the authorities. As usual, South Wales, with its vast mining work-force, was a critical area. Lindsay, the chief constable of Glamorgan, reported to the Home Office that he had been pressed by the coalowners on 7 April for a central military force to be stationed within the coalfield, as pumping was being prevented

[86] PP 1921 (39), xvi. 39.
[87] CAB 27/73 TC 24, STC 31 Mar. 1921; ibid. TC 25, 1 Apr. 1921.
[88] CAB 23/25, 17 (21): conclusions of meeting of 4 Apr. 1921.
[89] CAB 27/110, conclusions of Internal Protection Sub-committee, 4 Apr. 1921.

in some pits.[90] However, unlike their Scottish counterparts, Welsh coalowners opposed the use of troops or even the extensive use of volunteers for pumping, as this would be provocative and increase local tension.[91]

A significant development now took place which illustrated the increased powers which the Home Secretary could exercise over the provincial police. Shortt made enquiries of chief constables in the more rural areas as to the extent to which they would be able to lend police to chiefs of police in industrial districts.[92] The replies indicated that 350 men had been lent or promised to the West Riding and Glamorgan, about 470 more would be available for further coal-strike service, and 300 for a general strike. Dixon, of the Home Office, noted, 'I have reason to think that if need be a little inducement from the Home Office would bring up some more men'.[93] A Home Office letter was now sent to the deputy chief constable of West Sussex in the following terms:

> I am writing to confirm my message with regard to the situation in Glamorganshire on which I understand you have decided to send 100 men to aid the Glamorganshire force. The position reported to us yesterday was that the strikers had insisted on the stoppage of the pumps at the Glamorgan Colliery which is of vital importance. . . . The miners are reported to be determined: there is every prospect of serious trouble and the chief constable is very anxious to get your men if possible.[94]

The chief constable of West Sussex now assumed responsibility at once for taking a force of 100 of his men to South Wales without waiting for the authorization of his standing joint committee. This action was warmly commended by the Home Office.[95]

However, although these developments had taken place, the use of troops was not abandoned in South Wales. Shortt now agreed that, 'in view of the seriousness of the situation troops should be summoned'. The interaction between the Home Office and the War Office and the General Officers Commanding in Chief (GOCs in C) in this instance is of much interest. The War Office was

[90] Monmouthshire and South Wales Coalowners Association to Lindsay, 7 Apr. 1921 (HO 144/1746/417250/27).

[91] CAB 23/25, 22 (21) Appendix V, Cabinet conclusions, 8 Apr. 1921.

[92] Home Office minute, 7 Apr. 1921 (HO 144/1746/417250/20).

[93] Minute by Dixon, 9 Apr. 1921 (ibid.).

[94] Home Office to deputy chief constable of West Sussex, 9 Apr. 1921 (ibid. 45).

[95] Home Office to chief constable of West Sussex, 18 Apr. 1921 (ibid. 45).

informed that the chief constable of Glamorgan would be requisitioning troops. Further, GOCs were now instructed that troops could be moved in response to requisitions from the civil power at their own discretion without reference to the War Office.[96] The GOC Western Command, however, was very reluctant to allow his troops to be used in a policing role in South Wales. He did dispatch three companies of the Yorkshire and Lancashire Regiment to Cardiff but as 'these troops were not sufficient to enable guards to be placed at the pit heads . . . they would be retained in Cardiff and would stand by there'.[97] Lindsay insisted that troops should be sent to Tonypandy, at the heart of the Rhondda mining community, 'in view of the certainty of serious rioting following the endeavour to start the pumps'.[98] Eventually on 9 April 100 troops were indeed sent to Tonypandy, the Cabinet fearing 'that unless the disturbed areas in South Wales were taken in hand, serious trouble would arise'.[99] The chairman of the Glamorgan Standing Joint Committee, Lieutenant-Colonel Sir Rhys Williams, a Coalition Liberal MP, assured the reluctant Colonel Thompson, the officer in charge, that he would take 'all responsibility for the consequences of moving the troops up to Pontypridd and [he was] satisfied that it would have an excellent effect on the strikers to do so'.[100] It was reported by the Home Office on 11 April:

> The situation is good everywhere in the district. There are large crowds about but everything is quite quiet. Pumping is being carried on at practically all pits except Mardy. . . . The presence of troops at Tonypandy has had an excellent effect and good use has been made of flying squads of police lent from West Sussex and Wiltshire who have been moved about the district a good deal with the result that the miners do not really know how many police are available.[101]

At the same time, miners in Abertillery reaffirmed a previous decision not to allow safety men to operate the pumps in the

96 Minute by Dixon, 8 Apr. 1921 (HO 144/1746/417250/27).
97 CAB 23/25, 22 (21), Appendix VIII, Cabinet conclusions, 9 Apr. 1921.
98 Lindsay to Dixon at Home Office (telegram sent 10.15 a.m.), 9 Nov. 1921 (HO 144/1746/417250/31).
99 CAB 23/25, 22 (21), Appendix VIII.
100 Dixon to Home Secretary, 11 Apr. 1921 (HO 144/1746/417250/31).
101 Home Office report for Sir George Beharrell's bulletin, 11 Apr. 1921 (HO 144/1746/417250/99A).

mines, and this resulted in additional police and naval men being sent there. The admiralty was now asked to 'form a battalion for service on land from such naval ratings as were available, this battalion to be under the Army command in Wales' for service in the mining valleys.[102]

The War Office was alarmed at this widespread use of troops for protection purposes in South Wales. If the threatened Triple Alliance strike occurred, there would be no mobile reserve available should a large-scale disturbance occur. Now some significant new developments took place. The committee on internal protection which had been set up at the beginning of the strike advised the Cabinet to mobilize the reserve forces and also to set up a new force called a 'Defence Force' in which ex-servicemen and Territorial soldiers would be invited to enlist.[103]

On 8 April Lloyd George made a statement to the Commons. He argued that, if the threatened strike by the Triple Alliance took place, it would be necessary to enrol volunteers to carry out essential services. These volunteers would need protection. No less essential was the maintenance of law and order. The police, even when strengthened by special constables, were insufficient to give protection and to preserve order

> in view of the very large number of points that require protection, and of the organized character of the interference with the voluntary workers. They are entitled to look to the Government for protection and help from the Armed Forces of the Crown in their difficult task. This protection the Government has decided to afford them. It is therefore proposed to make a special appeal to patriotic citizens to enlist in an Emergency Force, recruited not for the purpose of interfering in any wage dispute, but solely to support the police. . . .[104]

The Defence Force was a thinly disguised form of Territorial Army. It would be recruited and administered by the War Office for ninety days and be subject to the Army Act. Its members would wear military uniform and would be armed. Another line of

[102] CAB 23/25, 22 (21), Appendix VIII, Cabinet conclusions, 9 Apr. 1921; *Daily Herald*, 13 Apr. 1921.

[103] CAB 27/110, Internal Protection Sub-committee, 4 Apr. 1921.

[104] CAB 23/25, 22 (21), conclusions of Conference of Ministers, 9 Apr. 1921; *Parl. Deb.*, 5th ser., 140, 696–7 (8 Apr. 1921).

physical defence for the existing industrial order was thus created.[105]

Negotiations between the government and miners broke down, and on 12 April the Triple Alliance announced a general strike for 15 April. The government now intended 'to use the fullest powers of the state to protect workers who remained at work in any of the services essential to the life of the community'.[106] By 12 April it was stated that 17,000 reservists had reported present, while 40,000 men had been reported officially as attested in the Defence Force. One of them in Durham was a future prime minister, Anthony Eden.[107] Preparations had also been made to draw special constables recruited from rural areas into disturbed areas.[108] Chief constables and GOCs in C were issued with instructions to keep in the closest touch with each other, while chiefs of police were told to communicate to the latter daily particulars of the places at which they feared rioting and disorder.[109] Three hundred troops had arrived at Pontypridd on 13 April, although all was reported to be quiet and the pumps to be working.[110] Additional naval ratings were moved to Glasgow, Newcastle, and other centres of industry in Scotland, the north of England, and South Wales. By 14 April, then, there was a formidable naval and military presence throughout the land, to be used 'as a second line to the police' in preserving law and order, and maintaining essential services if necessary.[111]

Then, on the evening of 14 April, there came a dramatic turn of events after a meeting of MPs with Frank Hodges, secretary of the MFGB. On 'Black Friday', 15 April, the Triple Alliance called off its

[105] The Cabinet agreed to this proposal of the Internal Protection Committee, even though almost every opinion previously given on the subject of auxiliary forces used in civil disputes had stressed the necessity of keeping them away from military control.

[106] CAB 23/25, 18 (21), conclusions of meeting of 12 Apr. 1921.

[107] CAB 27/73 TC 31, STC, 12 Apr. 1921; CAB 23/25, 23 (21), Conference of Ministers, 13 Apr. 1921; Robert Rhodes James, *Anthony Eden* (1986), 62.

[108] CAB 23/25, 22 (21), Appendix I, conclusions of conference of 5 Apr. 1921.

[109] HO 158/22 (377,100/279), 14 Apr. 1921.

[110] Summary of reports received from the police on the coal strike 1921 (HO 144/1746/417250/99).

[111] Notes on the Intelligence Organization for Emergency Home Defence 79/1421 Appendix, June 1921 (WO 32/5314). The Army was told to take no part whatever in an industrial dispute and that 'the legal powers of the army are practically nil so long as there is a policeman available'.

threatened strike, leaving the miners to fight on alone. Suddenly, the crisis was over. The STC now demobilized that portion of its organization put into force to meet a threatened Triple Alliance strike. They were thus denied the opportunity to test their long-prepared emergency procedures to the full. Thomas Jones, the deputy-secretary to the Cabinet, ironically commented: 'The Strike Committee very sick. They had been waiting for two years to press the button. They had pressed it. . . . But Jim Thomas upset it all.'[112]

The government's attention now focused entirely on the miners' stoppage. The state of emergency was renewed three times more until 26 July when the Emergency Regulations were allowed to lapse after the more or less return to full-time work in the mines. The STC remained in charge of affairs, issuing daily bulletins to the Cabinet on the state of public order in the provinces. Now police, backed up by the reservists and the Defence Force, were used freely for protection duties in the mining areas.

On 7 May 1921 the Home Office issued a highly secret circular to chief constables of port areas at the suggestion of the National Council of Port Labour Employers that they should now requisition troops if they had not already done so: blackleg labour needed to be protected as 'it is . . . essential to the life of the country that the loading or unloading of coal should not be stopped'.[113] There can be no doubt that these instructions were followed up.

Thus the Home Office encouraged provincial police chiefs in the mining areas to adopt an aggressive stance towards the national coal strike. However, even Troup became alarmed at the paranoia exhibited by Lindsay in Glamorgan. The chief constable reported that he had been sent police amounting to an additional 449 men from West Sussex, East Sussex, Wiltshire, Dorset, Devon, Cardigan, Gloucestershire, and Norfolk, and he used these men to protect collieries and reinforce his own police. However, they were almost always backed up by troops. For example, after disturbances at the Ferndale Collieries, Lindsay established

> a strong post of the York and Lancaster Regiment at Pontypridd as trouble

[112] Thomas Jones to Bonar Law, 24 Apr. 1921, quoted in *Thomas Jones: Whitehall Diary*, ed. K. Middlemas, i (1969), 153.

[113] Home Office Circular Highly Secret, 7 May 1921 (HO 144/1746/417250/114).

was anticipated. . . . This force speedily grew into a whole battalion . . . and after the hostile demonstrations against the Cymmer collieries and two collieries at Ynyshir it became necessary to establish posts of the above Regiment both at Cymmer and Ynyshir, the former supported by 50 of the Norfolk Constabulary, and the latter by 50 of the Gloucester Constabulary.[114]

When the chief constable of Glamorgan heard that the Army Reserve was to be disbanded in June 1921 (perhaps because of a threatened mutiny at Newport, Monmouthshire), he quickly wrote to the Home Office warning of

the serious consequences which will probably accrue in this district from the above step. . . . The disloyal agitators have, ever since the commencement of the Strike, stated that should food run out 'we will not starve while there is food in anyone's house or shop'.

With plenty of police and military in the district to prevent looting, the only alternative for the strikers would be for those who can find employment to go back to work. . . .[115]

Troup wrote to General Romer of the War Office that Lindsay was 'rather an alarmist': Romer replied (ironically perhaps) that he did not 'know how Lindsay ever sleeps! it must be a fearful existence he leads'.[116] In fact the troops in South Wales were not greatly affected by the disbandment of the reservists and remained there until the end of the strike.

One particular novelty during the strike, the Defence Force, met with an extremely fierce reception from the left. Its very existence marked a new departure in government policy towards strikers. The Manchester Labour Party, for example, condemned the government for forming a 'White Guard' for the protection of blacklegs. It was 'more likely than anything else to cause unnecessary bloodshed and provoke civil war'.[117] The large number of special constables who enrolled for service in the strike were seen as a class force—a direct menace to organized labour. They were free from popular control, while citizens had no appeal about their behaviour save to Whitehall.

[114] Statement by Captain Lionel Lindsay on coal strike 1921, 21 July 1921 (HO 144/1746/417250/178).

[115] Lindsay to Home Office, 3 June 1921 (ibid. 152).

[116] Troup to Romer, 4 June 1921; Romer to Troup, 6 June 1921 (ibid.)

[117] Daily Herald, 15 Apr. 1921.

The actions of the chief constables of Glamorgan and Monmouthshire in requisitioning naval and military assistance caused further angry protest. There were bitter condemnations from Labour MPs in the Commons about the presence of naval ratings in Abertillery, marching through the town with fixed bayonets, accompanied by machine guns.[118] The Labour members of the Monmouthshire Standing Joint Committee protested about the importation of both police and naval ratings, and demanded their withdrawal, claiming that local police had handled the situation admirably.[119] On the other hand, the chief constable of Monmouthshire insisted that the naval ratings had been imported with the approval of the chairman of the standing joint committee, Sir Henry Mather Jackson (who was, in fact, a powerful railway and coal magnate), and said that naval ratings would be withdrawn only if miners would undertake not to interfere with pump men.[120] In Glamorgan the Rhondda UDC protested bitterly about the importing of additional police, and even more of troops, redolent of the bitter confrontational atmosphere of 1910. They pressed Lindsay in vain to withdraw them.[121] In fact, as has been seen, troops from the Lancashire and Yorkshire Regiment remained in the Rhondda, or the valleys near at hand, until the end of the coal strike.

The chief constable of West Sussex had been encouraged by the Home Secretary to lend police to Glamorgan in the strike, doing this without waiting for the authorization of his standing joint committee. He claimed that he had received the grateful thanks of the Welsh coalowners as his men had 'arrived in Glamorgan in the nick of time, . . . giving protection to officials who were working the pumps. . . . Hundreds of thousands of pounds damage were saved by their presence'.[122] He was specially commended by the Home Secretary for his prompt action here, and Lindsay again obtained the reinforcements he demanded.

In many ways, then, the miners' strike in 1921 marked another important episode in the history of police organization. In particu-

118 Parl. Deb., 5th ser., 140, 1579 (18 Apr. 1921).

119 *Daily Herald*, 5 May 1921.

120 Ibid., 14 Apr. 1921.

121 Ibid., 11, 14 Apr. 1921.

122 Chief constable of West Sussex to Dixon, 14 Apr. 1921; Home Secretary to Mr Williams, chief constable of West Sussex, 18 Apr. 1921 (HO 144/1746/417250/45).

lar, it revealed starkly to police authorities in mining areas, many of whom had a Labour majority for the first time, the extent of the autonomy of the county chief constables and of Home Office powers over the provincial police since the Police Act of 1919. The *Daily Herald* condemned as 'astonishing' the fact 'that local authorities throughout the country should have allowed such gross and unwarranted interference with the privileges of local government'.[123] The Labour Party complained that the powers given to the Home Secretary to make regulations under the Police Act for borough as well as county forces enabled him to 'dictate to and override local authorities who prior to the passing of the Act were responsible for the control and regulation of their respective police forces'.[124] In self-protection, the chairman of the Manchester Watch Committee circularized other borough watch committees in 1921 to the effect that

> numerous communications have . . . been issued by the Home Office tending to curtail the autonomy hitherto enjoyed by Police Authorities. As a result of these communications and the new conditions they indicate the Manchester Watch Committee have become strongly impressed with the necessity of greater solidarity between police authorities throughout the country with a view to their being able to make united and direct representation to the Home Office on all questions affecting police administration.[125]

The Association of Municipal Corporations and the County Councils Association now set up police committees to consider questions of joint concern relating to the management and control of the forces, but these proved relatively powerless in the face of growing Home Office authority and increasingly independent stands taken by chief constables with Home Office support.

The maintenance of law and order during periods of industrial unrest assumed wholly new dimensions after the war. With the government determined to employ all the resources of the state to contain disorder, both police and troops were central to its emergency planning. The War Office was now reluctantly

[123] *Daily Herald*, 12 Apr. 1921.
[124] *Labour Party Annual Conference Report* (1921).
[125] Chairman of Manchester City Watch Committee to clerk to Liverpool City Watch Committee, 12 Apr. 1921: Liverpool City Watch Committee Minutes 1921.

reconciled to contingency schemes for troops to be used in a policing role during an emergency; this was despite the fact that their being used for policing purposes under governmental direction was contrary equally to the common law and the instructions contained in the *King's Regulations for the Army* and the *Manual of Military Law* for the use of the military in aid of the civil power, and to the basic instincts of army commanders. The calling up of reservists and the recruitment of the Defence Force were also contrary to all previous practice. And yet, in spite of the distinct traditions governing the army and differentiating its role from that of the police, by 1921 the principle that the armed forces could be used for policing purposes by the government was more entrenched than ever before. Internal security, so Field Marshal Sir Henry Wilson recorded shortly before his murder by the IRA in 1922, was now 'a foremost preoccupation' for the army. The Emergency Powers Act 1920 also drastically altered the position of the armed forces. They could now be used as much for the maintenance of essential services—as strike-breakers in effect—as for the preservation of law and order. The new role for the armed forces in labour troubles was unnatural and disagreeable—but it also seemed to be inescapable.

More important for the long term, perhaps, the Home Secretary had notably increased his financial control and general influence over the provincial police, as a result of the passing of the Police Act 1919 and the recommendations of the Desborough Committee. He now had new powers to make regulations for borough as well as for county forces. The status of chief constables, meanwhile, had been subtly enhanced. The main importance of the national coal strike of 1921, from the police point of view, was that it revealed starkly the ways in which Home Office authority over the provincial police had been extended compared with pre-war years. The Home Office was making a determined attempt to achieve a co-ordinated response to industrial unrest, and to undermine the element of accountability and local democratic control.

After the collapse of the coal strike in July 1921 the main phase of acute industrial conflict began to subside. Unemployment rose to well over a million; trade-union funds and membership began to decline; and from 1922 a period of markedly fewer strikes began. Even so, fears of nation-wide confrontation remained vivid in the mind of the governing élite. Nationalizing tendencies within the entire police system, and their association with a complex emergency apparatus directed against strikes that threatened vital supplies continued unabated, with profound effects for the nature, style, and public reputation of the law enforcement agencies throughout the land.

5

Towards a National Police Force: The general strike and after, 1923–1939

DESPITE the declining number of industrial disputes from 1922 onwards, successive governments continued to believe that a Triple Alliance or general strike remained a live possibility. The Supply and Transport Organization (which had been run down in 1922) was, therefore, secretly revived by Baldwin's Conservative government in the summer of 1923, with again the use of police and troops central to contingency plans.[1] On the intelligence and surveillance side, intelligence investigations into potential labour unrest, developed during and immediately after the First World War, continued as a major feature of the police response after 1922. As Director of Intelligence, Basil Thomson had, from 1919 onwards, made widespread use of plain-clothes police, CID officers, agents of various government departments, or military intelligence specialists, for purposes of industrial espionage. The Special Branch, indeed, was expanded in 1920 so that it could cope with the increase of work resulting from post-war industrial problems. The weekly reports from the Special Branch (which Thomson eventually left in November 1921 after a dispute with Lloyd George and Horwood, the newly appointed Commissioner of the Metropolitan Police who accused him of empire-building) continued to spread a mood of alarm about the extent of revolutionary activity throughout the land. In 1923 Sir Wyndham Childs, Thomson's successor as the head of Special Branch, and known as 'Fido' for his loyalty to authority, revealed that, during a dock strike that summer, his officers had been able to intercept communications between the London strike committee and the local Communist Party.[2] Throughout the 1920s and 1930s, indeed, the development of intelligence, both civil and military, became increasingly sophisticated and widely used.

[1] CAB 24/161 CP 314, memo. by Sir John Anderson on future of Supply and Transport Organization, 5 July 1923; CAB 23/46 42 (23), 31 July 1923.

[2] Trevor Barnes, 'Special Branch and the First Labour Government', *Historical Journal*, 22, 4 (1979), 943.

After the Armistice the War Office once again began its industrial intelligence operations.[3] From 1923 onwards there is also evidence that MI5 became involved in similar work; this called for a new type of agent who could infiltrate the unions without arousing suspicion.[4] The Special Branch also remained busy, using plain-clothes men to penetrate labour organizations such as the NUWM in the 1920s and 1930s. How effective all these activities were is open to dispute. In 1924 a Cabinet committee concluded that the intelligence services' view that Communists were active in fomenting strikes was much exaggerated.[5] Nevertheless, in the absence of a political police on the European model, these various intelligence organizations were a vital arm of the police and governmental responses to working-class challenges after the war.

The Home Office continued to work towards achieving a national police response to the threatened unrest. It sought a position where, in the words of the new permanent under-secretary, Sir John Anderson, the police forces, while remaining under local contol, could 'act together in case of need in co-operation with one another and with the Home Office as units in one great national service'.[6]

A major blow to obtaining a co-ordinated police response in the event of an industrial emergency appeared to have been struck by the financial 'axe' resulting from the Geddes proposals. The Geddes Committee on governmental economy which reported in January 1922 demanded reductions in spending in all government departments and public services. As far as the Home Office was concerned, it was decided that a lower standard of police expenditure was imperative. There should be a 5 per cent reduction in the strength of all police forces (the target was raised to 7 per cent in March 1923) and a 12½ per cent reduction in police expenditure.[7] As a result of this aspect of the Geddes axe

[3] War Office to home GOCs in C, 3 May 1921, no. 23A Appendix A, Annexure no. 3, and 11 June, ibid., Annexure no. 2 (WO 32/5314).

[4] Deacon, *Secret Service*, pp. 255–6.

[5] CAB 24/166 CP 273 (24), Industrial Unrest Committee, meeting of 15 Apr. 1924.

[6] Sir John Anderson, 'The Police', *Public Administration* 7, 2 (1929), 200–1.

[7] *First and Second Interim Reports of the Committee on National Expenditure*, PP 1922 [Cmd. 1581], ix. 1; PP 1922 [Cmd. 1582], ix. 173; HO 158/23 (400,519/34), 24 Mar. 1922.

(somewhat neglected by historians), there was difficulty in sustaining the numbers of the regular police during the inter-war period. Both provincial forces and the Metropolitan Police had problems in even keeping their numbers up to the reduced level prescribed by the Geddes Committee, and were forced to lower physical and educational standards in a period of maximum unemployment. Indeed the question of maintaining the police force up to establishment level continued throughout the inter-war years during which the ratio of police to population was much reduced.[8]

The Home Office made renewed efforts to ensure that chief constables would be able to obtain the manpower they required should an industrial emergency occur. The Desborough Committee had recommended that the special constabulary be further developed, but, as has been seen, recruits were few in industrial areas where they were most needed. Special constables had been sworn in under the temporary legislation introduced at the beginning of the war, but there was subsequently general uncertainty as to under which acts of parliament they would be operating. Fresh legislation had been urged to make their legal position clear.[9] The 1923 Special Constables Act, passed in the face of much Labour and police-authority opposition, gave permanent effect to the wartime provisions. Special constables could now be sworn in and used for day-to-day policing purposes, while the Special Constables Order, made under the authority of the Act, authorized the chief constable *inter alia* to nominate, appoint, control, and direct all special constables enrolled and provided the machinery for the local authorities to pay allowances to cover wages lost or other expenses incurred by the recruits. Compulsion had now been applied to police authorities to fund special constables who enrolled. The Home Secretary voiced the familiar view that the public had a duty to assist the police. He quoted from the Report of the Desborough Committee:

> the maintenance of public order and the suppression of all forms of violence are matters in which every member of the community is deeply

[8] *Annual Report of HM Inspector of Constabulary*, PP 1926 (2), xv. 206–7; Note by Receiver of Metropolitan Police, 25 Feb. 1925 (HO 45/20064/47244/1); see Appendix, Table 3.

[9] *Annual Report of HM Inspector of Constabulary*, PP 1922 (5), x. 311.

concerned. . . . The citizen has been and still is required to take his part in the preservation of the peace and the suppression of disorder.[10]

There now seemed no reason why special constables should not enrol in considerable numbers for service in an emergency or for day-to-day policing duties.

The preservation of emergency anti-strike machinery was not diminished by the coming to power of a Labour government under Ramsay MacDonald in early 1924. The Supply and Transport Organization, indeed, was reactivated by Labour during a dock strike that February. Fortunately the strike lasted for only ten days, food was never scarce, and there was no need to proclaim a state of emergency.[11] Josiah Wedgwood, Labour's chief civil commissioner in 1924, tried to remodel the emergency planning system and to eliminate the air of secrecy that surrounded it. A code of emergency regulations drawn up in February 1924 excluded the provision of 1921 that servicemen should be employed on 'services of vital importance to the community'.[12] But this was mere window-dressing. It was still recognized that troops would be used to maintain essential services and supplies in an industrial emergency, while all GOCs in C were instructed by the War Office to bring up to date their lists of officers and civilians available for army or intelligence work.[13] The Labour government, in fact, did proclaim a state of emergency during the London transport strike on 28 March; but it was soon revoked on 1 April when the strike was called off.[14] However, there was so much opposition aroused within the parliamentary Labour Party to the emergency organization that there were no more STC meetings during the time when the Labour government was in office. The Campbell case, which involved alleged Communist attempts to undermine the loyalty of the army, eventually caused the downfall of the ministry on 4 November.

[10] *Parl. Deb.*, 5th ser., 162, 944 (9 Apr. 1923); HO 45/20012/435162/17 contains report of Standing Committee B on the Special Constables Bill 1923; *The Times*, 1 May 1923.

[11] Jeffery and Hennessy, *States of Emergency*, p. 80.

[12] 1924–6: Home Office memos. on the Emergency Regulations, February–June 1924 (HO 45/12640/453900/8–10).

[13] CAB 24/167 CP 344, memo. by First Lord of the Admiralty on use of naval personnel in industrial disputes; War Office to GOCs in C, 24 Jan. 1924, Appendix C, Annexure no. 2 (WO 32/5314).

[14] Jeffery and Hennessy, *States of Emergency*, pp. 84–5.

The most important feature of these industrial difficulties during the short-lived first Labour government of 1924, from the point of view of the police, lay elsewhere. This was the attempt by Arthur Henderson, Labour's Home Secretary and a most powerful trade unionist, to get away from the use of troops to maintain law and order during strikes. He circulated the provincial police authorities with a General Mutual Aid Agreement, which he urged them all to enter into. This agreement embodied in one document standard terms governing the loan of men from one force to another, to enable men to be transferred swiftly to or from other areas in an emergency with the assent of the police authority.[15] This principle had been recommended by the Desborough Committee in 1919 and would make nation-wide collaboration by police forces more feasible especially if, as Henderson had emphasized, police authorities delegated to the chief constable the decision whether forces should be lent or borrowed. Over the next eighteen months this was to have its effects.

However, the fall of the government and the subsequent general election brought the Conservatives back into office with Baldwin again as prime minister. His Home Secretary was Sir William Joynson-Hicks, a passionate, almost fanatical, anti-socialist. Now the major strike expected by the government seemed imminent, with the continuing crisis in the coal industry. In the spring of 1925 Joynson-Hicks pushed ahead with emergency plans and encouraged other departments to do likewise. Then the ban on police recruitment imposed by the Geddes economies was lifted for police authorities near coalfields and ports. They were circularized that all vacancies in their forces should be filled.[16] But circumstances were more complicated than Joynson-Hicks's simple-minded approach suggested. Many authorities were uncertain from where this additional expenditure would be paid. In any case, the difficulty of obtaining suitable recruits for the force continued. There were said to be 3,000 in the First Police Reserve and 100,000 special constables registered. But the latter were untrained and 'of doubtful value'. The General Mutual Aid Agreement between police forces, launched by Henderson under the 1924 Labour government, and now agreed to by all police authorities, was not scheduled to begin operation until October 1925, while in any case

[15] HO 158/24 (400,508/13), 6 Feb. 1924.
[16] HO 158/24 (481,507/5), 24 July 1925.

the entire system still remained cumbersome.[17] Sir Leonard Dunning, chief inspector of constabulary, now discussed with chief constables the problem of obtaining sufficient manpower in the event of an emergency. They jointly concluded that the protection of vulnerable positions could no longer be left to the discretion of chief officers of police.[18]

This apparent weakness of the civil forces, in the eyes of the Home Office, meant that the army would again be heavily relied upon in an emergency. However, as has been seen, during the post-war period the War Office had been trying to limit its obligations to the civil power. It wanted to return to the principle, laid down in the *Manual of Military Law* and the *King's Regulations for the Army*, that the armed forces would only aid the civil power as a last resort, when the police had been overcome. To this end, in July 1925, a highly secret memorandum was circulated by the War Office to the eight GOCs in C. This memorandum gave detailed instructions as to their duties in aid of the civil power. It emphasized that, apart from the protection by small guards of vulnerable points selected by the War Office (which included army stores, railway goods yards and chemical works, munitions plants, and petrol depots), all other units should be kept in mobile reserve. The commanders were warned, 'Such demands for guards, other than those ordered from the War Office and laid down in command schemes, should only be complied with after the most careful investigation by the local commander'.[19] In effect, the War Office was trying to ensure that military aid should only be provided on War Office terms.

The Home Office was now in a state of alarm. The army was anxious to avoid dissipating its troops; police could not be spared for convoy duties or protection of vulnerable points. Therefore, in the event of widespread industrial trouble, it might be necessary to consider calling up the reserves or else enrolling a special Defence Force such as was constituted during the 1921 coal strike. These actions, however, were felt to be too dangerous.

That month another industrial crisis was averted, or at least

[17] CAB 24/174 CP 390, arrangements for dealing with industrial emergencies, 6 Aug. 1925; minute by Joynson-Hicks on mutual aid between forces, 1920–30 (HO 45/17913/400508/62).

[18] Dunning to Anderson, memo. on protection of vulnerable points, 27 July 1925 (HO 45/24819/455395/4).

[19] Duties in Aid of the Civil Power, 6 July 1925 (WO 32/5314/23A).

postponed. A coal strike did not come about, since Baldwin compromised at the last moment and proposed a subsidy to the coal industry spread over nine months. The Prime Minister is said to have declared, 'We were not ready'.[20] On 31 July the owners lifted their lock-out notices. 'Red Friday' was hailed as a victory for the miners, a kind of revenge for 'Black Friday' four years earlier.

Even so, the clash with labour, or at least with its most militant elements, the miners, seemed close at hand. The government, therefore, spent that winter building up, perfecting, and even publicizing, its anti-strike apparatus. In August 1925 Joynson-Hicks received Cabinet authorization to increase the number of special constables, and he urged chief constables 'quietly to recruit'. The General Mutual Aid Agreement, which had now been agreed to and signed by all police authorities, came into effect from 1 October 1925.[21] In addition to these measures, strenuous efforts were made by the Home Office and the inspectors of constabulary to increase the regular police force. This matter was the subject of constant correspondence between the Home Office and the police authorities, with varied effect, as the future was to reveal.[22] On 20 November 1925 Ministry of Health Circular 636 was issued. This formally told local authorities about the emergency organization. The two principal agencies for the preservation of civil order in the event of a strike were said to be the police and the special constabulary.

However, more significant developments had taken place. In the autumn of 1925 the Home Office pushed the War Office much further than it had originally been prepared to go in the matter of internal protection. By March 1926 secret agreements existed between the Home Office (which, in effect, meant John Anderson) and the military authorities to keep detachments of troops available to protect convoys and vulnerable points 'provided we (the Home Office) do not say anything to lead the constables to think that troops will be readily forthcoming'.[23] The War Office remained as hesitant as ever about using soldiers as policemen. The Home Office, however, insisted that soldiers were basically citizens, albeit in uniform, and, therefore, had a common-law duty

[20] G. M. Young, *Stanley Baldwin* (1952), 99.
[21] Dixon, 'The Home Office', p. 199.
[22] *Police Review*, 8 Jan. 1926, p. 19.
[23] Minute by John Anderson, 27 July 1925 (HO 45/24819/455395/4).

to aid the civil power in maintaining order. What was less certain was whether or not troops in this kind of situation should or could act only when accompanied by a magistrate. In effect, the Home Office recommended that troops should act as if they were policemen, just the same.[24]

In the spring of 1926, although the industrial scene generally was tranquil, the labour trouble expected in the coal-mines could no longer be kept at bay. The Samuel Commission's report on the mining industry on 10 March recommended both an end to the subsidy and some reduction in miners' wages. Inconclusive negotiations between government, owners, and unions reached deadlock by the third week of April, and the owners then gave formal notice that wage cuts would begin on 1 May. On 30 April the existing coal agreement expired. Since the TUC General Council was seeking a settlement on the basis of the renewal of the subsidy, it was the government which was now on the offensive. It was decided to proclaim a state of emergency at midnight on 30 April.[25]

On 1 May the miners were formally locked out. The TUC General Council promptly accused the government of 'a declaration of war'. Baldwin then broke off talks with the TUC and a general strike was called on 3 May. As has been seen, it took place against a background of detailed and lengthy preparations by the government, army, and police. By contrast, the trade unions were largely unprepared. The Cabinet's Supply and Transport Organization, which was to get its first and only test, was fully mobilized on 2 May, with its directing committee afforced by the inclusion of Churchill and Birkenhead among its members. This committee met daily during the general strike and assumed full control of the emergency organization.

In the first few days the government moved calmly into action. Secret plans for the use of troops had been stepped up on 14 April. The Cabinet had sanctioned the spending of £10,000 by the War Office to secure the free movement of troops around the country.[26] Preparations had been made to move one battalion by

[24] Memo. by Mr Bingham and Sir Ernle Blackwell on the question of issuing further instructions to police and military on the use of Firearms by Police, military and civilians engaged on emergency duties in the General Strike, 5 May 1926 (HO 144/22936/257009/26).

[25] CAB 23/52 19 (26); conclusions of meeting of 28 Apr. 1926.

[26] Jeffery and Hennessy, *States of Emergency*, p. 105.

road from Tidworth to South Wales and three more by sea, two from Devonport to Lancashire and one from Dover to Scotland. This move was made on 1 May. By 3 May battleships and cruisers were sent to ports around the country; four more battalions were moved by road to the north as a general reserve, with another two-and-a-half battalions reinforcing the troops in London. An announcement in the press was issued, stating that troops 'were intended for protection purposes only and not for taking sides in the strike'.[27]

However, the police and special constables were to maintain order, in the first instance. Chief constables were now circularized that troops should only be requisitioned as a last resort, and would only be available for the protection of vulnerable points if a Triple Alliance strike occurred. Any requisition for either military or naval aid should be communicated at once by telephone to the Home Office. Police authorities should make every effort to build up their regular police and to enrol special constables. National police preparations were now masterminded by the police department of the Home Office under Arthur Dixon. Provincial chief constables were emphatically reminded by the Home Office of the details of the emergency organization, and told to keep the Home Office and police liaison officers informed daily about developments of the strike in their areas.[28]

Significant developments in the area of mutual aid now took place. Two new Emergency Regulations, issued under the Emergency Powers Act 1920 (in addition to those previously issued in 1921) increased the Home Secretary's power over the provincial police. The first gave the Home Secretary the power to lend provincial police from one part of the country to another, usually up to 10 per cent of the aiding force; the cost of this was to be paid by the aided force under the General Mutual Aid Agreement. The second gave the police full power without being sworn in when they were moved from one county to another, as, for example, when escorting convoys; the cost to be paid by their own police authority. Chief constables had long been pressing the Home Secretary to take measures of this nature. As early as 1920

[27] CAB 27/260, STC, 3 May 1926; ibid. 29 Apr. 1926.

[28] HO 158/25 (449,000/47), 16 Apr. 1926; HO 158/25 (455,395/16), 19 Apr. 1926; HO 158/25 (449,00,57), 30 Apr. 1926; Dixon, 'The Home Office', pp. 235–51.

the Central Conference of Chief Constables had urged the Home Secretary to adopt the recommendations of the Desborough Committee and to take power to require any force to send men up to 15 per cent of its establishment to aid another force on standard terms of loan.[29] Both these regulations significantly interfered with the established principle that the preservation of law and order rested with the local police authorities; they also considerably increased their financial obligations. In fact, the lending of police by one area to another was made easier by the existence of the large special constabulary force which now enrolled.[30] Special constables were mobilized on 1 May and the Commissioner of the Metropolitan Police and the Home Secretary issued special appeals to citizens to enrol. On 10 May, for example, the Home Secretary appealed through the government-run *British Gazette*:

Give the Government enough Special Constables to enable us to allot two to every vehicle that is, or thinks it is, in danger, thus releasing the regular police for sterner work . . . most men can spare four or five hours out of the twenty-four to do a constable's beat.[31]

These appeals then met with a good response, and order was maintained by police and special constables in most parts of the country. The special constabulary was particularly widely used. During the strike it increased in number from 98,000 to 226,200 by the time the strike ended, for the whole of England and Wales.[32] Thus it far outnumbered the regular police force. Mounted special constables proved especially useful to reinforce the ordinary mounted police. In London there were four troops of mounted special constables with 25 men in each.[33] In Newcastle there was a mounted section of 46, a light car section of 350 to supervise convoys, a heavy lorry section of 40, and a motor-car section of 80 to patrol the city carrying dispatches and messages. In addition, 60 special constables carried out point duty, 8 formed an intelligence section, 12 a depot section, while 910 were employed

[29] Dixon, 'The Home Office', p. 199; also e.g. chief constable of West Sussex to Home Office, 14 Apr. 1921 (HO 144/417250/1746/45).

[30] Dixon, 'The Home Office', p. 250.

[31] *British Gazette*, 10 May 1926.

[32] *Parl. Deb.*, 5th Ser, 197, 2177–8 (7 July 1926).

[33] General strike arrangements regarding communications and transport (MEPO 2/3135); report on the activities of the special constables in the general strike to the Commandant-in-Chief of the Metropolitan Special Constabulary, 28 Oct. 1926 (MEPO 2/1838).

in reserve as a foot section for the purpose of reinforcing the rest if the emergency became acute. No less than 487 uniformed specials were employed here. The chief constable felt that the police and special constables maintained a total ascendancy over the situation from the outset. 'The whole organization as here set out would have rendered it unnecessary to draw from other forces or introduce the military for a period of three months.'[34] So valuable were the services rendered by special constables felt to be that, when the general strike ended, the government took the very unusual step of sending to each individual special constable who gave his service during the emergency a copy of the letter of thanks signed by Prime Minister (Stanley Baldwin) to the Home Secretary.[35]

But the regular police were the mainstays of public order. For example, in London John Anderson now reported that regular police were protecting the power stations on which the broadcasting services depended, while police protection had also been provided at eight power stations where naval ratings and civilian volunteers had been introduced. A special service of 100 buses, with police escort and with police on the buses as patrols, had been started from Chiswick after the complete stoppage of both the London underground and bus system.[36] Chief constables made free use of the General Mutual Aid Agreement. In Durham, for instance, on 10 May when there was interference with road traffic, 125 police were borrowed from the West Riding, 50 from Lincolnshire, and 47 from Norfolk.[37] There were many examples of local police initiative during the strike. In Preston and Burnley the Lancashire county force rendered prompt assistance and it never became necessary to call upon the military at all.[38] In Llanelli the Carmarthenshire county police drafted in large numbers of their own men from outlying parts of the county, while 100 Glamorgans lay ready in reserve. Cardiff City police held 75 men

[34] Special constabulary appointment and control 1923–9, memo. by the chief constable of Newcastle on the duties of special constables during the general strike, 28 May 1926 (HO 45/13364/447130/112).

[35] Dixon, 'The Home Office', p. 248.

[36] CAB 27/260, STC, 4 May 1926.

[37] CAB 27/332, Home Office Situation Report, no. 9, 10 May 1926; STC Daily Strike Bulletin, 11 May 1926.

[38] Police liaison officers' reports on the situation in the general strike, May 1926 (HO 144/6902/493562).

in reserve to help the Glamorgan police in the mining valleys.[39]

The general strike further confirmed the authority of the Home Office over the provincial police and troops. If the local authorities did not comply with Home Office directives, they could and would be overridden. One example was at Hull. Here there was a disturbance outside the City Hall on 7 May, when several hundreds of strikers attempted to block the path of buses and trams driven by volunteers. The chief constable was said to have been hampered from requisitioning military aid by the attitude of the mayor.[40] On 8 May, however, the captain of the *Ceres* was informed that 'disaffected strikers had burned and wrecked some trams driven by volunteers. . . . He took immediate action. He marched some of his men in full marching kit with rifles and bayonets and lined them up. He called on the mayor and made a speech on the mayoral balcony explaining his duties. He declared that, if another tramcar was assaulted, he would put a naval party on all trams and naval ratings would drive them.' No further damage was reported.[41] Arrangements were now made by the Home Office to reinforce the police force here, and 173 extra police were drafted into Hull.[42]

The South Wales police liaison officer reported that, because it was not acceptable to swear in special constables in some areas, there was a resulting lack of strength on the part of the police.

> A quiescent attitude was adopted and Councils of Action were enabled to coerce and intimidate traders. The adoption of the line of least resistance in Police Forces where Labour dominated the County Councils or Watch Committees was taken up by the Civil Commissioner and in one instance (Swansea) the Police Authority upon being pressed borrowed 50 men (and 50 more in readiness) from the County of Glamorgan in order to preserve the peace during the unloading of foodstuffs by volunteer labour.[43]

At Lincoln the chief constable was actually said to be 'a consistent friend of labour'. He refused to allow mounted police to enter the city, and the Strike Committee provided the whole of the special

[39] Ibid.

[40] CAB 27/260, STC, 9 May 1926.

[41] R. Rhodes James, *Memoirs* (1969), pp. 251–2.

[42] CAB 27/332, Home Office Situation Report, no. 9, 10 May 1926; STC, Daily Strike Information Bulletin, 11 May 1926.

[43] South Wales police liaison officer's report (HO 144/6902/493562).

constabulary with his agreement.[44] Here the alleged lack of strong action by the police was to lead, after the strike, to an inquiry by the inspector of constabulary. The outcome was to be the resignation of the chief constable of Lincoln, as well as the chairman of the local watch committee.[45]

Although the police, reinforced by the special constabulary, were responsible for the maintenance of law and order during the strike, chief constables acted in liaison with the armed forces throughout. In fact twenty-six battalions, about a quarter of the army's strength, were called out on emergency duty during the general strike. In London, for example, where six battalions of troops were stationed, a colonel commanding one of the regiments of foot guards worked alongside the Metropolitan Police. Police Headquarters, London District, was in turn kept in close touch with Scotland Yard, while MI5 lent London District twelve trained officers to work with army intelligence. Emergency schemes of a detailed nature had long been in existence for the military protection of the capital. In 1926 these schemes were now put into effect: the Civil Defence Scheme, the London Electric Power, and the Whitehall Defence Scheme. They included plans 'to assist the police at any point at short notice in case of riot, etc.' and also in the protection of 'supplies and communications'.[46] The basic army policy in London and elsewhere was to keep as many troops as possible in mobile reserve, unlike the policy of committing most of the garrison to special guard during the strikes of 1919.[47] However, as the strike progressed into its second week troops were very much in evidence guarding vulnerable points and convoys, especially in London. Indeed, it was in the capital that the most intensive use of the army took place. By the end of the first week of the strike sixteen vital points in the capital were being guarded by naval ratings, while a battalion of Scots Guards had been sent to Deptford and 200 ex-cavalrymen and polo players from Hurlingham and elsewhere had been enrolled as additional mounted police.[48] A platoon of the 3rd Grenadier Guards had been sent to

[44] M. Morris, *The General Strike* (1976), 55.

[45] Home Office minute on question of inquiries into the conduct of police (HO 144/20729/697140/14).

[46] Jeffery and Hennessy, *States of Emergency*, p. 115.

[47] Report on the general strike 1926 as it affected troops in the London district (WO 32/3455).

[48] Metropolitan Police Daily Newsheet, no. 3, 6 May 1926 (MEPO 2/3134).

guard the Shellmex Petrol Depot at Fulham and a company of Welsh Guards was dispatched to the Lots Road Power Station.[49]

In the general strike the docks at once assumed a dominating importance, and military liaison with the dock police now took place. Troops were often used to accompany food convoys: for example, on 7 May the Rolls Company was called upon to carry out an escort to Thameshaven where the police were said to have experienced serious trouble the day before, failing to get a convoy away, and one policeman had had his ear bitten off.[50] The most noted use of troops in London in the general strike, however, occurred on 8 May. The Cabinet agreed to provide the army with as many armoured cars as were available and approved the opening up of the London docks, previously closed by pickets, by a military force commanded by Lord Ruthven. On the night of 7–8 May the 1st Guards Brigade (comprising four battalions) was moved by lorry to a temporary camp in Victoria Park.[51] The Victoria and Albert Docks were opened at 4 a.m. on 8 May with as much show of force as possible; the first convoy left the docks escorted by twenty armoured cars. It consisted of 100 lorries each carrying two armed soldiers. Convoys like this continued from the docks for the remainder of the strike. If Churchill had had his way, he would have used machine guns and tanks as well as armoured cars for this enterprise.[52]

In addition to the use of the army in this way in the general strike, the navy now played a vital role. Its use illustrated the many-sided involvement of the services during the emergency and the liaison of the armed forces and chiefs of police. The navy was used on a massive scale both to maintain services and to undertake limited protection duties. It had been used in this kind of role before—for example, at Liverpool and Hull during the dock and seamen's strikes in 1911; in the Yorkshire miners' strike in 1919; and to pump water from Scottish mines flooded in Fifeshire during the national coal strike in 1921. But the use of the navy in 1926 was much larger than that of other forces. This was partly because many of the anti-strike plans were concerned with the safeguarding of the flow of essential materials and foodstuffs and

[49] WO32/3455, Section II, General Policy.

[50] Ibid. Narrative of Strike: Summary of Second Offensive Period, 7–17 May 1926.

[51] Jeffery and Hennessy, *States of Emergency*, p. 121.

[52] Rhodes James, *Memoirs*, p. 243.

protecting the ports, and the navy obviously had to be used for this purpose. In addition, it was felt to be more acceptable to the general public than were troops, because it was usually unarmed. Historically the navy, 'Jolly Jack Tar', had always been more popular than the notion of a standing army. There was also another element of the navy's role in the general strike as noted by a contemporary:

> It was a struggle of quite a different character from any in which the navy, trained for sea service, had hitherto taken part. . . . This emergency revealed once more the mobility of naval power and the element of surprise which is its not least valuable element, for ships can be moved by sea without attracting much attention.[53]

This verdict was amply borne out between 3 and 12 May 1926.

At the beginning of the strike battleships were sent to the Clyde, the Mersey, and Rosyth, and cruisers and destroyers to other harbours. The way in which the naval ratings operated and the close liaison they maintained with the police is well documented in the Admiralty papers.[54] HMS *Ramillies*, for example, sailed from Plymouth to Liverpool on 3 May. The naval officer in charge at Liverpool had been handed the Civil Unrest Schemes which had been prepared by the Admiralty on 2 May, and on 3 May had met the chief constable and civil commissioner to discuss the assistance which the navy might give. The *Ramillies* arrived in Liverpool on 4 May when the situation was reported to be quiet and orderly. The commander of the ship, Captain Wigram, wrote that

> but for the presence of *Ramillies* many harbour services such as the ferry service which is considered of primary importance would have broken down. The general opinion seemed to be that should the seamen and firemen fail to carry out their duties these could be carried out by naval ratings. There was little object in striking and generally they appeared glad of this excuse for not doing so. In Liverpool the general situation was quiet and orderly and the civil organization had been very carefully thought out.[55]

On 5 May two other ships arrived in the area and their commanders were in communication with the local chief constables of

53 Archibald Hurd, 'The Navy on Active Service', *Fortnightly Review* (July 1926), 90–1.

54 Civil Unrest, General Strike 1926 (ADM 116/2317, 2437, 2438, 2439).

55 Report from commander of HMS *Ramillies* on the proceedings of the ship in the recent industrial emergency for 3–21 May 1926 to the commander in chief at Plymouth (ADM 116/2439).

Manchester, Lancashire, and Cheshire. Their deterrent and protective value was emphasized. The *Wessex* was used similarly at Manchester to protect the docks and ship canal.[56]

A different series of events occurred at Southampton. On 5 May the staff of the White Star Line were met and threatened at the docks by pickets after they had unloaded mail in the *Majestic* and helped her sail. Captain Carrington, the naval officer in charge at Southampton, felt that protection for naval ratings here would be best served by the police, 'but I am of the opinion that the Police Force here although very efficient is not strong enough numerically to give the display of force necessary to discourage the strikers and encourage the would-be workers'. He was convinced that troops should thus be sent, since 'the knowledge of the presence of a body of armed men although kept more or less in the background is required to give the necessary feeling of security to would be workers'.[57] Destroyers were kept ready at Portsmouth, and the admiral in charge was in touch with the colonel commanding the troops in the Southern Area regarding the transportation, at short notice, of troops to Southampton. The police force was, however, able to provide the required protection for the naval ratings, and on 10 May there were reported to be in Southampton 200 borough police, 300 special constables, 40 regular dock police, and 150 special dock police.[58]

At Avonmouth, another large port, fear of disorder was apparent. The naval officer here asked the chief constable to arrange for the accommodation of 29 officers and 1,000 men if reinforcements to this extent was necessary.[59] HMS *Windsor* and HMS *Caledon* arrived here on 5 May. The senior naval officer contacted the commander of the *Windsor*. The object of naval assistance, he reminded him, was 'the effective protection of voluntary labour and goods. You must use your discretion as to the nature and extent of the assistance necessary. . . . Conflict with the civil population should be avoided wherever possible.'[60]

[56] Diary of events of naval officer in charge at Liverpool in the general strike (ibid.).

[57] Report on the situation in Southampton, 5 May 1926 (ADM 116/2438).

[58] Report on the situation in Southampton, 10 May 1926 (ibid.).

[59] Captain G. W. Campbell (naval officer in charge at Avonmouth) to commander in chief at Portsmouth, 4 May 1926 (ADM 116/2439).

[60] Senior naval officer at Avonmouth to commanding officer of HMS *Windsor*, 6 May 1926 (ibid.)

In Cardiff the chief constable reported that three warships had had 'a steadying effect' on dockers and transport workers.[61] A cruiser and a submarine arrived at Cardiff on 6 May. On 7 May the naval commander prepared a scheme for the defence of the docks here. Plans had been made to arm the seamen with rifles had they been needed for the maintenance of law and order. When food was being unloaded by volunteer labour, the number of police was reduced from sixty to ten and no untoward scenes occurred.[62] At Newport, after trouble with the power men, naval ratings were continuously employed during the strike. The military authorities supplied the guards at Pembroke Dock, and the power station at Pembrey, while the Cheshire Regiment was brought into barracks at Cardiff. Although it was never actively used, it made its presence felt by marching through the streets daily for exercise. In South Wales, perhaps because of this military and naval presence, the police were said to have kept the situation well in hand.[63]

The extensive use of troops and naval ratings for the maintenance of essential services and more particularly in a policing role for the protection of vulnerable points and convoys now posed major problems for the War Office. Although there was little disorder, once such protection had been given it was almost impossible to withdraw it. If a serious riot occurred in a particular locality there would not be enough troops in mobile reserve to provide assistance. In addition, the use of troops for the protection of convoys raised major problems which had no precedent, especially about the legality of the use of firearms by soldiers in this sort of situation.[64] The Cabinet itself shared these fears, especially after the TUC intensified the stoppage on 7 May. The idea of bolstering the available security forces with new strength emerged.

A significant development took place. Cabinet discussion now centred on the possibility of the formation of a third force, such as the Defence Force which had been formed in 1921, to get away from the use of troops in the protection of convoys and vulnerable points. This idea of a Defence Force, although favoured by Churchill, was overruled in Cabinet. Instead the Cabinet decided to raise a

[61] South Wales police liaison officer's report (HO 144/6902/493562).

[62] Diary of Commander T. B. Drew, naval officer in charge at Cardiff (ADM 116/2439).

[63] South Wales police liaison officer's report (HO 144/6902/493562).

[64] Memo. by Mr Bingham and Sir Ernley Blackwell (5 May 1926) (HO 144/22936/257009/26).

new body consisting of units of the Territorial Army, ex-servicemen, and other suitable and loyal candidates. This new force differed radically from the Defence Force which had been instituted in 1921 in the national coal strike and which was recruited and administered by the War Office and subject to the Army Act. It would be recruited and equipped by the War Office but placed under the control of chief constables for use in collective units. The new force would be called the Civil Constabulary Reserve (CCR) and its members would be sworn in as special constables. They were to wear plain clothes, but to be armed with brassards and steel helmets, and carry truncheons. The Exchequer would meet the cost.[65] Recruiting began on 10 May; within two days it was reported to the Cabinet that the CCR numbered 11,025 in London and 6,800 in the provinces.[66] However, in its brief period of existence it was not felt to have been very effective. Where the CCR was used, its members were said to have been looked upon as strike-breakers and therefore to have been a provocation to the unions. Because of this, in fact, the use of troops for escorts and protection duties continued as before: the formation of this force was thus counter-productive.

The TUC General Council was divided within itself, and the general strike was called off at noon on 12 May. By 16 May most people had resumed work. The Cabinet at once called a halt to the enlistment of volunteers; chief constables were told by the Home Office to stop recruiting for the CCR which was disbanded on 15 May; the Supply and Transport Organization was wound down, and troops withdrawn from docks and other key centres.[67]

Overall, as will be seen, the peaceful character of the general strike was felt to be testimony to the effectiveness of the policing methods adopted. Troops had no occasion to come into physical contact with strikers throughout and a mood of self-satisfaction permeated Whitehall.[68] However, the national coal lock-out continued for another six months, until the start of November, when the miners eventually went back to work, defeated. The

[65] CAB 27/260, STC 24, 7 May 1926; CAB 24/179 CP 189, Report of Inter-departmental Sub-Committee on CCR 8 May 1926; CAB 23/52 26 (26), conclusions of meeting of 7 May 1926.

[66] CAB 24/179 CP 197, 3rd Report of the Inter-departmental Sub-Committee on CCR, 14 May 1926.

[67] Ibid. CP 199 (26): 4th Report of the Inter-departmental Sub-Committee on CCR, 14 May 1926.

[68] Critchley, *History*, p. 199.

Emergency Regulations, therefore, remained in being. The STC played little part now, and protection and the maintenance of law and order were provided solely by the police, aided by special constables. Daily reports of the strike situation continued to be sent by chiefs of police to the Home Office. County chief constables continued to act in virtually autocratic fashion, while those in the boroughs were encouraged to act similarly, with the backing of the Home Office. When the return to work began in the summer and autumn of 1926, the Cabinet instructed that protection was to be given to everyone who went to work. Joynson-Hicks inquired of chief constables whether they were satisfied that 'in the present situation the police now under your control are sufficient to enable this object to be fully carried out'. He told them that ample police were available in other parts of the country to ensure proper protection for miners wishing to go to work. Arrangements could be 'made for you to have such further reinforcements, if any, as you may desire'. Contingency plans had been made to overrule police authorities who refused to accept reinforcements. Joynson-Hicks told the Cabinet that 'Chief constables are in the best position to judge of the local situation and the necessity for and effect of introducing "foreign" police'.[69]

Throughout the miners' strike, however, the Home Office found that the necessary measures for national co-ordination could be adopted without any recourse to the compulsory powers acquired under the Emergency Regulations in 1926. Indeed, there was no occasion to use these powers during the general strike nor during the stoppage in the coalfields. Some hundreds of men were borrowed by Derbyshire (595), Nottinghamshire (385), the West Riding (350), and Glamorgan (447), and small contingents by two or three other forces. But these transactions were all made voluntarily, the Home Office acting as a sort of 'broker' on the basis of data which had been collected showing which forces were able to spare men and to what extent.[70] The daily information given to F

[69] Home Office circular to chief constables to ascertain the possible sources of help, 30 Aug. 1926 (HO 45/17913/400508/61); Home Office memo. as to cases where police authorities may be unwilling to take the necessary steps, 12 Oct. 1926 (HO 45/17913/400508/50); CAB 24/181, CP 364 (26), 27 October 1926: memo. by Joynson-Hicks on strength of police forces in coalfields.

[70] Dixon, 'The Home Office' p. 250; for example, see 'Additional Police for Glamorgan', Home Office memo. on arrangements for loan of 405 men, 20 Oct. 1926 (HO 45/17913/400508/5A).

Division of the Home Office by chief constables enabled the department to establish a broad picture of the operational situation relating to the strike. Thus the Home Secretary had no need to adopt an overtly political stance in relation to the direction of the police as the coal strike progressed: F Division 'directed' operations without any compulsion being applied. In all, police were imported by nine forces in disturbed areas from over thirty other areas at a cost to the local police authorities of £96,000 during the period May–December 1926.[71]

On balance, Home Office officials now believed a similar course to that pursued in 1926 should be adopted in any future emergency, so long as Home Office relations with the county and borough police forces remained as satisfactory as they were in 1926. A. L. Dixon pointed the moral, as his department saw it. The police service, he argued, had clearly developed

> as a piece of operational organization. In this respect the integration of the Police in the long continued preparatory measures and the functions they undertook when the emergency took place was, in reality, no more than the culmination of a process that had been going on for 10 years or more. . . . By further developing and strengthening the links which had been forming between the Home Office and the Police these experiences established the Service in what was virtually a new, and certainly important, role as an executive Force, efficient, trustworthy, versatile and ready at call to guide, assist or restrain the civil population in a wide variety of ways.[72]

Thus the use of police in the coal strike in 1926 was a significant breakthrough since, for the first time in many years, the police had coped alone in the maintenance of law and order in a national strike. It showed that the Home Office's attempts since 1908 to centralize the police force operationally had at last borne fruit. In an emergency the provincial police were able to operate as a centrally controlled force, and a traditional objective of law enforcement had therefore been achieved.

Yet, although the Home Office expressed gratification at the way the emergency machinery had operated during the general strike, at a different level serious problems continued to arise. There was now growing tension between local police authorities and the

[71] *Parl. Deb.*, 5th ser., 203, 531, (3 Mar. 1927).
[72] Dixon, 'The Home Office', p. 251.

Home Office and more particularly between local police authorities and their chief constables, especially in industrial areas where the Labour Party dominated. There was much local resistance to the authoritarian approach of the Home Office and chief constables here. Police authorities now vehemently questioned the borderline between the enforcement of law and order and those logistical issues involved in the management of police resources which were legitimate matters for political concern and financial control. This exercise in national co-ordination had serious consequences for the local control of the police.

The system of mutual aid that operated during the general strike and coal strike of 1926 indeed raised critical questions about the control, finance, and accountability of police forces. In terms of the function and activities of F Division of the Home Office, the police authorities had been entirely excluded. They were at no time consulted, even though the use of F Division's co-ordinating activities had impinged significantly on their own responsibility to provide an adequate and efficient force for their areas. F Division had responsibility to co-ordinate the police response and received information from chief constables to enable it to do this. Thus it is not surprising that there was no record of the Home Secretary having to use the Emergency Regulation which increased his powers in this area. The influence he could already exercise over F Division and its civil servants meant that he did not need to do so.

Not only were police authorities excluded from any say as to the way in which the police response to the strike of 1926 should be co-ordinated. More important, the financial accountability of local police forces had been severely undermined. Neither the local police authorities nor the County Councils Association and the Municipal Corporations Association had been told anything about what the police response would cost. The Home Secretary's sanctioning of the large amount of expenditure for police provision was even more puzzling as the police had so recently been subjected to the Geddes economies. Chiefs of police had been given *carte blanche* to incur any expenditure felt to be required notwithstanding the current financial constraints being imposed on the police forces. Both central and local government expenditure was concerned here. The County Councils Association wrote to Joynson-Hicks in 1926 that its police committee felt that all extra costs incurred by police authorities as a result of providing additional police in cases of national emergency should be borne wholly by the national Exchequer. But the under-secretary of state replied that the Home Secretary held out no hope of the government assenting to this. Nor did it do so.[73]

Thus, during the course of the general strike and coal strike of 1926 significant changes had taken place in the relationship between the Home Office and the local police authorities and between the latter and their chiefs of police. The Home Secretary had called into question the function of the police authorities by curtailing their role. The police authorities' financial control over their police had been eroded, since chief constables were allowed to judge expenditure, and the financial accountability of the force had been thus undermined.

Although there was nothing police authorities could do about the change in their position *vis-à-vis* the Home Office, there were now examples of police authorities trying to discipline or even dismiss chief constables for their actions in the troubled months of 1926. Not surprisingly, the most remarkable illustrations of this demand for accountability can be found once again in the South Wales coalfield, in the counties of Carmarthenshire, Glamorgan, and Monmouthshire. Not only were these counties uniquely militant in the general strike in 1926; in addition, serious industrial disputes continued to reverberate in these areas, even in the depressed years that followed, right down to the famous 'stay-down' stoppages successfully directed against Spencer-style company unionism in Monmouthshire and Glamorgan in 1934 and 1935. These examples of conflict between chief constables and local police authorities in this period, therefore, merit detailed discussion.

In Glamorgan, in 1926, the Labour members of the standing joint committee disputed the right of Lindsay, the chief constable of Glamorgan, to borrow police from other police authorities, to help keep order in the coal strike of that year. Complaint was also made about the body of special Police Reserves raised by the chief constable during the strike. When he notified the committee of his action in incurring extraordinary expenditure, the standing joint committee, according to one later account,

[73] Clerk to Leicestershire Standing Joint Committee to Clerk to Denbighshire Standing Joint Committee, 19 Jan. 1927 (Denbighshire Standing Joint Committee Minutes and Correspondence).

saw it as a fit occasion to attack the Chief Constable personally for his action. Instead of dealing with the matter of cost, time was given solely to acrimonious discussions between the Magistrates' representatives and the County Council members on the committee, some of the latter being actual miners leaders involved in the disturbances.[74]

Indeed the support of Sir Rhys Williams, a magistrate and the chairman of the standing joint committee, and the other magistrate members of the committee was to be invaluable to Lindsay here as it had been in the national miners' strike in 1921. In Carmarthenshire, meanwhile, the Labour and Trades Council pressed the standing joint committee to ask for the resignation of the chief constable, Picton-Phillips, because of the anti-Communist crusade he was conducting in the Amman valley and his actions in the general strike, including the strengthening of the police force. Again, it was unsuccessful.[75] In Monmouthshire the Labour majority on the standing joint committee fiercely attacked Victor Bosanquet, the chief constable, for borrowing police during the general strike and the coal strike, and for breaking up meetings and processions. As they were legally entitled to do, they demanded his resignation 'in as much as his actions in times of emergency are calculated to disturb the peace of the county'.[76] The local Tory press commented that this was a 'Socialist Plot': owing to Labour opposition no police reserve had been maintained in the county during the general strike and coal lock-out, while the recruitment of the ordinary force had been suspended. The Conservative *Western Mail* wrote that it was

important that the experienced officials who are placed at the head of the police forces of the country should have a free discretion as to the measures which have been taken for the preservation of public order. The law abiding inhabitants of Monmouthshire may count themselves lucky that the conduct of the police in regard to the repression of crime and the preservation of public order is subject to the law of the land and the supervision of the Home Secretary and not subject to the control of the representatives of a political party. The Home Secretary alone has the power to compel a chief constable to resign.[77]

74 W. C. May, *Recollections and Reflections of a County Policeman* (1979), 132.

75 *Police Review*, 6 Aug. 1926.

76 Monmouthshire Standing Joint Committee Minutes, 23 June 1926 (County Hall, Cwmbran).

77 *Western Mail*, 25 June 1926.

The Home Secretary flatly refused to agree to this resolution requesting the dismissal of the chief constable, and to the non-filling of vacancies within the force. However, the standing joint committee decided to confirm it.[78] The *Western Mail* observed that this showed the need for reform of the policing of the country as a whole.

> Monmouthshire is not the only county where attempts have been made to gain control over the administration of the law by particular parties or factions. . . . The solution of the problem lies in the standardisation of the whole police force of the country: the organization of the force as a national service on national lines and administered directly by the state.[79]

Although he was now 67, Bosanquet refused to resign, but the county council members of the standing joint committee, described by the chief constable as 'my little lot of Communists', persisted in demanding that he did so. However, the Home Office now showed its financial power over the provincial police authorities. It refused to issue a certificate of efficiency for the force for the year up to September 1926, and withheld the police grant until the police force was increased.[80] This case was said by the *Police Review* to be unique in police history. The matter was finally settled after a visit by representatives of Monmouthshire Standing Joint Committee to the Home Office.[81] According to the *Police Review*, the Home Office, in intervening here, recognized that, if such a resolution as had been adopted by the Monmouthshire Standing Joint Committee had been allowed to succeed, a serious blow would have been struck at the position of chief constables, and the efficiency of the police forces throughout the country.[82]

It was not accidental that early in 1927 the Police (Appeals) Act was passed. This act stated that any police officer was entitled to appeal to the Home Secretary against the penalty of dismissal or enforced resignation. By Section 2(2) of this Act, the Home Secretary may '(a) allow the appeal; or (b) dismiss the appeal; or (c) vary the punishment' and may for the purposes of deciding the

[78] Ibid.; *South Wales Daily News*, 21 June 1926.

[79] *Western Mail*, 26 June 1926.

[80] Bosanquet to Dixon, 11 Oct. 1926 (HO 45/17913/400508/50). *Western Mail*, 9 Dec. 1926.

[81] *Police Review*, 31 Dec. 1926.

[82] Ibid., 17 Dec. 1926.

appeal direct that an inquiry be held.[83] The right of appeal against the decision of a chief constable had long been pressed for by the rank and file of the force. It was highly significant that, of the appeals made to the Home Secretary under the Police (Appeals) Act between 1927 and 1935, only one appeal, and that from a chief constable, was allowed out of 103.[84] This appeal also arose indirectly out of circumstances connected with the miners' strike in 1926.

In the borough of St Helens in Lancashire friction between the watch committee and its chief constable, A. R. Ellerington, had been building up since 1918. It reached a climax in 1926 when police were drafted from Liverpool to help the St Helens force with industrial troubles. The committee objected to the presence of the Liverpool police and the way in which they exercised their powers. However, after an inquiry by Sir Leonard Dunning, the Home Office told the committee that the Liverpool men should remain. Meetings of the committee became more acrimonious in 1927. Its members complained of the way the chief constable responded to them, of his conduct before the magistrates, his dealings with members of the force and the Police Federation, and of his behaviour towards the general public. Finally, they attempted to dismiss the chief constable. Ellerington then appealed to the Home Secretary under the Police (Appeals) Act 1927, and was reinstated after an inquiry by Sir Henry Maddocks KC and Sir Leonard Dunning, chief inspector of constabulary.

This, however did not end the matter. The watch committee now produced statements, some of which suggested misconduct on the part of the chief constable, and it consulted the Home Office as to the form of inquiry by which they should be investigated. Joynson-Hicks then decided on an inquiry under the Tribunals of Inquiry (Evidence) Act, largely to secure that the evidence given might be on oath. This inquiry was conducted by T. Hollis Walker KC, the recorder of Derby, and C. de Courcy Parry, an inspector of constabulary. They explored the feud in detail. Although the evidence was loaded against the chief constable, they came to the conclusion that the chairman and other members of the watch committee who worked with him had baited the chief constable, and generally the inquiry found wholly in his favour. It expressed doubt 'as to whether the Chief Constable of a borough should be at

[83] Police (Appeals) Act 1927, 17 & 18 Geo. v, c. 19.
[84] See J. M. Hart, *The British Police* (1951), 77.

the mercy of a temporary majority of a Watch Committee acting perhaps on party lines, either in reference to breaches of discipline in the force, or in regard to his own tenure of office'.[85] The Home Secretary then called upon the St Helens Watch Committee to accept this report, to recall the chief constable to duty (he had been suspended), and to restore and maintain proper relations with him, so that a certificate of efficiency could then be granted by the Home Office. Very reluctantly, the St Helens Watch Committee had to give in. The effect was to show that watch committees in boroughs, like standing joint committees in the counties, were unable to dismiss a chief constable if the Home Office chose to support him.

After the defeat both of the general strike and of the national coal strike in 1926, the prospect of further major industrial unrest declined considerably. However, the government kept up its contingency plans for future crises. The STC remained in being. The STC was, so John Anderson declared: 'unanimously of opinion that for the present it was sufficient that preparations should be made as for the contingency of an industrial dispute and not as for the possibility of another attack on constitutional government'.[86] As before, the committee included the use of police, troops, and naval ratings in its plans to deal with labour.

The War Office was not happy about the way in which troops had been used in the general strike. It was, as ever, anxious to limit the liability of the army for internal order in industrial disputes. The general view of the Army Council was that the way in which troops had been used in the general strike for protection duties should not be repeated, as it had severely strained the constitutional usage.[87] One of the lessons of the strike had been the moral value of a formed body of troops in a disaffected area even though no actual disturbance broke out. Troops, even when acting as an escort to convoys, were still acting as a tactical reserve of police. Yet the governing principle of the employment of troops during civil unrest was that they should be retained in reserve for as long as

[85] See correspondence relating to St Helen's Oct.–Nov. 1926 (HO 45/17913/400508/52); *St Helens County Borough Police Force, Reports to the Secretary of State for the Home Department*, PP 1928 [Cmd. 3102], xii. 49.

[86] CAB 27/260, STC, 24 Mar. 1927.

[87] Note on the Principle of the Employment of Troops in Aid of the Civil Power, 28 Jan. 1927 (WO 32/3456).

possible and only aid the civil power when the police were overcome. This policy was much more likely to be capable of practical application if there was available, for the regular constabulary, a first reinforcement in the shape of a CCR.[88] The formation of such a reserve in the general strike in 1926 was regarded by the Army Council as a partial recognition of the fact that the provision of a reserve in support of the civil power was primarily the duty of a civil authority. The Home Secretary and many chief constables also felt that the CCR should be kept in existence for use in an emergency. It had the advantage that it was funded by the Exchequer, for use by chief constables, and, unlike the police who usually operated singly, it could be used in groups and could therefore protect vulnerable points more easily.[89]

At the beginning of 1927 the STC discussed the possibility of creating a body of whole-time special constables in the form of the CCR, to reduce the calls on troops. The STC now appointed a Protection Sub-committee to inquire into the possibility of raising such a force.[90] Joynson-Hicks proposed that the Home Office would undertake the recruitment of the force and its command, if the War Office would accept responsibility on the equipment side. By the end of 1927 it was agreed that there was no intention of enrolling this force at present, but only of making paper plans, so that a scheme for the recruitment of the Civil Constabulary Reserve would be ready if the government decided to use it. The War Office assented to this proposal, although it had originally wanted the formation of such a force to be entirely in the hands of the Home Office.[91]

In 1932, as the Home Office had still made no preparation, the CIGS agreed that the War Office would give the Home Office assistance with the organization, recruitment, and administration of the CCR on the condition that, after its formation, its use would be entirely a matter for the Home Office and the police.[92] This was agreed to, and by December 1932 a secret pamphlet had been drafted by the War Office for the formation of a CCR in the

[88] Note by the Adjutant-General to CIGS, 12 Feb. 1927 (WO 32/3456).

[89] Home Office minute on the formation of the Police Reserve, 1946 (HO 45/20536/658780/11).

[90] STC minutes, 17 Feb. 1927 (ADM 116/3494).

[91] CAB 24/189 CP 257 (27), joint memo. by Home Secretary and Secretary of State for War, 10 Nov. 1927.

[92] Notes by CIGS, ? April 1931 and 26 July 1932 (WO 32/3513).

metropolis. By April 1935 a similar scheme for the provinces had also been worked out.[93] In practice, the Home Office had again succeeded in underlining the War Office commitment to aid the civil authority, at least for the moment.

However, the central role of troops was still seen as a strong probability in the case of a major strike. Indeed in 1927 the STC agreed that the Army Council should be kept informed that it was likely that 'there would be a small number of vulnerable points for which it would not, in fact, be possible to provide adequate protection by regular police or any auxiliary police which might be available'.[94] Troops should, therefore, be earmarked with this possible purpose in mind. The Adjutant-General was now reconciled to the fact that he could not 'refuse to consider in advance plans for the employment of troops in an area like the docks'.[95] Between 1927 and 1929 the London Dock Defence Scheme was drawn up by the Protection Sub-committee of the STC in consultation with the Port of London Authority and other port employers. As soon as a stoppage began, the docks would be sealed off and only entrances essential to working would be left open. These would be guarded by a strong force of police. The army would provide two infantry battalions and armoured cars for escorting convoys.[96] The Committee felt that it would be of great advantage in an event of such magnitude as a dock strike if an adequate military force could be made available from the beginning of the period. At the time when volunteer labour was working the docks

> the employment of an adequate military force should be regarded as an integral part of the protection arrangements. . . . the first moves should be made under cover of an overwhelming show of force. . . . It is doubtful whether any body of unarmed police even if supported by a mounted detachment could produce the necessary effect and in any event this could not be secured without employing police in such numbers as seriously to cripple their activities in other directions. It is to be remembered in this connection that the most successful efforts to remove goods by convoy from the docks will be stultified if the vehicles conveying the goods . . . are held up . . . if it is to be solved to any effective degree the Police must be everywhere and be ready to concentrate at any point and

93 CCR Formation Instructions, Dec. 1932 (HO 45/20536/658780/5).
94 STC minutes, 17 Feb. 1927 (ADM 116/3494).
95 Minute by Adjutant-General, 12 Feb. 1927 (WO 32/3456).
96 CAB 27/261 (24) 8, STC, 28 May 1929.

that they cannot therefore immobilize any considerable numbers of men on the protection of the Docks or of convoys without seriously interfering with these other equally important duties elsewhere which only they are competent to perform. For this reason we have come to the conclusion that the employment of troops should form part of the measures for protection from the commencement of the third stage.

The committee did, however, agree that the question whether the employment of troops was necessary or desirable 'must remain for decision when the occasion arises'. The new London Dock Scheme was completed by the STC by May 1929.[97] Thus if a major strike in this area occurred there could be no doubt that troops would be used again, as in the general strike, in a policing role by the Home Office.

Nevertheless, one clear conclusion emerging from the general strike and miners' lock-out was that the main responsibility for the preservation of law and order in any future industrial emergency could be borne by the police. This was in large measure because the government visualized that no future general strike would be likely to occur and that a single-industry crisis was most probable. The Home Office now concentrated upon building on the experience of the use of police in the general strike and coal strike. By 1928 all police authorities had agreed to the renewal of the General Mutual Aid Agreement for a further indefinite period. The Home Office was in constant communication with individual authorities to keep up force numbers.[98] However, although police recruiting was only curtailed between 1922 and 1925, it remained difficult to recruit suitable men for the force, while the prevailing economic climate made most police authorities reluctant to increase their forces to any large extent; Home Office pressure for the amalgamation of the smaller borough police forces with those of the surrounding counties during the inter-war period met with no marked success. Indeed, the ratio of police to population became increasingly unfavourable in the later 1920s and 1930s.[99]

[97] Ibid.

[98] Home Office to Receiver of Metropolitan Police, 22 Aug. 1928 and correspondence (HO 45/17913/400508/62); Home Office to Clerk to Monmouthshire Standing Joint Committee, 26 Apr. 1927 (Monmouthshire Standing Joint Committee Minutes); Dixon, 'The Home Office', p. 195.

[99] *Report of the Committee on the Police Service*, Part II, PP 1920 [Cmd. 574], xxii. 539; *Report from the Select Committee on Police Force (Amalgamation)*, PP 1931–2 (106), v. 123; and see Appendix, Table 3 below.

One of the main lessons of the general strike, from the police point of view, however, was that a large number of special constables had enrolled during the time of crisis. The Home Office now made an effort to ensure that this unpaid volunteer force was not allowed to lapse. A major criticism of the special constables who had enrolled in such great numbers was their lack of organization and control. Police authorities were now instructed by the Home Office to maintain an adequate special constabulary and to give it periodic instruction in police duty.[100] In order to overcome suspicion which the special constabulary was said to have aroused among some sections of society, Home Office rhetoric now emphasized the common-law duty of all citizens to aid the police. The Royal Commission on Police Powers and Procedure which reported in 1929 emphasized that 'The Police of this country have never been recognised, either in law or by tradition, as a force distinct from the general body of citizens'.[101] Indeed, one of the inspectors of constabulary commented in his evidence before the commission:

> the experience gained by the Special Constabulary during recent years has had a widespread effect. . . .
>
> Earlier on, police activities may have been looked upon by the man in the street as the more or less routine happenings of a mysterious profession of which he knew little or nothing. As a result of a practical share in Police experiences some greater part of the community is now conversant with Police responsibilities and professional procedure. Practical experience is an acid test of difficulties and has settled many doubts.

He felt that, now ordinary people had had practical experience of police duty, they could go out and spread their own opinion amongst the rest of the community to the advantage of police.[102]

There was now a steady increase in the First Reserve, and also of special constables willing to enter into a three-year agreement.[103] During the general strike the special constabulary had expanded to 60,000 in the metropolis. It was felt desirable to increase the establishment of the uniformed special constabulary First Reserve

[100] See, for example, Manchester City Watch Committee Minutes, 1926–36, and Liverpool City Watch Committee Minutes, 1926–36.

[101] *Report of the Royal Commission on Police Powers and Procedure*, PP 1928–9 [Cmd. 3297], ix. 138.

[102] Ibid., *Minutes of Evidence*, Part I, p. 118, evidence of Major-General L. W. Atcherley.

[103] *Annual Report of HM Inspector of Constabulary*, PP 1927 (2), xi. 985.

on three-year engagements from 8,000 to 15,000, and this could be done from men enrolled during the general strike. They should receive peacetime training, and be employed as often as possible on ceremonial duties.[104] In 1934 it was proposed by the Commandant of the Metropolitan Special Constabulary Reserve to fix the number of this force at 12,500 uniformed men, to receive compulsory training, with the object of providing 'a more efficient force, better trained and more suited to the demands which might be made upon it during a period of national emergency'. The then Home Secretary, Sir John Gilmour, agreed.[105] In many provincial cities special constables were given some training in the 1930s to enable them to perform the work of the regular police in an emergency. In Manchester, for example, the special constabulary was highly organized by this time. In 1928 the force was grouped into seven companies, each with at least one commander, several sub-commanders, and, below them, sergeants and constables amounting to a total of 754 in all. The training of the force was carried on during the period 1 October–31 March by means of drill, lectures on police duties and the principles of first aid. By 1936 there was also a mounted detachment of special constables who

> patrol the main thoroughfares of the city and perform police duty generally. There are twenty horses attached permanently to the department. The detachment rendered invaluable service at various times during the year in connection with demonstrations and processions.[106]

Throughout the later 1920s and 1930s, indeed, the number of peacetime special constables remained high, although showing a decline from the massive numbers recorded during the general strike. In 1930 a total of 142,731 was registered for England and Wales, and numbers exceeded 100,000 for the remainder of the inter-war period.[107]

[104] Memo. on a conference at the Home Office on the Establishment of the Metropolitan Special Constabulary Reserve, 26 May 1926 (MEPO 2/1837); Home Secretary to Commissioner of Metropolitan Police, 22 June 1926 (ibid.); *Parl. Deb.*, 5th ser., 197, 2178 (7 July 1926).

[105] Minute on Metropolitan Special Constabulary Reserve Organization from Walter Allen, Commandant in Chief of the Metropolitan Special Constabulary Reserve to Commissioner of Metropolitan Police, 1934 (HO 45/17536/672294/1); F. C. Johnson (Home Office) to Walter Allen, 23 Apr. 1934 (ibid.).

[106] Chief constable's reports to Manchester City Watch Committee, 1920–39.

[107] *Annual Report of HM Inspector of Constabulary*, PP 1930 (40), xvi. 837; *Report of HM Inspector of Constabulary*, PP 1937–8 (53), xiv. 549.

In 1931 John Anderson reported that changes in police organization were going 'in the direction of increasing numbers, efficiency and co-operation as between one force and another'. The only problem which could arise which might affect the position materially was if there should be any question of modifying the present rates of pay.[108] In fact, in 1931 the May Committee on governmental economy recommended drastic cuts in government expenditure, notably in unemployment benefit, but also in the armed forces and the police. Police pay was to be cut by 12½ per cent in two annual instalments. Although these cuts were modified after the threat of reduced pay had caused a mutiny in the navy at Invergordon, this large reduction in pay was not acceptable to the police service. There were now protest meetings of the Police Federation and attempts to cause disaffection in the force.[109] The loyalty of the police was again suspect as it had been in 1918 and 1919. In 1934 Sir John Gilmour, the Home Secretary, actually tried to get the police included in the Incitement to Disaffection Bill on the grounds that 'A good deal of information has come to light recently which suggests that the Police Service contains at least a proportion of men who could not be relied on to withstand attempts to undermine their loyalty'.[110] Yet these fears proved groundless. Despite the pay cuts of the 1930s the police were in a better position than many other workers at this time. In fact their wages and clothing allowances, their subsidized housing and travel, all seemed to reveal a nexus of privilege which set them apart from the communities they policed.[111]

These measures taken by the Home Office in the years since the general strike ensured that, subject to fears about the effect of pay cuts, the internal coherence and co-ordination of the police were greatly reinforced. Internally, the force was well equipped to fulfil its central role in dealing with any future industrial conflict. There still remained, however, one important external constraint upon the police—the possibility of tension between chief constables and local police authorities anxious about accountability.

[108] CAB 53/22 COS 267, Home Office report to the Committee of Imperial Defence by John Anderson, 17 Apr. 1931.

[109] *The Times*, 2 Nov., 26 Sept. 1932.

[110] CAB 24/247 CP 53 (34), memo. by Home Secretary on the Incitement to Sedition Bill, 23 Feb. 1934.

[111] J. P. Martin and G. Wilson, *The Police: A Study in Manpower* (1969), 66.

One significant case heard in 1930 raised the central issue of the independence of the constable. Although technically concerned with operational questions, it had implications for wider policy-making and it is appropriate, therefore, to discuss it at this point. In the case of *Fisher* v. *Oldham Corporation*[112] it was sought to make the corporation of the borough of Oldham liable for damages for the actions of the local police. This was said to have been the first occasion in England when such an action had been brought. Fisher, a Plaistow timber merchant, had been arrested in London and taken to Oldham to be charged with obtaining money by false pretences. He had been detained for several hours, and then found not to be the man for whose arrest a warrant had been issued. When he was released he sued the corporation. His statement of claim alleged that the defendants acting through their watch committee were the police authority for the county Borough of Oldham and were the employers of the police for the said borough. McCardie J. first of all cited the relevant sections of the Municipal Corporations Act 1882 which provided that watch committees might frame such regulations as they should deem expedient for preventing neglect or abuse and for making borough constables efficient in the discharge of their duties. They might at any time suspend or dismiss a constable whom they thought negligent or unfit. Because of this, the defendants, having a duty to pay salaries or wages, and power to make regulations for and dismiss their police, were placed by the Act substantially in a master-and-servant relationship. However, as McCardie also pointed out, other statutory provisions had given the Home Secretary, as central police authority, a power to make regulations as to the government, mutual aid, pay, allowances, pensions, clothing, expenses, and conditions of service of the police. In addition, the Police (Appeals) Act had strengthened the power of the Home Secretary over the police. Taking these together with the common-law view of the status of police officers, it became clear that the police, in affecting the arrest and detention of the plaintiff, were fulfilling their duties as public servants of the Crown and that the corporation was not answerable in law for their actions. Thus McCardie found that 'a police constable is not a servant of the borough. He is a servant of the State, a ministerial officer of the central power, though subject, in some respects, to local super-

[112] [1930] 2 KB 364.

vision and local regulation.' The effect of this judgment was materially to strengthen the position of constables against their police authorities.

Although the Home Office's views and case law strengthened the position of the individual constable in his relation to the law, in the provinces police organization was so structured and so governed by hierarchical decision-making that it was very rare for a single constable to make a self-determined move. The dominant figure here was the chief constable in whom operational control of every police force was vested.

It was in counties like Glamorgan that the most critical cases occurred. In 1935, when Chief Constable Lindsay applied for reinforcements in anticipation of disturbances connected with the stay-in stoppage, the Labour members of the Glamorgan Standing Joint Committee questioned the need for these additional police. They alleged that the chief constable had no legal powers to act in this direction without the approval of the committee.[113] Lindsay replied that the only power the committee had over him was that of the control of any costs he would incur through the transportation of police to Taff Merthyr. A few days later, he applied for police reinforcements from outside the county. Even though the magistrate members of the standing joint committee proposed immediate action, the county council members argued that the strike was caused by the colliery company's refusal to recognize the miners' demands for increased wages. The chairman of the committee then asked the deputy chief constable, over the head of the chief constable, whether, in his opinion, there was no exaggeration in the application. The deputy chief constable considered that the reinforcement might be postponed for a few days, whereupon Lindsay, with the magistrates' backing, referred the problem to the under-secretary at the Home Office. The latter then placed 50 Birmingham police at his disposal. The chief constable was now able to borrow 50 policemen from the Bristol City force, 50 from Swansea, a further 50 from Birmingham, and 100 from Liverpool.[114] Labour and Communist members of the standing joint committee promptly refused to pay the bills for the borrowed police and any future expenses of the Glamorgan police in attending military drills. When the standing joint committee placed this

[113] *Recollections*, May, p. 292.
[114] Chief constable of Glamorgan to Standing Joint Committee, n.d. Dec. 1935.

case before the Home Office, however, it instructed the county treasurer to pay the bills, and he did so.[115]

Throughout the 1930s the Labour-dominated membership of the Glamorgan Standing Joint Committee had been pressing for the resignation of Chief Constable Lindsay, who was now elderly. In July 1936 they called for his resignation when he reached the age of 75. Labour councillors claimed that he had served the police service of Glamorgan badly, and had encouraged police brutality. Even the Home Office now suggested that Lindsay might resign, but he refused to do so until Labour allegations made against him were disposed of.[116] Eventually he did agree to go on 7 December 1936, after forty-five controversial years in Glamorgan.[117]

Although the experience of the general strike and coal strike in 1926 was extreme and transitory, episodes such as those mentioned above tend to confirm the wider pattern of the history of the police since 1919—diminishing local control over police operations, accentuated by the pressures arising from major industrial disputes. Yet nowhere was this officially admitted. One intriguing view of the Home Office outlook was expressed by Joynson-Hicks in 1926 when he coyly admitted that he exercised, as he put it, 'a curious kind of supervising power' over the provincial police. A later Home Secretary, Sir John Gilmour, gave his view in 1933. His department was 'always endeavouring to co-ordinate the work between Scotland Yard and the different authorities throughout the country'. There was also 'an increasing appreciation on the part of police authorities throughout the country of the necessity to co-operate with the Home Office, and an earnest desire on the part of chief constables to do so'.[118]

A left-wing Labour MP, Mr Rhys Davies, complained to the Speaker of the Commons in 1936 that, when matters of police administration came up under a provincial local authority, the town clerk invariably referred them to the Home Office. Yet in the House MPs were told that 'we must go to the watch committee or the standing joint committee'. The Deputy Chairman replied, in nineteenth-century terms, that the Home Secretary did not control the provincial police.

[115] *Recollections*, May, pp. 199–200.
[116] *Western Mail*, 28 July 1936.
[117] Ibid. 3 Oct. 1936.
[118] *Parl. Deb.*, 5th ser., 199, 734 (26 Oct. 1926); ibid., 279, 1813 (30 June 1933).

> [the Home Secretary] cannot give orders. The orders to them are given by the statutory authority, which is the standing joint committee in the case of a county and in the case of a borough . . . it is the watch committee. . . . The most that he can do is to circularize the local authorities and give them advice. . . . The only responsibility of the Home Secretary in respect of the provincial police is that he can inspect them and see that they are efficient.[119]

But it is clear from the record that in practice, as opposed to antique theory, successive Home Secretaries took a broad and buoyant view of their powers over the provincial police between 1919 and 1939. While they accepted the general concept of the independence of the provincial police authorities, at the same time they were often to advise them, to the point of overriding them altogether.

The final conclusion must, therefore, focus on the abiding power of the Home Secretary, built up relentlessly in the atmosphere of industrial confrontation that marked labour relations in the first three decades of the century. By the 1930s the central government had achieved a position of unprecedented power over the provincial police and their local authorities in emergencies. The St. Helen's case showed that borough, as well as county, committees were being undermined. As the powers of the central state increased, so did those of chief constables. Closer integration between the Home Office and the police sprang, not from any deliberately conceived policy on the part of the local authorities, but from the willingness of most chief constables to co-operate with the central government. A tacit consensus developed between the Home Office in the era of Troup and Anderson and chief constables as to what were their respective spheres of responsibility, and the nature of their coexistence. The effect was that police authorities were now confined essentially to providing and maintaining an efficient police force, whereas matters of 'policy' (defined by Troup as the 'means and methods' of carrying out police duties) lay beyond the sphere of local authority control.

By the end of the 1930s the avowed objective over the past thirty years entertained by leading Home Office figures like Troup and Anderson had been substantially achieved. In the provinces the central government had overriding power to ensure the effective assistance of one force to aid another in an emergency and the co-

[119] Ibid., 314, 1554 (10 July 1936).

operation between local forces. Behind them lay the brute force of central financial support. The armed services, brought in most reluctantly to aid the civil power, reinforced the Home Office's purposes still further. Removed from local control they had become an arm of the central state.

In 1939 the belief in local independence in the maintenance of law and order still endured, as it had done since the Middle Ages. The police system retained its formal county or borough structure. The view that everyday crime and disorder in a community could be most effectively dealt with by the police on the spot survived in large measure. Nevertheless, there had been significant changes. Chief constables now need pay little heed to their police committees. Nationally, parliament had scant influence over the determination of police policy. In place of the authority of elected representatives, there was a commitment to police autonomy with Home Office direction. After the accretions of legend have been peeled away, significant moves towards the nationalization of the British police were a decisive result of the labour troubles of 1900–39.

6

Picketing, Industrial Disorder, and the Police, 1900–1918

THE organizational framework within which the police acted, nationally and locally, has now been examined in detail. But it was through executive action that the main impact of the police upon labour relations was most acutely felt. In this and the subsequent two chapters, therefore, the nature and extent of police operations will provide the focus of attention, with particular emphasis on picketing and industrial disorder, and the control of demonstrations by the unemployed. It was in these key areas, above all, that the executive role of the police impinged upon the working-class movement, often with bitter consequences.

The years 1900–1918 have been shown to be a time of unusual strain and stress for industrial relations and the rule of law. As local and national disputes both became violent, it was on the picket line that disorder commonly broke out. Especially in the years 1910–12 a sequence of crises brought conflict between the police and labour on an unprecedented scale. Amongst the authorities, as has been seen, the Home Office devoted new energy to co-ordinating the activity of police forces, with very limited success. It also used troops on an unprecedented scale in a policing role. Now for the first time a co-ordinated national executive response was urged on the police (often backed up by troops) by the Home Office. The degree of success achieved by the department in this respect will emerge in the treatment below. Here, we will start by reviewing the legal and industrial circumstances which influenced official policy, and set out the stages by which procedures were developed and defined.

At the outset of the twentieth century picketing was still nominally regulated by Section 7 of the Conspiracy and Protection of Property Act of 1875. After outlining various forms of intimidation and annoyance, this section added a clause that was understood to legalize peaceful picketing 'in order merely to obtain or communi-

1. Police taking their meals in the colliery power house during the Tonypandy riots, November 1910.

2. Captain Lionel Lindsay, MVO, OBE.

3. Winston Churchill inspecting Imperial Service Cadets at Brighton, 1910.

4. Joynson-Hicks arriving for a Cabinet meeting during the general strike, May 1926, together with Mitchell Thompson, Cunliffe-Lister, and Hoare.

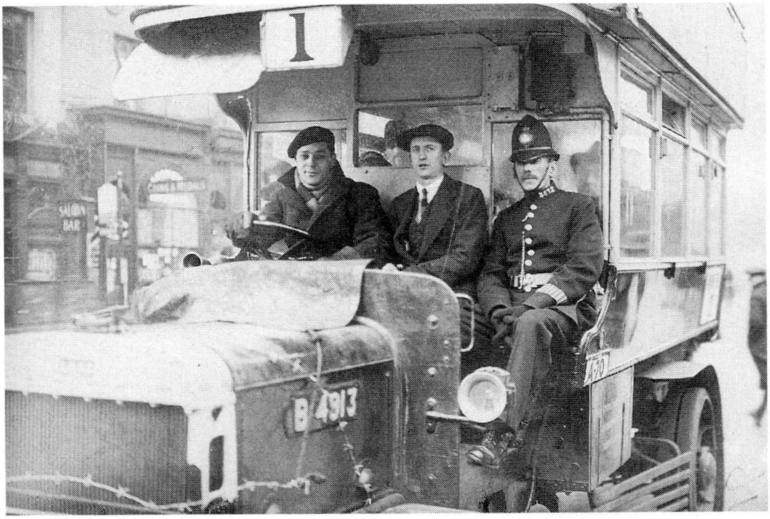

5. Volunteer drivers under police protection during the general strike, May 1926.

6. Naval ratings unloading their rations, guarded by soldiers, while protecting Neasden power station during the general strike, May 1926.

7. Police charge hunger marchers at Marble Arch, 1932.

8. Police keeping order in Trafalgar Square during a mass meeting of the unemployed, 4 March 1934.

cate information'.[1] But, as Lord Lindley remarked in the 1890s, 'you cannot make a strike effective without doing more than is lawful'.[2] As Kahn-Freund has written, 'it is here more than anywhere else that permissible economic pressure and impermissible physical force are liable to get mixed up'.[3] There was much uncertainty, not to say confusion, about the bearing of statute law on picketing as currently practised. Indeed, picketing presented unresolved problems to those who formulated rules and even more to the police who had to try to enforce them on the spot, in the circumstances of particular disputes. How much depended upon their judgement was soon to appear.

The difficulty of using the formal machinery of the law to regulate industrial disorder was demonstrated, for example, in the violent disturbances already described which occurred at the Featherstone Colliery in Yorkshire 1893. In the major strike which took place at the Penryhn slate quarries in North Wales in 1900–3 the methods adopted by the quarrymen in enforcing the collective decision not to allow blacklegs to work included boycott, picketing, and demonstrations along with 'attacks on individuals and

[1] Under Section 7 of the Conspiracy and Protection of Property Act 1875 an offence is committed by every person who,

> 'with a view to compel any other person to abstain from doing or to do any act which such other person has a legal right to do or abstain from doing, wrongfully and without legal authority,
> (1) Uses violence to or intimidates such other person or his wife or children, or injures his property; or
> (2) Persistently follows such other person about from place to place; or
> (3) Hides any tools, clothes or other property owned or used by such other person, or deprives him of or hinders him in the use thereof; or
> (4) Watches or besets the house or other place where such other person resides, or works, or carries on business, or happens to be, or the approach to such house or place; or
> (5) Follows such other person with two or more other persons in a disorderly manner in or through any street or road, shall on conviction thereof by a court of summary jurisdiction, or on indictment as hereinafter mentioned, be liable either to pay a penalty not exceeding twenty pounds, or to be imprisoned for a term not exceeding three months, with or without hard labour.'

[2] Quoted by K. W. Wedderburn in his evidence of 22 Mar. 1966 (31) before the Royal Commission on Trade Unions and Employers' Associations (HMSO 1966), 1304.

[3] O. Kahn-Freund, *Labour and the Law* (2nd edn., 1977), 261. The word picketing, as applied to industrial strikes, was first used in 1867 and applied to men stationed by a trade union to watch men going to work during a strike and to endeavour to dissuade them from doing so.

property'.[4] Women and children were prominent amongst those looting and catcalling. The day after the reopening of the quarry at Bethesda, in June 1901, a demonstration of 3,000 people was held; it ended with twenty people being summoned for threatening behaviour. Thereafter, demonstrations and processions marching around Bethesda and the neighbourhood became regular features of the strike. Outside the homes of blacklegs, these would stop for hooting, hissing, and sometimes the breaking of windows. There were frequent arrests for obstruction and insulting language. The authorities responded in August when fighting between police and strikers took place, by sending 200 infantry and 60 cavalry into Bangor, and moving 100 South Staffordshire and East Yorkshire Infantry and 30 dragoons to Bethesda. Even with the presence of troops in the vicinity, giving moral support to the police by their presence, minor incidents continued to occur. On 20 August some 50 cavalry were moved into the area when strikers attacked a public house where two non-strikers were drinking. At the end of the month twenty-six people came up before the magistrates charged with disturbing the peace and obstruction. Many further incidents followed, culminating in looting and a near riot on New Year's Eve 1900.[5] Eventually there were several prosecutions for riot at the Caernarfon Assizes.[6] Picketing here was not regulated by the law, but by the presence of a sufficient force of troops and police in the neighbourhood. It was seen as a simple problem of public order and treated as such.

There were many complaints about police conduct at Penrhyn, yet the strikers had no redress against the police. Throughout the strike, local Liberal voices such as the Caernarfon newspaper, *Yr Herald Cymraeg*, argued that the strikers and families were largely peaceful and that it was from the police, often emboldened by the presence of troops, that the main threat of violence came.[7] The general feeling of the Bethesda community seems to have been that police action was biased and over-zealous. Adding to the tally of policemen and troops in the district was only adding to the number of Lord Penrhyn's supporters. The police were variously criticized for want of tact, acts of cruelty and improper language,

4 Jones, *Quarrymen*, p. 232.
5 Ibid., pp. 238–44.
6 D. Williams, *Keeping the Peace*, pp. 240–1.
7 *Yr Herald Cymraeg*, 4 June 1901.

the giving of false evidence, and a general want of impartiality. The majority report of a sub-committee of the Caernarfonshire Standing Joint Committee, signed by five out of the seven members, severely condemned the police for their general behaviour.[8] Yet no inquiry into police conduct here was held: the chief constable merely claimed his statutory responsibilty for the discipline of the force and was supported by the magistrate members of his standing joing committee.

Although the police, often backed up by troops, seemed to have all the powers they needed to deal with picketing, and were to be unaccountable for their actions, Colonel Ruck, the chief constable of Caernarfonshire, was faced with complaints from the managers of the quarries over what they felt to be the inadequacy of police protection for blacklegs in the face of bitter hostility from pickets. Ruck, however, disagreed with the quarry management on two crucial points. He informed them that it was not the role of the police to initiate proceedings against those who embarrassed or insulted blackleg labour. Rather, it was the aggrieved persons who should do so. The police could act only if it was a case of unlawful assembly. There was little they could do about 'rough music'. Ruck also argued that the behaviour of some blacklegs had been offensive towards the strikers. The quarry manager, E. A. Young, overcame the problem of what he felt was police inactivity by prompting independent legal action by his blackleg workmen. Their costs were paid for by the quarry management, and civil proceedings now followed.[9]

The Penrhyn troubles illustrated graphically a theme that will recur in the subsequent discussion, namely that the law on picketing was notable for its non-observance and non-enforcement. The police had no powers of arrest for any of the offences specified under Section 7 of the Conspiracy and Protection of Property Act 1875. Although they could charge persons with offences under this section of the Act they were dependent upon evidence being forthcoming and this was often inaccessible after the event. In fact, the police tended to avoid prosecutions under the Act, as convictions were in any case very difficult to obtain. There was a major legal controversy at this time (including two conflicting decisions in the Court of Appeal) about what was

[8] Jones, *Quarrymen*, p. 252.
[9] Ibid., pp. 248–51.

peaceful picketing and what was not.[10] The main problem here was whether picketing ceased to be peaceful once the conveying of information to strikers became an attempt to persuade, perhaps in intimidatory fashion. It may be concluded that the Penrhyn strike provided further proof of the unsatisfactory nature of the law and of the overall guidelines that existed for the problem of picketing.

A new chapter began with the passage of the Trade Disputes Act 1906. This was originally a measure introduced by the Labour Party, which was taken up by the new Campbell-Bannerman Liberal government, and which rapidly became law. Section 2 of the 1906 Act replaced the proviso about attendance in Section 7 of the Act of 1875 by a wider one:

> It shall be lawful for one or more persons, acting on their own behalf or on behalf of a trade union or of an individual employer or firm in contemplation or furtherance of a trade dispute, to attend at or near a house or place where a person resides or works or carries on business or happens to be, if they so attend merely for the purpose of peacefully obtaining or communicating information or of peacefully persuading any person to work or abstain from working.[11]

Thus came into being what has been termed 'the modern right to picket'. Trade unionists, when on strike, were given an immunity from civil or criminal liability for 'peaceful persuasion'; but otherwise Section 7 of the 1875 Act remained law, and pickets were not exempted from the criminal law altogther. In the view of present-day legal historians, however, the 1906 Act basically confirmed the situation as it actually existed.

This new measure was directly in opposition to the findings of the Royal Commission on Trade Unions in 1906. It also conflicted with the advice of Sir John Walton, the Liberal Attorney-General, who felt that 'peaceful picketing' was not a concept that had much validity in itself. The Royal Commission in 1906 had argued:

> The truth is that picketing—however conducted—is always and of necessity in the nature of an annoyance to the person picketed. . . . It is obvious how easy it must be to pass from the language of persuasion into that of abuse, and from words of abuse to threats and acts of violence. A considerable proportion of the cases of physical violence which occur during times of strike arise directly or indirectly out of picketing.

[10] *Lyons* v. *Wilkins* [1896] I Ch 811; and [1899] I Ch 255.
[11] Trade Disputes Act 1906, 6 Edw. VII, C. 47.

It also added, significantly, that 'the real vice of picketing consisted in illegal intimidation'.[12]

These immunities conferred by Section 2 (1) of the 1906 Act were to cause endless debate and argument in subsequent years, both police and pickets being uncertain as to the precise effect of the law. It was said that trade unionists tended to believe that the Act gave them a licence to behave as they wished on picket lines. 'It was believed . . . that the protection afforded by the Act of 1906 upon an act done in furtherance of a trade dispute was sufficient to take it out of Section 7 of the Act of 1875.'[13] Conservatives claimed that the unions had been given extraordinary privileges, that police powers had been curtailed, and that the police were now powerless when confronted with organized labour. Conversely, the left tended to see this provision as an attempt to limit picketing practice, influenced by a wish to protect blacklegs. The police called upon to uphold these provisions were seen as being drawn into disputes on behalf of the government and employers. Thus, far from clarifying the position, the Act of 1906 seemed to have complicated matters further. It confirmed that picketing remained a social phenomenon for which it was particularly difficult to provide legislation. It was again to be evident how much its control depended on the judgement of the police.

In a dispute which occurred at the Hemsworth Colliery in Yorkshire in 1907 the police were said to have insulted and interfered with peaceful pickets, and used their batons freely while simultaneously providing protection for blacklegs.[14] The chief constable here, Captain Metcalf, agreed to hold an inquiry into police conduct with the approval of his standing joint committee.[15] He also told the Home Office that he had warned his police to be more careful in their attitude and conduct towards the strikers, and 'impressed upon them the necessity for the exercise of the greatest tact in their most difficult duty'.[16] But no national directives came from Whitehall. Although chief constables in the counties kept the Home Office informed about the industrial

[12] *Report of the Royal Commission on Trade Disputes and Trade Combinations* (Majority Report), PP 1906 [Cd. 2825], lvi. 15.

[13] *Parl. Deb.*, 5th ser., 419, 1837–8 (26 Feb. 1946).

[14] H. Smith to chief constable of West Riding, 8 May 1907 (HO 45/10367/156704/1).

[15] Home Office to Mr Potts, n.d. Sept. 1907 (ibid.).

[16] Chief constable of West Riding to Home Office, 6 Sept. 1907 (ibid.).

situation in their areas when strikes occurred, it is evident that the preservation of law and order in these situations was seen by the department as the responsibility of the local police authorities to handle picketing as they saw fit, and that no overview was provided by central government.

As has been seen, with the onset of major strikes during the 1910–12 period the Home Office was drawn into local industrial affairs in a significant way for the first time, with implications for the police. Picketing was regulated not by the law but by the presence of a sufficient number of police in an area. Frequently, these were not available in any number, as strikes were often nation-wide. Moreover, the cost of borrowing police, particularly for small boroughs, could be prohibitively expensive. To ensure a national response to strikes of this kind, the Home Office assumed national responsibility for the provision of police and, more particularly, troops. In addition, it now began to try to apply some coherence and precision to the law on picketing. Home Office direction with reference to the executive action of the provincial forces as well as the Metropolitan Police now came about for the first time, with startling consequences as will be seen.

It was in the coal-mining industry that the most desperate cases of disorder always arose. As has been seen in Chapter 3, the first case of extreme disorder came at the Cambrian Collieries around Tonypandy in the Rhondda valley, and also at the Powell Duffryn Collieries in the Aberdare valley in the autumn of 1910. These added important new elements to the story of picketing. On 7 November strikers in the Rhondda valley were said to have attempted to force officials, stokers, and others in the Glamorgan colliery Llwynypia to leave work. This led to serious rioting in Llwynypia and Tonypandy on 7–8 November. Meanwhile, in the Aberdare valley, on 2 November, a train carrying working colliers had been attacked by strikers between Aberdare and Cwmaman, while rioting occurred at Aberaman on 8 November. The police available were hopelessly inadequate. The chief constable, Captain Lindsay, had under his command for the protection of the collieries in the two valleys just over 100 foot and mounted men. The Glamorgans were reinforced on 7 November by thirty men from Swansea, sixty-three from Bristol, and fifty from Cardiff.[17]

[17] D. Evans, *Labour Strife in the South Wales Coalfield, 1910–11* (1911), 40.

On 7 November the picketing strategy pursued by the Cambrian strikers entered a new phase. By the evening of that day all ventilation and pumping work at the Cambrian Combine pits, with just one exception, had been suspended. Machinery had been brought to a standstill at the pits of Brittanic Merthyr and Glamorgan at Gilfach Goch. The same was true at the pits of the Naval and Cambrian companies at Penygraig and Clydach Vale. At the electric power station at Clydach Vale a crowd was alleged to have overpowered the police and manhandled some electricians there when they tried to escape. While Lindsay concentrated his resources on protecting some fifty or sixty officials and draftsmen at the Llwynypia Colliery of the Glamorgan company, the miners had succeeded in closing down completely pits at Clydach Vale, Trealaw, Penygraig, and Tonypandy. A major assault was made on the Llwynypia Colliery on the night of 7–8 November. The police dug themselves in, with such strength as they had, at the colliery pay office and the gateway adjoining. Ninety-nine foot and mounted police, under the personal command of Chief Constable Lindsay, defended the colliery. Thirty of them formed a double cordon across the entrance to the colliery yard; a further twenty-three guarded the power station. After the crowd outside had gathered to hurl first abuse and then missiles at the police inside the colliery premises, the police themselves, reinforced by men from Clydach Vale, began a series of increasingly violent baton charges around 11.30 p.m. The police were eventually successful in dispersing the crowd of strikers who fled in disorder just after midnight. The Rhondda crisis, however, had only just begun.[18]

At 1 a.m. on 8 November a serious disturbance began in Pandy Square, Tonypandy, where the strikers driven from Llwynypia had assembled. The police baton-charged the crowd and an hour's fight ensued. It is known that over sixty strikers were treated for injuries such as broken skulls and damaged bones; but probably a far greater number suffered in the fighting which lasted over three hours. In all between seventy and eighty police constables were engaged, and police casualties totalled thirty-eight. Lindsay, pressed by the coalowners, now applied for military assistance, as was seen in an earlier chapter. But before the Metropolitan Police who were dispatched actually arrived, about 9,000 miners marched, on the afternoon of 8 November, through Tonypandy,

[18] Ibid., p. 41.

Trealaw, and Llwynypia to the Glamorgan colliery where a one-and-a-half hour battle with the police resulted, unparalleled in its ferocity and bloodshed. The main object of the strikers, who were said to be armed with 'shafts, pick-axes, iron bars, pokers, barbed and plain wire ropes . . . cudgels as well as stones', was to capture the power house.[19] The colliery was held by 120 constables, again under the personal command of Lindsay. The crowd brought down the surrounding railings, then showered the police guard with stones and attacked the power house. The police forcibly cleared the crowd and there were many casualties on both sides. One account of the police attack described it as follows:

> With a dervish yell and batons drawn they dashed out between 80 and 90 strong from the colliery yard and cut a way clean through the densely packed mob. Their first purpose was to split up the crowd. . . . This purpose accomplished, the police . . . divided their party into two sections, one of which . . . set to work to drive the rioters in the direction of Llwynypia, and the other applied itself to the task of compelling the retreat of the mob towards Tonypandy. . . . Constantly the two sides were in furious combat. . . . Scores of the rioters were struck down like logs with broken skulls and left on the ground . . .[20]

In the opinion of one long-serving policeman present, no worse conflict between police and strikers had ever occurred.

There followed the sack of Tonypandy when sixty tradesmen's premises were pillaged: similar disturbances took place at Aberaman in the Aberdare valley. The *Labour Leader* described alleged police attacks on old men, women, and children at Aberaman, and deliberate assaults upon isolated individuals. Here, a crowd estimated at between 2,500 and 3,000 arrived at the power station. The miners swarmed over the fence between the towpath and the railway, charged across the track, and threw stones at the Glamorgan and Cardiff police assembled there. The police turned a hose-pipe on some boys when they called them to send out the colliery officials. The crowd then advanced on the power house itself. Superintendent Gill gave his men the order to charge, and the crowd were then batoned and chased by the police. Many leapt into the canal to save themselves from truncheon blows. The casualties, however, were not as serious as at Llwynypia where one man, Samuel Rayes, a miner, had died from injuries received,

19 Ibid., p. 45.

20 Ibid., pp. 46–7

another 500 also suffered injuries, and over 40 per cent of the foot constables and 16 mounted men were treated for wounds they had received.[21]

As has been explained previously, Churchill, the Home Secretary, now intervened dramatically in the dispute. The 300 Metropolitan Police, dispatched by Churchill, arrived in South Wales on 8 November. By 10 November the police in the area numbered 1,400 local, borrowed, and Metropolitan men, and troops reinforced the police presence; both police and troops were placed under the direction of General Macready by the Home Secretary. However, disorder continued and was often exacerbated by imported police. On 9 November the Metropolitans attacked some peaceful onlookers outside the Aberaman public hall, driving them to the sides of the main road where they were wedged together in a compact mass. Women and children present were screaming with terror. The police then charged across the road into the crowd which had gathered: 'they even had the horses' feet up on the entrance steps and the horses' heads into the entrance.'[22] In Clydach Vale on 15 November it was reported that the police had assaulted a picket. Macready was told that about sixteen men were on picket duty: 'a few hundred yards from the colliery entrance. . . . the sergeant on duty asked what they were doing; they said they were picketing the mine; he said, "I will soon shove you out of that", and got together a body of 20 constables and hustled them away.'[23] Strikers constantly claimed that the police did not act within the law and 'did not allow the pickets to interview men passing to and from their work'.[24] Conversely, Moylan of the Home Office intelligence service reported several complaints from men 'who have been stopped by pickets from going to work. They alleged that they have been threatened and intimidated, and that pickets of 12 men have stood in a line across the road and prevented their further passage.'[25]

The treatment of picketing remained a central issue for the authorities and the unions alike. On 16 November Lindsay, at the request of the Home Office, tried to clarify the position. He

[21] *Labour Leader*, 18 Nov. 1910; Evans, *Labour Strife*, p. 52.

[22] Aberaman Public Hall, Institute and Free Library Committee, to Home Secretary, 14 Nov. 1910, PP 1911 [Cd. 5568] lxiv. 28, no. 65.

[23] Macready to Home Office, report for 15 Nov. 1910 (ibid. 29, no. 68).

[24] Ibid.

[25] Moylan to Home Office, 16 Nov. 1911 (ibid. 31, no. 70).

circulated copies of Section 2 of the 1906 Act to all police officers 'with instructions to those in charge to impress on their men the necessity of strictly adhering to the law in regard to picketing'. He added on 18 November: 'the strikers are taking advantage of the Trade Disputes Act, 1906 to assemble in localities too numerous to be properly supervised by the police, for the purpose of committing acts of lawlessness, whenever there are not sufficient police to prevent them or local police to recognise them.'[26] Macready now took the situation in hand. He commented on 'the total ignorance of the law on the part of ordinary persons. That it is illegal to congregate in highways or on railway stations is quite a surprise to a striker.'[27] He also noted that the presence of women among disorderly crowds was an additional difficulty. This was a factor they were 'apt to exploit to the utmost, sheltering themselves behind the weaker sex with the certainty of attracting public sympathy should consequential injury, or worse, befall the womenfolk'.[28] Macready was thus compelled to intervene, and provide his own interpretation of the law. He told the local strike committee that it was within its rights under the 1906 Act to place pickets at mine entrances, but that, if more than six were present on any picket line, the police had orders to move them on for causing obstruction. He also instructed pickets to wear badges 'so that the police would be able to distinguish between pickets and the mob'.[29] But the basic dilemma of the impossibility of regulating picketing by the law remained.

This was again illustrated on 21 November when there was vigorous picketing of the railway stations in the Rhondda valley. Until now troops had been kept very much in the background. However the storming of signal-box cabins and the holding up of passenger and freight trains now made railway travel hazardous. Beasley, the manager of the Taff Vale Railway Company, told Lindsay that parties of pickets had insisted on making their way to Tonypandy, Dinas, and Llwynypia stations and had warned the station-masters there that, if they were prevented from reaching

[26] Chief constable of Glamorgan to Home Secretary, 18 Nov. 1910 (ibid. 32, no. 72).

[27] Memo. by Macready on certain points connected with the strike in South Wales, 5 Jan. 1911 (ibid. 48).

[28] Macready, *Annals*, i. 151.

[29] Ibid., p. 148. Macready to Home Office, report for 19 Nov. 1910 (PP 1911 [Cd. 5568], lxiv. 34, no. 76).

the platforms and examining the trains for blacklegs, they would bring down sufficient force to overwhelm the stations. That evening Macready received reports that Tonypandy station had been besieged by large crowds of strikers, and that the police were having much difficulty in clearing the station. The situation at Penygraig was equally serious. Every available constable in the Cambrian Combine area was now called out to prevent picketing of any railway traffic carrying blacklegs. At the same time Macready ordered Major Freeth to take half of his company of Lancashire Fusiliers, and march, accompanied by a magistrate, to Penygraig. A company of the West Riding Regiment was also sent to Penygraig at the same time by road, while two companies of infantry in reserve at Newport were also dispatched to Pontypridd.[30]

Before the troops arrived the fiercest fighting between police and strikers had now taken place. The Metropolitan Police drove the crowd from the approaches to Tonypandy station and, when they were stoned by the crowd, charged them repeatedly. The crowd retreated up the steep hills of Penygraig, and the police charged uphill after them. This went on for about an hour. Lindsay arrived at 9.30 p.m. with seventy more Metropolitan, Glamorgan, and Cardiff police, whom he divided into four groups. They charged up the side streets, where they were met with volleys of stones, bricks, and kitchen utensils. Major Freeth then appeared with his troops. According to the pre-arranged plan, they blocked the streets on the high ground, and 'by a little gentle persuasion with the bayonet drove the stone-throwers into the arms of the police'. By midnight, and after many more casualties, the disturbance was over.[31]

After this, the military were used to control the population more actively in South Wales. This move was endorsed by Chief Constable Lindsay, who tactfully wrote to Churchill on 23 November:

> I have, Sir, as you are well aware, fully shared your great anxiety as to the result of any action by the military, but now I am thoroughly reassured on this point, and feel sure that the very careful study of the situation by General Macready and all his officers will enable them to give us the very best possible help from the moral point of view . . . that nothing rash or

[30] Moylan to Home Office, memo., 22 Nov. 1910 (ibid. 38, no. 82).
[31] Ibid., Macready, *Annals*, i. 152.

risky will ever be attempted, and should the worst come to the worst they will completely save the situation.[32]

When the colliery at Gilfach Goch (which faced ruin if it was not restarted) was reopened on 25 November, the police force of forty was now supported by 100 men and four officers of the Royal Munster Fusiliers and five troops of cavalry. This parade of armed force, though not ordered to suppress a disturbance, was said to be in the interests of public order. The lighting of the fires was accomplished and pumping began at the pit with no disturbances occurring because of the presence of troops and police.[33] From now on, troops guarded this colliery from a camp on the nearby hillside. Captain Childs describes how, because he and his intelligence department were always anxious about the vulnerability of Gilfach Goch Colliery, Macready arranged to keep the local population alert by organizing demonstrations of the mobility of the troops. 'We worked out manoeuvres whereby cavalry and infantry used to arrive suddenly at Gilfach, in the early hours of the morning, having taken different routes. There was no question but that the population were impressed and we had no more serious rioting there.'[34]

However, the conceptual and practical difficulties of actually enforcing the law when mass picketing was taking place were now illustrated once again. For example, after the mass picket on 21 November, and the violence at Penygraig, the number of arrests was limited on the grounds that 'it was quite unsafe to make any more. The crowd would have attempted rescue, and the number of police necessary to take the captures to the police station would have weakened too seriously the force available for dealing with the crowd.'[35] Churchill now instructed Macready on 23 November about the procedure to be followed.

Arrest and prosecution should follow in all cases where evidence is forthcoming against lawbreakers. Cases of intimidation clearly going beyond peaceful persuasion, even if they cannot be prevented at the time, should be investigated afterwards with a view to the conviction of

[32] Chief constable of Glamorgan to Home Secretary, 23 Nov. 1910 (PP 1911 [Cd. 5568], lxiv. 40, no. 84).

[33] Moylan to Home Office, memo., 25 Nov. 1910 (ibid. 43, no. 87).

[34] Major-General Sir Wyndham Childs, *Episodes and Reflections* (1930), 90.

[35] Moylan to Home Office, memo., 22 Nov. 1910 (PP 1911 [Cd. 5568], lxiv. 38, no. 82).

offenders. The police should not hesitate to make arrests where *prima facie* case is disclosed and after every incident of disorder police inquiries and detective work should be rigorously prosecuted. This does not mean that pickets should be hustled or the police force be dissipated . . . and must not be thought in conflict with my general advice to the Chief Constable to go gently in small things. Behind the day-to-day maintenance of order . . . there must be a regular process of bringing offenders, particularly rioters and thieves, to justice.[36]

In fact there were no more disturbances, the military being much more in evidence guarding colliery premises and indulging in military drilling. The strike petered out by December. During the entire strike in the mid-Rhondda it was on only three occasions that local magistrates were called upon to deal with cases of intimidation. The first was not decided until 6 December. Perhaps because of the wish of the stipendiary magistrate, D. Lleufer Thomas, a progressive Liberal, not to arouse any more local ill-feeling, most of these cases were dealt with by fines and binding over; only two were awarded imprisonment. Troup of the Home Office, characteristically, disapproved of this leniency. Dealing with intimidation cases by 'mere binding over' 'cannot fail to give strikers the impression that the offence is trivial and they may commit it without risk'. However, he felt that the Home Secretary himself could 'hardly press for severity'.[37]

Following an initiative by Clement Edwards, Liberal MP for East Glamorgan, the Home Office now raised the possibility with the Lord Chancellor's department of appointing '1 or 2 specially selected J.P.'s at each of the village mining centres who would support law and order'.[38] However, Lord Plymouth, the Lord-Lieutenant, failed to appoint working-class magistrates, as was later confirmed when the matter arose again in 1917.[39] In fact, in 1911 over 530 persons were prosecuted for unlawful behaviour during the industrial strikes and were subsequently brought before the magistrates by the police, and fines and sometimes imprisonment of strikers followed. Significantly, however, only 16

[36] Home Secretary to Macready (telegram), 22 Nov. 1910 (ibid. 40, no. 83).

[37] Minute by Troup, 13 Dec. 1910 (HO 144/1554/199768/178).

[38] Home Office minute on appointment of Glamorgan justices of the peace (HO 45/10638/204636/1).

[39] Churchill to Lord Plymouth, 31 Aug. 1911 (ibid.); Lord Plymouth to Churchill, 6 Sept. 1911 (ibid.); correspondence between Clement Edwards MP and Home Office, 1917 (ibid. 2).

of these 530 were convicted for intimidation, while in the Aberdare Valley the number was a mere 22 convictions, none for intimidation.[40] This was the legal outcome of the Cambrian strike.

The extensive use of troops and borrowed police in South Wales in 1910 caused much outcry from leaders of the Labour Party. Keir Hardie and others launched a chorus of criticism in November 1910 which was to plague Churchill's reputation with the working class in the valleys down to the 1950s.[41] Hardie requested a local inquiry into the conduct of the police at Tonypandy and Aberaman 'in view of the indignation prevailing among the inhabitants of these districts'.[42] In the *Labour Leader* he attacked the use of mass charges by the police especially the Metropolitan and their attacks on solitary individuals. 'At Penygraig they actually broke into people's homes and half murdered the inhabitants who were at supper.' He believed:

> The average 'Bobby' is a decent enough chap in his own town. When, however, he is taken to another part of the country, kept on duty night and day, badly housed and plentifully supplied from some source of liquor, he naturally is full of resentment against those whom he believes to be the cause of all his woes and takes it out of them when occasion arises.

Hardie added that he had received evidence from impartial outsiders such as shopkeepers, ministers of religion, and others, and urged the Home Secretary himself to institute an inquiry into police behaviour.[43]

Yet no official inquiry into police conduct by either the chief constable, the standing joint committee, or the Home Office was undertaken. The Standing Joint Police Committee had no power to initiate any inquiry into police conduct. Lindsay, inevitably, refused to take action. In his position as chief constable, he was responsible for the discipline of the force. He now reported to Churchill that inquiries among the police confirmed that 'Mr Keir Hardie's attacks on the Police are groundless. . . . The grossly

[40] Evans, *Labour Strife*, p. 208. On this, see Appendix, Table 5 below.

[41] Memo. from Conservative Political Centre to all candidates and agents, 25 Jan. 1950 (Bodleian, Conservative Party Archives CC 02/1/16); *Parl. Deb.*, 5th ser., 20, 10–17 (15 Nov. 1911).

[42] *Parl. Deb.*, ibid., cols. 17–18.

[43] *Labour Leader*, 2 Dec. 1910; *Parl. Deb.*, 5th Ser., 20, 406 (24 Nov. 1910).

untruthful accusations against the Metropolitan Police' were 'quite in accordance with all the traditions of the worst class of the inhabitants of the district . . .'.[44] Instead, Macready produced a report of his own on the action of police and troops at Tonypandy. He was generally complacent about events. He quoted the views of middle-class people who thought the Metropolitan Police had 'acted with great patience under extraordinary provocation'. Some even believed the police had 'erred on the side of leniency' while 'The whole tone of the strikers . . . was one of aggression'.[45] The violence of the strike had largely been triggered off by 'the doctrine of extreme socialism preached by a small but energetic section'. He also praised the conduct of the Metropolitans in South Wales. The Metropolitan policeman had the advantage of 'being unbiassed and indifferent to what those around may think of him, however unpleasant his duties may be, while the local man cannot get away from the fact that his lines may hereafter be cast in the same locality'.[46]

When a case was brought before the divisional court by Councillor Thomas Bowen for assault by the local police on 8 November on the orders of Superintendent Gill, the court held that there was no evidence to connect the superintendent with the actions of his men. The *Labour Leader* commented bitterly:

> So it would appear that in future police may, with the cognisance of the officer in charge, run amok through an unoffending crowd and indulge in assault and battery to their heart's content. So long as the officer refrains from giving direct orders to perpetrate outrages, or so long as it cannot be proved that he has given instructions to assault, he can evade all responsibility and the law will hold him absolutely guiltless.[47]

Not only was no redress taken against police action, and no inquiry of any kind instituted. To add insult to injury, the *Police Review* reported that Lindsay declared that police who acquitted themselves satisfactorily in the strike would be considered favourably for promotion.[48]

[44] Chief constable of Glamorgan to under-secretary of state at Home Office, 30 Nov. 1910 (Glamorgan County Police Papers, Cardiff County Hall).

[45] Statements as to the conduct of the Police (PP 1911 [Cd. 5568], lxiv. 52 ff.).

[46] Memo. by Macready on certain points connected with strike in South Wales, 5 Jan. 1911 (ibid. 48).

[47] *Labour Leader*, 20 Jan. 1911.

[48] *Police Review*, 27 Jan. 1911.

In contrast to the behaviour of the police, the troops seem to have caused little trouble in South Wales. While their very presence aroused much resentment, especially that of the cavalry, Macready's troops were said to have behaved with firmness and tact.[49] It was later claimed by Mavis Llewelyn, a local girl, that the Durham Light Infantry had refused to come out against the miners as they themselves were all colliers' sons. She added, 'the police would do more dirty work than the troops would do'.[50] Gradually the unrest in the Cambrian pits died away, and the last of the Metropolitan Police were withdrawn from the area in February 1911. The bitterest memories of the strikers, in fact, concerned not the troops but rather the mineowners, the chief constable, and Metropolitan and other borrowed police, and Winston Churchill himself.

It can be concluded that the events which occurred at Tonypandy in 1910 were of major significance. Not only had Churchill completely overturned the established procedure of riot control. He had also inaugurated the principle of the central government giving instructions to the provincial police about their executive action in industrial disputes—particularly that to be associated with picketing. The police had been encouraged to follow central governmental instructions, yet were to be unaccountable locally or nationally for their actions. Their authority in combating embittered trade unionists had therefore been significantly reinforced.

The year 1911 was known in labour circles for 'the great unrest', and the trouble of the summer of that year as 'the general strike'. Indeed, disruption was much more widespread even than in the general strike of 1926. As has been seen, stoppages now took place on a national scale in the docks and railways, while conflict continued in the mining industry. The responsibility for the preservation of law and order was considered a national concern and treated as such. Troops were distributed round the country and were freely available for use in aid of the civil power. Police authorities were urged to do their utmost to preserve law and

[49] Home Secretary to chief constable of Glamorgan, 10 Nov. 1910 (PP 1911 [Cd. 5568] lxiv. 11, no. 31); R. Page Arnot, *The South Wales Miners: A History of the South Wales Miners' Federation* (1967), 204.

[50] Evidence of M. Llewelyn (ML 164) (South Wales Miners' Library).

order and encouraged to give protection to blacklegs whether disturbances had occurred or not.

During the seamen's and dock strike, the potential for violence was accentuated by the tremendous heat. In Cardiff, for example, on 17 August, at the beginning of the national railway strike the temperature reached 124.1 degrees in the sun. Disturbances occurred at Cardiff, Hull, and Salford. In Hull, mass picketing and intimidation were said to have been accentuated by the importation of 400 additional police. There was a more or less general strike by 27 June when non-union labour had unloaded the SS *Titania*, and dockers had picketed other works in the town.

> At Reckitt's factory 2,000 strikers forced the firm's boilermen to strike, . . . Initially, Reckitt's employees refused to leave and fighting ensued with a contingent of 30 Birmingham police who were guarding the premises. Property was damaged and by-standers were swept into the conflict as police determinedly baton-charged the crowd. . . . Throughout the city, work premises were now guarded in anticipation of a breach of the peace, rather than protection being given only in event of such breach occurring. . . . The business community universally felt that strike's extension was brought about solely by intimidation.[51]

Although a truce was concluded in Hull on 1 July, the rank and file repudiated the settlement, and eight hours of sporadic rioting ensued. It was said that only police intervention prevented arson. A force of 500 Metropolitan Police was now sent in to deal with the disturbances. The officer in charge of the Metropolitans in Hull reported on how he had used a plain-clothes police constable to patrol the town and to obtain information. The Leeds police, he commented, had 'made rather a bad name for themselves by the indiscriminate use of their truncheons'.[52]

In Cardiff, attempts were made to use non-union labour, often Chinese, to load and unload ships. On 18 July the use of non-union men to unload the SS *Annan* caused a fierce disturbance which the local police were unable to contain. The crowd set fire to some empty boxes and loose straw lying on the quayside. The Bute Dock police tried to extinguish it, but 'hostility to the police was first caused by turning the fire hose on the crowd' and a major bout

[51] K. Brooker, *The Hull Strikes of 1911* (East Yorkshire Local History Society Series, 35; 1979), 16.

[52] Report of officer in charge of Metropolitan Police at Hull, 2 July 1911 (MEPO 2/1467).

of incendiarism followed.[53] The head constable applied for the assistance of outside police on the same day, and 320 officers of the Metropolitans and 20 horses and 30 men each from Merthyr, Gloucestershire, and Monmouthshire were sent to help local police control the turbulent situation. But, notwithstanding the large number of police available, the agents of the SS *Annan* did not proceed to work on the ship. On 19 July a near general strike erupted in Cardiff in sympathy with the seamen. The head constable reported:

> Whilst the workers came out more or less voluntarily, there can be no doubt that very considerable influence was exercised by bodies of men and women going from place to place with a view to inducing those inclined to remain at work to join their ranks.
>
> This procedure on their part was probably regarded by them as peaceful picketing, but I am afraid that in the absence of the police they, in many instances went beyond what could reasonably come within the meaning of the term, although there was no personal violence.
>
> Many complaints were received by the police upon this question, and in every instance where it was possible police protection was given.[54]

There was further violence after 19 July, and disturbances which the local magistrate classified as 'riots' occurred on several occasions in the next few days, mainly concerned with attacks on local Chinese laundries. The Metropolitans were said by the *Labour Leader* to have 'run amok' on Friday, 21 July: 'Six or eight get into line and rush at top speed across the road to three or four civilians. . . . The great pace at which they come lends force to the charge. Then they thump and kick. This was their modus operandi in the principal streets of Cardiff when there was no semblance of riot on Friday night.'[55]

There were many recriminations about the conduct of the Metropolitan Police, 'Churchill's Cossacks' or 'Home Office Hireling Hooligans' as they were now called in the Labour press. The Cardiff Trades and Labour Council took evidence from those willing to come forward with complaints of misconduct against the Metropolitan Police and a good case for proof of violent behaviour was made out. However, the Home Office again refused to hold

[53] Chief constable of Cardiff's report on the seamen's strike, 10 Aug. 1911 (Cardiff City Watch Committee Minutes).

[54] Ibid.

[55] *Labour Leader*, 18 Aug. 1911.

any inquiry. The object of sending the Metropolitans, the Home Office observed, 'was to maintain the peace and prevent crime and outrage'. No question of the Metropolitans interfering in a trade dispute therefore arose.[56]

But capital as well as labour felt aggrieved by what had occurred. Although a mass resumption of work took place on the 31st, the shipping strike was generally successful. In many places complaints were now received by the Home Office from employers alleging that violence and intimidation had been rife and that the police had refused to take firm action. A deputation to the Home Office from the Shipping Federation complained that 'in the recent strikes, large numbers of workmen who had no dispute with their employers and no grievances were compelled by intimidation, and in some cases actual violence, to leave their work and take part in the so-called "General Strike" '. They attributed this partly to the insufficiency of police protection, partly to the licence given the strikers by the Trade Disputes Act 1906.[57] In reply, Churchill naturally supported the police action. The police force had 'acted with vigour and given all necessary protection'. As regards the provisions with regard to picketing in the Trade Disputes Act 1906, he pointed out that there was 'nothing in it which sanctioned intimidation or threats of violence'. However, he promised to consider 'whether any instructions could be given to the police which would assist them in distinguishing between peaceful persuasion by pickets acting within the law and the intimidation [*sic*] particularly . . . by crowds which it is their duty to repress'.[58]

On 11 August 1911, after discussion by the Cabinet and the approval of the Law Officers, an important Home Office circular was issued to chiefs of police. This was a significant landmark in official attitudes towards labour disturbances. It inaugurated a long series of Home Office circulars giving advice about executive action to the provincial police. It reminded them of the provisions of the 1875 and 1906 Acts with regard to intimidation and picketing. A feature of the recent strikes had been that large crowds of strikers had visited works where there was no dispute and had induced workmen who had no grievance with their

[56] Minute by Troup on Dock Wharf, Riverside and General Workers Union protest against importation of outside police and troops, 27 July 1911 (HO 45/10649/210615/104).

[57] Minute by Troup 3 August 1911 (HO 144/5491/212614/30).

[58] Home Secretary's reply to the Shipping Federation, n.d. August 1911 (ibid.).

employers to come out on strike. It was alleged that intimidation had taken place. The circular pointed out that the relevant sections of these acts gave no protection to intimidation or threats of violence; the duties of the police in dealing with these offences had not been in any way affected. The chief difficulty experienced by the police was to distinguish between peaceful picketing and that which amounted to intimidation. It was stressed that the number of pickets was crucial here although the Act of 1906 did not lay down any limit to the numbers involved. The circular continued:

> it is clear that where a crowd watching or besetting any works is so disproportionate in size to what is needed for lawful purposes as to exclude the idea of peaceful persuasion the Act of 1906 may cease to apply and the persons taking part in the demonstration would then become liable to be charged with watching or besetting under the Act of 1875.

It also proposed that official pickets should be badged by the union, and that the police should communicate with strike leaders to this effect.[59]

The issue of this important circular to the provincial police was of major significance. Until this time, apart from the incidents at Newport and Tonypandy in 1910, the preservation of law and order had been a local affair of little concern to the Home Office. Now for the first time the Home Office was attempting to get a uniform executive response from the police by issuing specific and detailed instructions. This important document, in effect, redefined Section 2 (1) of the Trades Disputes Act 1906. The police were now encouraged to interpret the Act as extending their own powers. The circular also endorsed the opinion of Walton, the Attorney-General in 1906, that picketing was not lawful unless exercised for the purpose of peaceful persuasion: this process of persuasion would be regarded as evidence of intimidation or coercion if not one, but a dozen men went on this mission. A large crowd was in itself evidence of intimidation.[60] The new circular was said by Troup to be based on the results of Home Office research into the way in which strikes in 1910 and 1911 had been conducted. Macready himself ironically commented that it would be 'of the very greatest assistance to Chief Constables, especially those who are afraid of responsibility in dealing with strikers'.[61]

[59] HO 158/15 (212,614), 11 Aug. 1911.
[60] *Parl. Deb.*, 4th Ser., 163, 1421 (1 Nov. 1906).
[61] Macready to Troup, 5 Aug. 1911 (HO 144/5491/212614/30).

In addition to these instructions to the police, the military were now encouraged to take stronger action. As has been seen, before the railway strike troop movements were centrally co-ordinated and the Army Regulation requiring their requisition from a civil authority was suspended. The common-law powers and duties of the military to assist the civil power, with or without civil sanction, were now re-emphasized by the Law Officers while the Home Office circular of August 1911 about picketing was also issued to army commanders who were sent to strike areas.[62]

Now the spotlight moved on to Liverpool. As has been seen the mayor had requisitioned troops and had the aid of a host of borrowed police. Thus fortified, the railway companies induced the police to make an attempt to reopen Brunswick and Edge Hill stations. Convoys of provision wagons were successfully escorted by police and the Warwickshire Regiment to wholesale markets nearby, unmolested by strikers. But serious trouble took place on 13 August—'Bloody Sunday' as it became known.

This was greatly to inflame the temper of the strikers in Liverpool. A meeting of the National Transport Workers' Federation drew 90,000 people to St George's plateau. Although the socialist, Tom Mann, persuaded the head constable of Liverpool to keep the police and the troops which had been requisitioned out of sight, 100 Royal Warwickshire were stationed in St George's Hall, along with a large number of police. All went reasonably well until, at the end of the meeting, the police removed some boys sitting on the window sill of the North Western Hotel. There now began a scene of 'indescribable savagery and anger'.[63] The head constable, Leonard Dunning, called out some of the Police Reserves, and they began to clear Lime Street, where they were met with showers of missiles. The police then drove the meeting from the plateau, which caused immense violence. The troops appeared, the Riot Act was read, and the plateau was eventually cleared by force.

The Liverpool Strike Committee now appealed to all transport workers to assist the railwaymen and dockers. They should protest against the bringing in of the military and the savagery of the

[62] Troup to Solicitor-General, 9 Aug. 1911; Macready to Troup, 5 Aug. 1911 (HO 144/5491/212614/1).

[63] *Labour Leader*, 18 Aug. 1911.

police by showing industrial solidarity and stopping work.[64] On 15 August, after another disturbance, troops fired into a crowd. In Vauxhall Road a detachment of Scots Greys and some men of the Warwickshire Regiment, who were accompanying five prison vans filled with men and women arrested during the riots, was attacked with a fusillade of stones. Some constables drew their batons and for a moment the crowd was driven back. But two men had got in front of the crowd and were both shot dead; another three were wounded.[65]

There were many demands for an inquiry into the conduct of the police on 'Bloody Sunday'; yet both the watch committee and the Home Secretary refused to hold one. On balance, the authorities expressed themselves satisfied. The head constable of Liverpool believed that 'both military and police behaved admirably, and the experience of working with the former has been valuable to the officers of the police, who will call them out more readily in future'.[66] Churchill supported him to the hilt: 'You should not hesitate to apply to me for any further aid you may require. . . . You will be promptly supported by the Government.'[67] King George V wanted even sterner action. He telegraphed Churchill that Liverpool was experiencing a revolution rather than a strike. He therefore strongly deprecated 'the half-hearted employment of troops. They should not be called upon except as a last resource but if called upon, they should be given a free hand and the mob should be made to fear them'.[68]

On 17 August there was a complete railway stoppage at Liverpool. *The Times* reported that in that turbulent city 'the position is steadily going from bad to worse. . . . . There have been riots and bloodshed.' The local justices telegraphed the Home Office for additional military force to protect those wishing to work. Nevertheless, it was still difficult to get blacklegs to report for work, while only 100 naval personnel were available for protec-

[64] Ibid.

[65] *Parl. Deb.*, 5th ser., 29, 1990 (16 Aug. 1911).

[66] Head constable of Liverpool to Home Office (telegram), 15 Aug. 1911, PP 1911 (323), xlvii. 697–8.

[67] Home Secretary to Lord Mayor of Liverpool (telegram), 16 Aug. 1911 (ibid. 698, no. 7).

[68] K. Rose, *George V: A Biography* (1983), 342.

tion of the docks. The raw industrial power of the strikers largely prevailed.[69]

Now at 5 p.m. the same day the national railway strike began. The railway companies were given *carte blanche* to call upon troops and so had an absolute guarantee of an adequate, if restricted, train service. Troops with ball and cartridge and naked bayonets, so the *Labour Leader* bitterly commented, could be used at the employers' whim wherever picketing appeared to be effective.[70] The War Office told general officers in command of strike areas that troops should be used to escort essential trains through disturbed areas, and to protect major signal boxes. In effect, the policing role of troops was explicitly confirmed:

> In order to cope successfully with cases where obstructions are placed in the way of trains . . . it is essential that wherever possible arrests should be made and the culprits brought to trial. In order to facilitate this, escorts should wherever possible be accompanied by at least one member of the Civil Police.[71]

At Stafford, for example, the head constable reported on 19 August that the appearance of officers and men of the West Riding Regiment 'promptly altered the whole tone of the strikers; . . . my police had no difficulty whatever in keeping the crowd away from the important signal box'. The head constable of Nottingham wrote that the knowledge that the troops 'were within easy reach of Nottingham and Derby, and available, was a most important factor in the preservation of order'. At Lincoln, on 18 and 19 August, serious rioting occurred around the railway station. The police made baton charges to disperse the mob but on 19 August, when the troops arrived, no further disorder occurred. At Chesterfield, after serious rioting around the railway station on 19–20 August, fifty men from the West Riding Regiment were called in:

> The bugle was sounded, after which the Mayor read the Riot Act Proclamation. . . . The Mayor then authorized the officer in command of the Yorkshires to act, and he determined at first to charge with fixed bayonets. The soldiers charged up the hill at the double and formed a

[69] Railway strike, Aug. 1911, confidential memos. and reports; head constable of Liverpool to Home Office, 17 Aug. 1911 (HO 45/10658/212470).

[70] *Labour Leader*, 25 Aug. 1911.

[71] War Office circular on protection of railways by the military, 19 Aug. 1911 (HO 45/10658/212470, no. 4).

cordon across the street. The crowd again collected, but was dispersed by the police after a baton charge.[72]

The most disastrous episode of the strike occurred in Llanelli in South Wales, on 19 August. After repeated disturbances at the railway station an attack was made by a crowd of strikers on a train which had passed through Llanelli station completely unprotected. This occurred at a railway cutting sloping on either side to a considerable height near the station. The train had been obliged to slow down so that the next set of gates might be opened. A number of men ran up to the engine and manhandled the driver, who was said to have been drunk. They put out the fire, let off the steam, and put the vacuum brake out of order. The train was completely immobilized. Eighty of the Worcestershire Regiment were quickly on the scene followed by three magistrates; they were stoned by crowds from the embankments. The troops had no success in attempting to pacify them. The Riot Act proclamation was read. Eventually the officer in charge gave one minute's warning of an order to fire. However, before the minute was up a single shot rang out, followed by five rounds. In the garden of No. 6 High Street, two men were killed. Two others were wounded by bullets and the crowd fled.[73]

Now violent rioting and looting continued in the vicinity for many hours; troops and police were outnumbered and the situation was explosive. Hopkin describes how crowds advanced on a train which was now drawing in:

There was near hysteria when it was realised that the train contained kit and provisions for the soldiers of the Devon Regiment. Kit-bags were torn open, and the personal belongings of soldiers triumphantly scattered along the line. After the coaches had been ransacked, they were systematically wrecked, their windows smashed and the doors torn from their hinges.

Almost immediately looting began, though quietly at the outset. Some people made off with blankets and provisions, while others exhilarated by

[72] Memo. on the effect of the presence of troops on rioters 1911 (ibid., no. 9).

[73] For a fuller account see D. R. Hopkin, 'The Llanelli Riots, 1911', *Welsh History Review*, 11. 4 (Dec. 1983), 488–515. There is a discrepancy between the account of the chief constable and that of a newspaper report which stated that a shot was fired before the minute promised by the military commander had elapsed. The chief constable's report stated that the minute's warning of the order to fire was observed; see chief constable of Carmarthen's report on Llanelli riots 1911 (10 Oct. 1911), Carmarthen Standing Joint Committee Minutes.

the ease with which it might be done, turned their attention to other targets nearby. A warehouse was raided and fires started. . . . As dusk gathered, the looting intensified. When darkness fell the fires of dozens of looted trucks could be seen for miles around. Large crowds gathered to watch the spectacle. Truck after truck was broken open and goods taken away: sacks of flour, tubs of butter, sides of bacon, crockery and enamel ware, bamboo tables and miscellaneous household goods. Women changed to new clothes on the spot. Children were kitted out with ill-fitting garments. A truck of bonded spirits was discovered and thereafter, throughout the night, men and women could be heard in the adjoining fields crying out in their drunken revelry. Altogether ninety-six trucks were looted and many of them gutted by fire.

At around 10 p.m. the military decide to intervene. Troops and firemen advanced on the scene when suddenly two huge explosions rent the sky. An unfortunate arsonist, whose charred body was later discovered under a burnt-out truck, had inadvertently set fire to a cylinder of detonators. The blast killed three other people nearby, while a further eleven were taken to hospital with serious burns and injuries. Even so the looting along the railway sidings continued until the early hours of the morning.[74]

Much later in the evening, reinforcements of 350 Sussex troops arrived and cleared the railway lines. Order was eventually restored at 2 a.m. the next morning when news began to spread that the railway strike had been settled.[75]

On 19 August the railway strike was declared to be at an end. Churchill now encouraged chief constables and police authorities to take firm action against rioters and looters in disturbed areas. The Home Office was told that in Cardiff there were thirty-one serious cases pending after the recent riots in the dock strike, ranging from assaults on the police to attempted murder and arson. The town clerk here instructed Counsel 'to attend the various prosecutions for riot at Quarter Sessions and watch the interests of the police and corporation'.[76] After the Llanelli troubles the chief constable of Carmarthenshire received a telegram from the Home Secretary to the effect that 'in cases where rioting has been accompanied by looting of shops or warehouses or railway waggons he deems it very important that

[74] Hopkin, 'Llanelli Riots', pp. 498–9.

[75] Ibid., p. 500.

[76] Replies to Home Office telegram to chief constables on the action of the strikers and the measures taken by the police to keep order, 20 Aug. 1911 (HO 45/10656/212470); Cardiff Watch Committee Minutes, 20 Sept. 1911.

enquiries should be made by police as to persons who have committed larceny or received stolen property and that where they can be traced prosecution should immediately follow'.[77] Police raids were now conducted in particular areas of Llanelli and a total of twenty-three men and one woman appeared at the local magistrate's court between 22 and 25 August, charged with looting. All but three were sent for trial at the Carmarthen Assizes and received heavy sentences.[78] In spite of this, those charged with riotous behaviour were felt to have been given lenient treatment. When Churchill heard that the man prominent in inciting the crowd to riot at Llanelli was charged with being drunk and disorderly and fined 25*s*., he pressed for severe measures to be taken.[79] The chief constable reassured the Home Secretary in a telegram that 'The man referred to as fined for drunkenness was also fined for assaulting police, he was severely truncheoned, he and others will be charged with inciting to riot if the evidence which is now being collected justifies it.' He added, 'People who might are naturally afraid to give evidence'. The latter was indeed the case. Only nine individuals were brought to court for riotous behaviour. They were summarily dealt with by magistrates and fined 20*s*. each.[80]

There were many protests at the conduct of the police, backed up, as they were, by troops in many areas. But, as usual, demands for inquiries into police conduct met with little success locally and none nationally. The Home Office was at pains to refute any allegations that the intervention of troops during the strike, for instance at Liverpool or Llanelli, had led to riots or a breakdown of order. A memorandum from the department pointed out that in every case rioting had begun before the troops had arrived on the scene:

> For the rest, if the numerous reports received from the various centres of disturbance are examined, it will be found that, when the full facts are ascertained, there is no ground for the suggestion that the presence of

[77] Home Office to chief constable of Carmarthen, 21 Aug. 1911 (HO 45/10655/212470/222).

[78] Hopkin, 'Llanelli Riots', pp. 501–5 and 514–15.

[79] Home Office to chief constable of Carmarthen (telegram) 23 Aug. 1911 (HO 45/10655/212470/222).

[80] Chief constable of Carmarthen to Home Secretary, 23 Aug. 1911 (ibid.); Hopkin, 'Llanelli Riots', pp. 504–5 and 514–15.

troops led to riot. . . . On the other hand there are many cases in which the arrival of the troops stopped the riot, sometimes by the action they took, sometimes by their mere presence.[81]

But, whatever the justification offered by the Home Office for the dispatch of troops around the country in 1911, the fact remained that their actions had caused widespread revulsion among the public. Indeed, at an inquest later in the month on the shooting of the two men at Llanelli, the jury brought in a verdict of justifiable homicide. But they added the rider, 'We think it would have been better if other means than the order to fire had been adopted . . . for the purpose of dispersing the crowd'. A verdict of justifiable homicide was brought in at about the same time in respect of the two men who were shot dead by troops at Liverpool during the disturbances of 15 August.[82] In fact, it was later revealed that Richard Spiers, a private in the Worcestershire Regiment, had refused to shoot to kill at Llanelli. Although this story was denied by the military authorities, Home Office papers contain evidence of its truth. Spiers was said to have been caught at New Radnor where he was living 'chiefly on nuts, apples and blackberries', and was later court-martialled.[83] Beyond that, no official action was taken, by civil or military authorities, to respond to public reactions to the handling of the strike.

As has been seen, industrial unrest continued to plague the government in 1912, with the national miners' strike and the Port of London dock strike. Picketing continued to pose a major problem for the police. McKenna, the new Home Secretary, issued instructions to the Metropolitan Police that they should make full use of the law on street obstruction in dealing with pickets who tried to obstruct the free passage of the street. They were reminded that pickets were not entitled to congregate in unlimited numbers and told to ensure that they did not obstruct the public highway. Pickets should be orderly and not use abusive language, or threatening behaviour, or cause intimidation by sheer numbers.[84]

[81] Memo. on the effect of the presence of troops on rioters, 1911 (HO 45/10658/212470, no. 9).

[82] D. Williams, *Keeping the Peace*, pp. 32–3.

[83] Ibid., p. 182. For the case of R. Spiers, see *South Wales Press*, 27 Sept. 1911 and HO 45/10656/212470/352.

[84] Memo. by Troup on a question to be asked by Lord Charnwood in the House of Lords, 22 Jan. 1913 (HO 144/5491/212614/34).

These instructions proved to be very effective in stimulating police action. In the dockyard area of Rotherhithe, for example, the police dispersed a crowd of 3,000 people who were trying to prevent vans from leaving the docks on 11 June. There was much violence but that on the part of the police far exceeded that of the crowd. There were many demands for an inquiry into police conduct and for once, the Home Secretary now agreed to one.

This took place under a Metropolitan magistrate, Chester Jones, who heard evidence from twelve members of the public and forty-three police officers.[85] He found that the police action in clearing a large crowd at Mill Pond Bridge was broadly justified because of the size and threatening character of the mass of people involved. On the other hand, his inquiry is notable for being more critical of police methods than was customary. In the subsequent pursuit of individuals, after the crowd had been dispersed, cases were heard in which the police had severely rough-handled a number of quite innocent people. A shop keeper named John Herbert Marney had been putting up the shutters of his shop when he was struck several times by a policeman with his rolled-up cape; his little finger was broken. His wife was also assaulted by the police. Walter Albert Maxwell and his brother, two local residents who had not been part of the original crowd, were beaten up by police in the forecourt of their home. A coal porter, Frederick John Edwards, who was apparently saying goodnight to some friends, was struck on the face by a policeman with his cape, without any provocation. Other accusations were not substantiated. Even so, Chester Jones's conclusion was that, while it was necessary for the police to clear the crowd, 'in the subsequent pursuit some members of the Police Force employed were guilty of excesses, and some persons have undoubtedly a right to complain of the treatment they received'.[86] Complaint, however, was the only redress available to the members of the Rotherhithe community thus abused. There is no evidence of any police officers being in any way disciplined, or even rebuked, after these unpleasant episodes.

However, although instructions could be given to the Metropolitan Police about the way the police should react to

[85] *Report by Mr Chester Jones on Certain Disturbances at Rotherhithe on June 11th 1912 and Complaints against the Conduct of the Police in Connection therewith*, PP 1912–13 [Cd. 6367] xlvii. 297.

[86] Ibid. 302.

picketing, there can be no doubt that Home Office pressure for a more aggressive action towards picketing in the 1910–12 period had some influence with the provincial police. When the Home Office had brought to its attention the fact that the head constable of Chesterfield had broken up pickets and charged them with unlawful assembly, H. B. Simpson now noted:

This is an excellent example of what can be done under the Common Law to put down the abuses that arise from picketing. It might have been difficult to prove intimidation against individuals: to charge the ring leaders with unlawful assembly not only avoids this difficulty but also allows of an interval before sentence is passed during which angry passions may subside. . . . It is hoped that the Police Authorities will take example by Chesterfield.[87]

Subsequently in the Cornish Clay Pit strike, in 1913—a very violent episode in this traditionally peaceful region—the chief constable of Cornwall issued a proclamation to the effect that peaceful persuasion in trade disputes was perfectly lawful, but that anything in the nature of unlawful assembly was punishable in the courts. As a result of this proclamation, John Fischer Williams, a Liberal barrister sympathetic to labour, alleged in a letter which was passed on to the Home Office: 'in the St. Austell district wherever four or five strikers are gathered together (meetings of three are permitted) in circumstances which seem to the policeman on the spot (often imported from South Wales) suspicious, the police lay-on with their batons and "disperse the mob" '.[88] Williams (whose home was in Cornwall) added that 'the police—good natured and civil enough men in their way—look on the strikers as natural enemies and jump at any occasion of hammering them with batons—not such a difficult task for athletic well-fed policemen'.[89]

One familiar outcome of the Cornish Clay Pit strike was a renewal of protests against police brutality by the Labour Party and the TUC. J. R. Clynes, MP, at the annual TUC Congress, moved and carried a resolution which protested at the violent conduct of police imported into Cornwall during the clayworkers' strike—

[87] Minute by H. B. Simpson, 1 May 1912 (HO 144/5491/212614/29).

[88] Mr Fischer Williams to F. D. Acland at Foreign Office, 2 Sept. 1913 (HO 45/10710/24202/19).

[89] Ibid.

especially that of the notorious 'Glamorgans' from South Wales. The Home Secretary was urged to institute an inquiry.

> Surely such a picture as that justifies the strong censure of the police. . . . We know that policemen, in their private capacity are pretty much like ourselves, but in the discharge of their public duties they are changed into the instruments of the master-class, and are specially imported into districts not to preserve the peace, but to repress the activities of the strikers. . . . The whole police system is in jeopardy, on account of the flagrant manner in which it has been abused in the interests of the employers in connection with these disputes. . . . in Cornwall. The police inspector, seeing that there were men acting as pickets in connection with the strike, determined that their number should be reduced, and actually took upon himself to bring the number of pickets down to three. Now surely this is no part of the duty of a police inspector. . . . It is bad enough having to put up with new interpretations of old Statutes, but to have a fresh form of public control imposed by police inspectors upon Trade Union pickets is an intolerable position. . . .[90]

But, predictably, no inquiry into the behaviour of the police here was ever held.

Yet, in spite of the mobilization of the resources of the state in 1911–12, many of the strikes which took place had still been successful. This was said by the Home Office and police to be mainly because of effective intimidation. Some local pressure was now put on the government to modify, even to repeal, the Trade Disputes Act 1906, and to devise legislation to discourage intimidation. In Liverpool, for instance, after the railway strike in 1911, it was reported that intimidation had been rife in every direction. The mayor forwarded to the Home Secretary resolutions passed by the executive committee of justices:

> That the Home Secretary be informed 1) that in the opinion of the Committee the present position in Liverpool does not justify any relaxation of the military and police precautions here; that 2) having regard to the manner in which the so-called 'peaceful picketing' has been carried on in this city during the last few days, and the wholesale personal intimidation of workmen which is now rife in all parts of the City, and also to the fact that owing to such intimidation it is almost impossible to obtain evidence which would justify prosecutions under the Conspiracy and Protection of Property Act 1875, the Committee trust that Parliament will

[90] *TUC Annual Conference Report* (1913), p. 238.

not adjourn until additional and adequate powers have been given to the Justices to enable them to prevent intimidation and to deal with the present disorder.[91]

He added that the committee believed that the present forms of picketing and intimidation were 'almost the sole factors in preventing a universal settlement of the existing trade disputes in this City'.[92] Again, a memorial from the Leeds Chamber of Commerce called for a Royal Commission to investigate the working of the Trade Disputes Act 1906.[93] King George V himself asked the Prime Minister to devise legislation to discourage both picketing and intimidation. Asquith replied, however,

I see little prospect of any practical scheme of legislation which would command anything like general acceptance being devised between now and the autumn sittings. In regard to picketing, I expressed my own opinion that the existing law if properly enforced, is quite strong enough to deal with the cases of intimidation and that the difficulty (which would be at least equally great if the law were strengthened) is in procuring the evidence necessary to convict.[94]

In spite of this, Home Office researches were now stepped up as to the working of the Acts of 1875 and 1906, with regard to police effectiveness in controlling picketing. The new Home Secretary, Reginald McKenna, on the suggestion of Troup, sent a circular at the end of 1911 to forty-three boroughs and cities. This asked watch committees to let him have their experiences in regard to picketing and for particulars of cases in which problems had been met by the police in obtaining evidence to justify proceedings for intimidation and molestation under the 1875 Act and in obtaining convictions.[95] The replies to the circular generally showed that intimidation was a problem and very few proceedings had in fact been taken under the Conspiracy and Protection of Property Act 1875, mainly because of the difficulty of the police in obtaining evidence.

[91] Lord Mayor of Liverpool to Home Secretary, 21 Aug. 1911 (PP 1911 (323), xlvii. 698, no. 10).

[92] Ibid.

[93] Memo. from Leeds Chamber of Commerce to Home Office, 26 Oct. 1911 (HO 144/5491/212614/8).

[94] CAB 37/107/107, Asquith to George V, Sept. 1911.

[95] Home Office circular 1911 to chairmen of 43 watch committees (HO 144/5491/212614/8).

In reply, a deputation from the Liverpool, Birkenhead, and Bootle justices mentioned two cases of great difficulty with regard to picketing which they regarded as typical. The first was when a workman's house was picketed in his absence. This was a very subtle form of intimidation, and the police held that they could not interfere with the picket. The other case was where the picket was supported by a large crowd in the background, and the police could obtain no evidence of intimidation. The Merseyside justices alleged that there was 'a good deal of misunderstanding existing both in the minds of the police and the magistrates as to the effect of the Trade Disputes Act'. Although some of this misunderstanding had been removed by the Home Office circular of 1911, 'they were not, however, satisfied that even when the law was sufficiently understood it was sufficient to prevent cases of intimidation'.[96]

Another form of intimidatory behaviour was condemned by the head constable of Leeds, who wrote to the Home Office:

> the real difficulty that the Police have to contend with in these strikes is due to the large crowds composed of sympathizers with the strikers. . . . It is perfectly true that the Trade Disputes Act of 1906 in no way justifies peaceful picketing in these numbers and in this manner but I am afraid there is an impression among the public that it does, with the result that much resentment is felt towards the police when any action is taken to disperse these crowds, so much so that we cannot but feel . . . that it is like setting a spark to gunpowder to attempt it, and that to do so is likely to bring about the very result that we wish to avoid, namely a grave breach of the peace.[97]

At Leeds, in 1911, the main charges made by the police related to assault, persistently following, disorderly conduct, malicious damage, unlawful wounding, and throwing of missiles. Intimidation had not been proceeded with.[98] The head constable of Bradford reported that during 1911 no proceedings had been taken for offences under the 1875 Act and emphasized the difficulty for the police in enforcing this Act. The Birkenhead town clerk, in similar vein, gave a list of cases under the 1875 Act where

[96] Merseyside justices' report to Home Secretary, 15 Dec. 1911 (HO 144/5491/212614/8).

[97] Head constable of Leeds to under secretary of state at Home Office, 8 Dec. 1911 (ibid. 8b).

[98] Head constable of Leeds to Home Secretary, 8 Dec. 1911 (ibid.).

witnesses had been afraid to give evidence.[99] However, where prosecutions under Section 7 of the 1875 Act had taken place, and where evidence had been forthcoming, they had been successful. Indeed, when cases involving picketing came before the courts, judicial decisions now showed that the term 'peaceful persuasion' was being strictly interpreted in the courts. If any magistrate or judge felt that there was any element of threat in any picketing, the picket necessarily lost the protection afforded by the Act of 1906.[100]

In the light of the replies to the Home Office circular, Troup at the Home Office agreed that a change in the law was theoretically desirable: 'If Parliament would restrict the number of pickets by a definite rule, require them to wear distinctive badges, and give power of immediate arrest for intimidation, the hands of the Police would be much strengthened, without any detriment to the picketing that is really peaceful.'[101] However, he felt the case made out was too weak for parliament to consider a change in the law. In addition, even if police powers were strengthened with regard to intimidation, there would be little change in the situation since there were far too few police to provide the kind of protection employers desired. If the police failed it was usually not because of any defect in the law but because 'it was impossible for them, whatever their numbers, to be present at all places and times where and when intimidation might occur'.[102] With regard to mass picketing, the Law Officers had ruled in 1911, and the police had been circularized to this effect, that a large crowd itself was evidence of intimidation and should be broken up and the ringleaders charged.[103] The replies to the circular to watch committees had confirmed that much could be done under the ordinary law of the land to prevent picketing or make it ineffective, without having recourse to the Acts of 1875 or 1906.

In both the national miners' strike and the Port of London dock strike of the spring and summer of 1912, the police were accused,

[99] Head constable of Bradford's report to Home Secretary, Dec. 1911; Town clerk of Birkenhead's report to Home Secretary, Dec. 1911 (ibid. 19).

[100] See, for example, *Conway* v. *Wade* [1908] 2 KB 844; *R.* v. *Baker* 7 Cr App (1911) 89.

[101] Minute by Troup, 31 Jan. 1912 (HO 144/5491/212614/16).

[102] Memo. by Troup on a question to be asked by Lord Charnwood in House of Lords, 22 Jan. 1913 (ibid. 34).

[103] Minute by Troup, 25 Nov. 1911 (ibid. 11).

simultaneously, both of offering too much protection for blacklegs and of allowing too much intimidation and violence. In the Commons, Bonar Law quoted a letter from the proprietor of a London wharf complaining that dockers during the recent strike were 'in fear of their lives. The police inspectors deplore the weakness of the Home Secretary. They are not allowed to break up huge processions formed specifically for intimidation.'[104] In a letter to *The Times* in reference to the attitude of the government towards trade unionists in respect of picketing and strikes, Sir Robert Anderson, an ex-Metropolitan Police official, strongly implied that the police in the metropolis were hampered in their duties by orders from the Home Office.

> I speak with knowledge when I say that the working officers of the Force are becoming demoralized. To any one who knows the men of the Metropolitan Police the facts make it as clear as light that they are afraid to act, believing that if they do their duty they may incur Home Office censure instead of, as in former days, receiving commendation and reward.[105]

Troup responded with a memorandum on the general principle of protection which was approved by the Prime Minister and the Home Secretary. In this, he confirmed that the police authorities were still within their rights in using their discretion as to the amount of protection given in any particular circumstance. There was nothing in either the county, borough or Metropolitan Police acts to suggest that 'constables are to be allocated for the protection of individuals who apprehend or say they apprehend special danger'. Indeed:

> the protection which the police can give to persons working during the strike must depend on their resources and on the degree and imminence of the danger of violence and intimidation. It is impossible to have a constable in attendance day and night on every workman for the purpose of protecting him from all possibility of interference. To do this the number of the police force would require to be three times as great as that of the workers.

Many watch committees or police chiefs wrongly believed that they might be held liable for neglect of duty if they failed to provide

[104] *Parl. Deb.*, 5th ser., 39, 977 (12 June 1912).
[105] *Police Review*, 26 June 1912.

protection for individual workmen whenever they asked for it.[106]

One interesting request came from the chief constable of Cornwall, who, as has been seen, adopted aggressive tactics during the Cornish Clay Pit strike in 1913. He now asked the Home Office to redefine the law of unlawful assembly, and this was seriously considered there.[107] H. B. Simpson of the department noted that 'it may be well to consider whether in fact a more precise statement of the law should be drawn up in order to assist any police authority who thinks it desirable to issue one'.[108] Leonard Dunning, an inspector of constabulary, agreed:

> The police like many other people, are altogether in a fog as to the extent which the law of unlawful assembly has been modified by the Trade Disputes Act, and a claim that a number of people are assembled for the purpose set out in Section 2 (1) makes them hesitate to deal with the assembly as the surrounding circumstances may justify their doing.[109]

But Troup moved cautiously when a draft circular on the law of unlawful assembly was drawn up by Simpson. Any circular would not be of much practical assistance to chief constables and

> It shows . . . how impossible it is to state the law as to unlawful meetings in any clear and definite shape which would assist the police. . . . The fact is that in dealing with disorderly crowds the Police have in practice to rely on other powers than the old law of 'unlawful assemblies'.

He recognized the point at which a lawful and unlawful assembly merged and at which it became necessary for the police to intervene was a difficult one; but felt it must be left to the discretion of the chief constable.[110]

Initiatives were now taken in parliament. In the spring and summer of 1912 and again in early 1913 attempts were made by Unionist MPs to limit the powers of pickets. Lord Claud Hamilton introduced a bill to make picketing unlawful, while Lord Robert Cecil introduced another measure to restrict picketing.[111] Neither, however, was given any support by the government. An amend-

[106] Home Office memo. on general principle of protection by Troup for use of Home Secretary in the debate of 12 June 1912 (HO 45/10675/218781, no. 22).

[107] Minute by H. B. Simpson on Cornish Clay Pit strike: action of chief constable, 22 Sept. 1913 (HO 45/10710/242402/19).

[108] Ibid.

[109] Minute by L. Dunning on the above, 27 Oct. 1913 (ibid.).

[110] Minute by Troup, 27 Jan. 1914 (ibid.).

[111] *Parl. Deb.*, 5th ser., 34, 463 (20 Feb. 1912); ibid., 12, 2971 (6 Aug. 1912).

ment to the Trade Union Bill 1913, which reversed the 1909 Osborne judgment on the unions' political levy, tried to limit peaceful picketing to two pickets only; but this was easily defeated. In the House of Lords, Lord Charnwood asked for a more satisfactory regulation by statute of the use of pickets and urged that the organizations which employed them should be made responsible to the courts.[112] Lord Nunburnholme alleged that the police 'winked at the breaches of law' because of the lax approach to the Home Office over the past two or three years.[113] The department, therefore, had to respond to political criticisms that it had erred on the side of leniency.

In defence of the existing Acts of 1875 and 1906, a Home Office memorandum by one of its legal advisers declared that the experience gained during the strikes of 1910 and 1911 showed that there had been a widespread misunderstanding as to the effect of the Trade Disputes Act of 1906. However:

> the Home Office has not had brought to its notice any instance in which the Trades Disputes Act has enabled a successful defence to be set up to a charge of intimidation. . . . The principal obstacle to the effective administration of the law is the difficulty of obtaining evidence of offences but where evidence has been forthcoming there has been no difficulty in securing the conviction and punishment of offenders.[114]

Troup added:

> It is not of course suggested that the law as it stands is perfect and that no improvements would be made if it again came under revision by Parliament. But the chief obstacle arises not from the law, but from the inherent difficulties of the situation—the difficulty of inducing persons who are injured or threatened to give evidence and the impossibility of supplying police protection to every individual workman in his own home and in going to and returning from work.

He concluded:

> Nevertheless, under the existing law much can be done by discreet and firm police action, and by taking proceedings as occasion requires under the provisions of the general law as to threats, as to the use of abusive

[112] Ibid., House of Lords 13, 394 (22 Jan. 1913).

[113] Ibid., 413.

[114] Home Office memo. by J. F. Williams, dated 20 Jan. 1913, on debate on Lord Charnwood's Bill (HO 144/5491/212614/34).

language in the streets, as well as, occasionally, under the special provisions of the Conspiracy and Protection of Property Act 1875.[115]

Thus, by the eve of the war the Home Office itself endorsed the view of police authorities that picketing could not be regulated by the law specifically designed to deal with it, and that the police should concentrate on using the ordinary criminal law to control its conduct.

The First World War brought no great changes. During the war the 1915 Munitions of War Act forbade all strikes and Regulation 42 of DORA made picketing illegal. Nevertheless, strikes did take place, mainly in the engineering and shipbuilding industries, in Sheffield and particularly in Clydeside in Scotland. There was also an official miners' strike in South Wales in July 1915. The police were told by the Home Office in 1916 to give what protection they could to workers, and to prevent picketing. But picketing, as a fact of industrial life, continued as before.[116]

The pre-war phase of industrial unrest, therefore, ended with the definition of unlawful picketing, and its appropriate method of handling by the police during industrial disputes, as uncertain as ever. The Trade Disputes Act of 1906, Section 2 (1)—seen by the trade unions as their *magna carta*—far from clarifying the way in which pickets were allowed to behave, had proved, in fact, to be a major hazard for both police and trade unionists alike. Some police chiefs and many employers of labour supposed that the Trade Disputes Act had limited the powers of the police in relation to maintaining law and order, and preventing intimidation. The Bradford Chamber of Commerce wrote to the Home Office on 30 May 1913 complaining that the Acts of 1875 and 1906 had given the unions a position of 'complete irresponsibility'. Moreover, they had created 'a privileged class not subject to the ordinary laws of this realm'.[117] Certainly, the evidence from industrial disputes down to 1918 did show the intrinsic difficulty of regulating picketing by statute. Formally, picketing was regulated by Section 7 of the 1875 Conspiracy and Protection of Property Act, and by Section 2 of the 1906 Trade Disputes Act. In practice, though, the

[115] Minute by Troup on the above, 21 Jan. 1913 (ibid).

[116] Law Officers' opinion on picketing, 19 Feb. 1916 (HO 45/10804/308532/1).

[117] Bradford Chamber of Commerce to Home Secretary (telegram), 30 May 1913 (HO 45/10704/238840/1).

law relating to picketing was conspicuous for its non-application. Picketing was controlled not by the letter of the law but by the sheer physical presence of a sufficiently large number of police. The problem of intimidation, its identification in specific cases, and general control remained as grave as before.

With the onset of major national strikes in the 1910–12 period, the Home Office, as has been seen, now took a direct interest in the preservation of law and order locally. It came to interfere directly with the established principle that law and order was essentially the responsibility of the local police authorities. From the time of the troubles at Tonypandy in 1910 onwards, police chiefs were given detailed executive instructions from Whitehall about more effective ways in which picketing should be handled. The outcome was vigorous, sometimes violent, action by the police themselves, often made more effective because they were backed up by troops. This kind of response provoked a bitter outcry from the labour movement, political and industrial, and led to frequent but unavailing demands for inquiries into police conduct.

There was much pressure from industrial employers and Conservative politicians, and from many police authorities themselves, to reform the law on picketing and intimidation, and further to increase police powers in this area. The ineffectiveness of measures adopted to deal with intimidation, especially of blackleg labour, led to anxiety and resentment. But the Home Office, Troup especially, saw little hope of improvement. The inherent problem remained of obtaining evidence in cases of intimidation on the picket line or elsewhere because of the unwillingness of witnesses to come forward. There was a limit to the amount of protection employers could expect for their workmen. The police themselves preferred to invoke the ordinary criminal law to deal with unlawful picketing; the Home Office urged the police simply to take more vigorous action under the ordinary law of the land as it stood.

In the face of an apparent mounting threat from militant trade unions during the strikes of the pre-war period, a threat which the First World War was only to reinforce, the police and the Home Office thus turned their backs on the sophisticated novelties of labour law along the models of 1875 or 1906. They resorted instead to the most traditional remedies and interpretations. It was an outcome that left police, employers, politicians, and trade unionists all dissatisfied, and in many cases aggrieved, with the government searching with growing desperation for some kind of enduring solution. It did not bode well for the handling of renewed, intensified labour troubles, or the future course of police executive action, in the post-1918 era.

7

Picketing, Industrial Disorder, and the Police, 1918–1939

THE industrial conflict which marked the years immediately before the First World War continued to erupt with equal ferocity in the years following it. The outbreak of major post-war strikes led the Lloyd George government and its successors to prepare for a possible crisis of a magnitude hitherto unknown in British labour history. The first post-war trial of strength came in the spring of 1921 with the nation-wide mining lock-out. This was followed by sporadic industrial disputes, sometimes alarming in their violence, culminating in the 1926 general strike. Thereafter, down to 1939, there was industrial confrontation on a lesser scale, mainly concerned with non-unionism (or perhaps company unionism) in South Wales, and the stay-down demonstrations of the 1930s. It is against this background of present, or potential, unrest that the operations of the police and their executive activities must be seen.

After the war, and in the light of the Russian revolution, the government proposed a far tougher policy towards industrial troubles. The Lloyd George government vigorously advocated that protection should be given to any man who remained at work during a strike. Employers were to be told that the government was behind them 'with police and if necessary troops',[1] and perhaps civilian auxiliaries as well. A Home Office memorandum of August 1919 struck the new note of the time. It emphasized the urgency of magistrates reading out the Riot Act proclamation to avoid confusion in times of disturbances. It added:

> This is perhaps more than ever necessary, now that in times of industrial disturbance there may be present, not only a mob of strikers and sightseers, on the one hand, and the magistrates, military, police and perhaps special constables on the other, but also certain citizens who have volunteered to assist the authorities to carry on during an emergency.[2]

[1] CAB 27/59 Industrial Unrest Committee, 19 July 1919.

[2] Admonitions to crowds by justices during riots, Aug. 1919 (HO 45/10990/111765/2).

The police themselves remained detached from the trade union movement, especially after the failure of the NUPPO strikes on behalf of police unionization in 1918–19. Police powers with regard to picketing had, indeed, been increased during the war years. In addition, the DORA regulations, which extended police authority more broadly, had come into force. The police were openly urged to take a more vigorous attitude towards pickets. As a result, many on the left feared that police authority was not only being inexorably reinforced, but being put to political and partisan use. The threat of a state police on continental lines seemed to be approaching ever nearer.

It was recognized by the government that industrial disputes had changed significantly in character since the war. They were now conducted on far wider and different lines, with the element of class confrontation more pronounced. The nature of the task which police and troops were, therefore, being called upon to perform had also changed. In the immediate post-war years, although physical violence was comparatively rare, the intensity of the struggle, the high degree of organization among the unions, and the solidarity of the spirit of resistance enhanced the potential dangers to the state if trouble occurred.

The industrial crisis which engulfed the government after the war called for a swift and effective response by the police, often backed up by troops, and free from the shackles of democratic control. As noted previously, the government acquired far more influence over the administration of the provincial police after 1919, through the increased grant and the use of Home Office regulations. In addition, Home Office rhetoric from Anderson and others and later case law now came to stress the independent nature of the office of constable.[3] The effect of this was to emphasize the autonomy of the police as against their police authorities. The constable's office, not the power of the police committee, became the defining feature of the relationship. The legal status of the constable did not change. Rather, his common-law status was elevated and reaffirmed, with the suggestion that the constable was a servant or employee of the state. So far as troops were concerned, the duties of army commanders, when

[3] Evidence of L. Dunning before the Desborough Committee, PP 1920 [Cmd. 874], xxii. 665; John Anderson, 'The Police', pp. 192–3; PP 1928–9 [Cmd. 3297], ix. 138; [1930] 2 KB 364.

aiding the civil power, were to use their own discretion as to the action to be taken by their men. In fact, the duty of individual soldiers, as citizens with a moral duty to uphold the authority of the state, was also re-emphasized at this time. Protection was to be given, jointly, by police and troops, in guarding key installations before any disorder occurred. However, it is noticeable that during the post-war strikes of the 1919–26 period the troops were never in the forefront when disorder took place. Although their very presence gave moral support to the police, it was the latter, assisted by special constables and other auxiliaries, who kept order throughout, sustained, as has been seen, by the new stream of directives emanating from the Home Office and central government.

The use of both police and troops in this way was made easier by the passage of the Emergency Powers Act 1920, and the Emergency Regulations issued under it in 1921 and 1926 when states of emergency were declared. The regulations introduced under this Act 'for the preservation of the peace' and 'for any other purposes essential to the public safety and the life of the community' provided a blanket cover for military operations aimed at maintaining essential services. They also meant markedly increased police powers. The police were now allowed, with the approval of the Home Secretary, to prohibit marches and meetings; they were granted wider powers of arrest without a warrant, and leave to enter and to search premises. It was an offence to do anything likely to cause disaffection or to hinder the implementation of the emergency measures. Peaceful picketing, indeed, still remained lawful. But the very existence of these broad powers given to the police and their military allies markedly extended the ways in which trade-union activity could be controlled and curbed.

The most severe test of these powers was the national miners' lock-out which began on 1 April 1921, with a threat of a Triple Alliance strike in the background. A state of emergency, as noted, was declared under the Emergency Powers Act, and Emergency Regulations promptly introduced. Special constables were enrolled. Troops, reservists, and a Defence Force were called up, and police action was co-ordinated by the Home Office to cope with any possible disorder. Daily reports were forwarded by chief constables about the state of public order in their areas to the Home Office, which now involved itself directly in the day-to-day preservation of order in the strike.

Since there was much fear of flooding in the pits and the destruction of colliery workings, the police were encouraged to give full protection to those safety officials who continued to work. They were reminded of the Home Office circular of August 1911 dealing with picketing, which emphasized that a large crowd was itself evidence of intimidation. 'On this occasion it is not desirable to make arrangements with strike leaders as to the number of pickets or the wearing of badges but any picket likely to cause intimidation by their [*sic*] numbers should be broken up.'[4] On 3 April it was reported from Wrexham in North Wales that:

> An attack was made by a crowd of about 50 strikers on a pit of the Wrexham and Ackton Colliery at Gwersyllt. . . . The police beat it off and no damage was done . . . the men at work, though frightened are still carrying on. The police think there may be another attack tonight but do not anticipate anything with which they will be unable to deal.[5]

However, on 6 April a police constable was badly injured at Burnley, trying to prevent intimidation of those men still working. At Pontefract and Featherstone in Yorkshire the chief constable reported on 8 April that 'A mob of several hundred men has been parading . . . trying to induce men who are working pumps to come out. They met with very little success.' At the New Monkton Pit, also in Yorkshire, 'a crowd of about 50 men approached with a view to trying to bring out the pumpmen but finding the police there they withdrew'. In Derbyshire the police escorted blacklegs to and from their homes.[6]

However, here and elsewhere, the Home Office became increasingly concerned at what it regarded as successful forms of intimidation being adopted. At the March Lane Colliery in Derbyshire about 100 miners were working with police protection at the start of May; but 200 striking miners then went to the colliery and persuaded them to stop work. The next day only about 14 of the original 100 were working. The Home Office complained that, in this case, the police were not doing their duty, as laid down in

[4] HO circular, 5 May 1921, in HO 144/1746/417250/108.
[5] CAB 27/80, STC, Daily Strike Bulletin, 4 Apr. 1921.
[6] Ibid., 6 Apr., 8 Apr., 7 May–25 June, 6 June 1921.

the Home Office circulars of 1911 and 1921. It forcibly reminded the chief constable here that these circulars had made it clear that a crowd of this size was not protected by the Act of 1906 and could be charged with watching and besetting under the Act of 1875 as it constituted intimidation.[7]

As always in a mining dispute, it was in South Wales that the most intensive police activity took place, even though there had been few disturbances. In part this was because of the determined attitude adopted by Lindsay, chief constable of Glamorgan. As has been seen, Lindsay and Bosanquet, the respective chief constables of Glamorgan and Monmouthshire, were not slow to apply for troops, while Lindsay also had a large squad of 449 borrowed police at his disposal. He posted them variously at Tonypandy, Fernhill, and Bute Collieries where the manager and the loyal workmen believed that this show of force 'restored confidence in that part of the Rhondda which it passed through'. Troops from the Yorkshire and Lancashire Regiment, along with fifty men from the Norfolk constabulary and also fifty from the Gloucestershire force were actively employed in the Rhondda, Rhymney, and Aberdare valleys, and in the Gilfach Goch district.[8] Nevertheless, mass picketing by Welsh miners intensified (as it did in other coalfields), mainly organized by George Dolling and A. J. Cook, two leading left-wing district officials of the South Wales Miners' Federation (SWMF).

Reports to the Home Office about the conduct of the strike sent by Chief Constable Lindsay show the way in which Home Office advice about more belligerent conduct by the police was interpreted, and how the powers given to the police under the Emergency Regulations were used to break up pickets and intimidate the strikers generally. Lindsay reported that on 2 May a force of eighty police, led by himself, stopped a procession of strikers from interfering with men still at work at Cymmer Colliery. Even so, 'the officials were intimidated and left the pit'. On 3 and 4 May the chief constable went on to Ynyshir Colliery in the Rhondda with 100 police, where they protected miners going on morning shift. Nevertheless, 'The officials came from so many different directions that it was impossible to give them adequate

[7] Minute by Troup on disturbances at Marsh Lane Colliery, Derbyshire, 5 May 1921 (HO 144/1746/417250/108).

[8] Statement by Lindsay on national coal strike, 21 July 1921 (ibid. 178).

protection . . . [they were] jostled and hooted on their way to the pit head and threatened with direst reprisals for their loyalty'. On 6 May a large procession formed up to march to Llwyncelyn, where the safety men were being picketed. This consisted of a large crowd headed by a brass band. Lindsay now appeared on the scene with a force of 200 police, composed of men from the Glamorgan, West Sussex, and Wiltshire forces. He ordered the procession to halt; the police then assembled at the colliery in the famous 'Macready formation' familiar from 1910—a deep and formidable front with protected flanks supported by a similarly deep and powerful group bringing up the rear. 'Without waiting for orders, [they] went straight to the column of strikers and drove them roughly back. They drove them right through Porth, through Cymmer and a second time through Porth, taking the names of the most prominent leaders.'[9] To one of the police involved, 'the keynote of the value of tight formation is mobility with power to move in, over and through every yard of any given locality carrying the tight formation to close quarters and supplying the tangible human element which makes rioters run.'[10]

Lindsay himself felt that this procession was 'the acme of defiance of the law of the land' and took steps to issue summonses to the leaders in charge of it.[11] By the end of May over 500 summonses had been served by the police for prosecution under Emergency Regulation 19 (relating to acts likely to cause sedition) in South Wales alone. In some cases as many as twenty summonses were served on a single individual.[12] On 16 May A. J. Cook, the miners' agent at Porth (and a Communist), had his house raided by the deputy chief constable and a number of police officers. The house of John Thomas, secretary of the Unofficial Reform Movement, was also ransacked and much correspondence removed. The *Daily Herald* claimed angrily that the police were using the Emergency Regulations to initiate a reign of terror in South Wales.[13]

Lindsay, however, reported to the standing joint committee in Glamorgan in June:

[9] Ibid.

[10] May, *Recollections*, p. 78.

[11] Statement by Lindsay on national coal strike, 21 July 1921.

[12] *Parl. Deb.*, 5th ser., 142, 1286 (2 June 1921); A. Horner, *Incorrigible Rebel* (1960), 55–6.

[13] *Daily Herald*, 16, 25 May 1921.

our strong reinforcements have enabled us to prevent the rioters from doing permanent damage to any of the collieries by preventing officials from working . . . and has also enabled us to get good evidence in a very much larger number of serious cases of riot, intimidation, unlawful assembly than we have ever had during any other industrial crisis.

He argued that 'the Emergency Regulations, issued to meet the present emergency, by placing more power in the hands of the authorities, have even in this short time, produced a most marked effect for the good and these Regulations will, I am sure, always be a powerful factor in the interests of law and order'.[14] He complained, when the Home Office withdrew the Regulations on 3 July, that it had done so 'long before we were safely through with our labour troubles, as usual without consulting the opinion of those on the spot who were best able to judge'.[15] A lengthy report was sent by him to the Home Office, which detailed the role of 'violent extremists' in South Wales and their alleged plans for setting up a revolutionary government. There were, he reported, continual attempts at organized attacks on loyal workmen in the Rhondda, Rhymney, and Aberdare valleys. Although he had been told that it 'would be far better to offer no opposition whatever to the forces of disorder for fear of bringing on the "bloody revolution" predicted on all sides', he had been able to 'keep the upper hand in the cases of organized attacks . . . but of course not to prevent wholesale terrorism of peaceful citizens'. It might be, however, that local miners were 'frightened by the violence of the Extremist Programme'. During the miners' stoppage, 'the forces of the Crown stood by helpless, while the most precious law of the land, viz. that the liberty of the subject shall not be interfered with', was flagrantly broken. Large bodies of police and troops could deter such men from 'committing acts of terrorism for the moment but it is only the certainty of exemplary punishment that will cause these terrorists to desist from their criminal conduct'.[16]

However, although a vigorous stance had been adopted in South Wales in 1921, neither Lindsay nor the Home Office was complacent about the way in which the dispute had been conduc-

[14] Lindsay's report to the Glamorgan Standing Joint Committee, June 1921.

[15] Lindsay to Colonel Deverell (HQ Welsh Area), 30 July 1921 (HO 144/1746/417250/178).

[16] Statement by Lindsay on national coal strike, 21 July 1921 (ibid.).

ted in the courts. For example, eighty-nine members of the SWMF who had marched to the Maerdy Pit on 5 May were charged by the police with intimidation under Section 7 of the Act of 1875, but most of these cases which relied heavily on police evidence were withdrawn. The stipendiary magistrate applauded the fact that the stoppage had been 'characterized . . . by a singular absence of disturbances or intimidation'; however he did declare that in thirteen of these cases from Maerdy a *prima facie* case had been made out for the grave offence of riot, and in two of these cases for unlawful assembly, and they were committed to the Glamorgan Assizes.[17] After incidents which occurred at the Standard Colliery, Ynyshir, on 3 and 4 May when intimidation was said to have been carried out by a procession led by George Dolling, Samuel Jones, and Thomas Jones, 142 people had been charged with intimidation under the 1875 Act. The charges were subsequently withdrawn by the police. However twenty-three people including these three were charged with unlawful assembly and also were committed to the Glamorgan Assizes.[18]

Lindsay's response was one of anger that so many of the 'accused were let off'. He hoped that 'no such disastrous compromise will be come to in the cases to be heard at the present Assizes', adding that, 'should the cases be withdrawn, it will give fresh courage to the disloyalists'.[19] Lindsay's report was presented to Sir Edward Morley Sanson KC, the leading police counsel, and had the desired effect. Even when seventy-two people were convicted at the riot trial at Swansea, Lindsay was not satisfied. He wrote to Troup claiming that there was much local indignation in South Wales about the leniency habitually shown by the courts towards 'disloyal agitators and intimidators [*sic*]'. He added that, 'While the number of convictions gives great satisfaction, it is felt that the sentences were light and the rebukes administered by the judges were mild.'[20] In fact, all those committed to the Glamorgan Assizes received considerable sentences. Cook, for instance,

[17] Minute by Troup, 6 June 1921 (ibid. 150); minute by Dunning, 13 June 1921 (ibid.); particulars of offences committed and proceedings taken for unlawful assembly, Maerdy, 5 May 1921 (ibid.); *Daily Herald*, 25 May 1921.

[18] Ibid. 25 May 1921; particulars of offences committed and proceedings taken for unlawful assembly, 1921 (HO 144/1746/417250/150).

[19] Statement by Lindsay on national coal strike, 21 July 1921; Lindsay to Troup, 8 June 1921 (HO 144/1746/417250/152).

[20] Lindsay to Troup, 6 Aug. 1921 (ibid.).

received four months' imprisonment and Dolling, two months.[21]

Even though there were many convictions for riot in the 1921 coal lock-out the Home Office, too, was far from satisfied. Perhaps this was because riot is a risky crime from the point of view of the prosecutor. There is every chance of an acquittal or of a lenient sentence, for it is no easy task to identify those chiefly responsible for or even those participating in outbreaks of disorder. This was further confirmed in the miners' strike of 1984–5. In addition, since they are major offences, riot, rout, and unlawful assembly can only be tried on indictment at the assize court. It was preferable to rely upon speedier summary crimes of public order which could be dealt with in courts of summary jurisdiction.[22] Although the police were now using the Conspiracy and Protection of Property Act of 1875 to bring charges, the difficulty of getting some magistrates to accept police evidence over charges of intimidatory behaviour proved a major stumbling block. Dunning, one of the inspectors of constabulary, protested that 'the settlement of an industrial dispute ought not to be accepted as a sufficient reason for letting persons who have committed crimes in the course of a dispute go unpunished'.[23] Troup himself noted that in this dispute, although charges of riot and unlawful assembly were proceeded with, 'charges of intimidation seem to be dismissed'.[24] He deplored the restrained approach of local Liberal magistrates like Lleufer Thomas (Pontypridd and Rhondda) and Llewelyn Williams, the recorder of Cardiff (a former Liberal MP), 'but we cannot get rid of them'.[25]

There was, of course, another side of the story. The state had been mobilized against the miners; there had been much violence and major sentences for riot inflicted. The miners were, perhaps, less hostile to the troops themselves than to the government's policy and the borrowed police. As Abe Moffat, the Scottish miners' leader and a Communist, later stated: 'They can draft in as many troops as they like but they can't produce coal. So we adopted the attitude of creating friendly relations with the soldiers; we invited them into miners' homes and to any socials or

[21] Horner, *Incorrigible Rebel*, pp. 55–6.
[22] For fuller details see D. Williams, *Keeping the Peace*, pp. 236–43.
[23] Minute by L. Dunning, 13 June 1921 (HO 144/1746/417250).
[24] Minute by Troup, 6 June 1921 (ibid., 150).
[25] Minute by Troup, 4 Mar. 1917 (HO 45/10742/263275/219).

dances.'[26] David Watts Morgan, a Welsh mining MP, even observed that the military had helped in relieving distress and in arranging football matches and concerts.[27]

The Defence Force met with a predictably fierce reception from the left. Its very existence seemed to mark a new departure in government policy towards strikers. On the other hand, a military officer commanding troops in Lancashire commented: 'My own experience of the Defence Force . . . from 12 April to 19 July 1921 was that there was never the slightest probability of its services being needed and that the strikers treated it with amused friendliness but not with awe.'[28]

On balance, it was the police, especially the borrowed police, who were most strongly criticized by Labour MPs for their conduct during the 1921 miners' strike. The existence of the Emergency Regulations, it was felt, gave the police *carte blanche* to behave how they pleased and created an inflamed atmosphere in mining districts.[29] It was always in South Wales that labour relations seemed to be most tense, and here the police were more ardent in their duty than in any other coalfield in England and Wales. A combination of anti-Communist hysteria amongst the authorities and the greater political commitment and militancy of the miners, dating from pre-1914 days, contributed to this alarming mood of tension and confrontation between workers and police.

The coal stoppage lasted from 1 April to 4 July, but the only outcome was an unhappy return to work on the existing wage system on a district basis, with many wage reductions in consequence. In some South Wales lodges the strike went on for some weeks more, until the end of August. It was an unmistakable defeat for the miners, and an apparent vindication of the policy of the authorities.

Between 1922 and 1926 there were further industrial disputes in engineering and shipbuilding, the docks and coal-mining, and several of these should be highlighted. In each case, the police were much involved in protecting blacklegs against pickets. Again the law of picketing was notable for its non-observance. Disorder

26 Quoted in Morris, *General Strike*, p. 86.
27 *Parl. Deb.*, 5th ser., 142, 1287 (2 June 1921).
28 Note regarding formation of Defence Force, 13 Sept. 1925 (WO 32/2674).
29 *Parl. Deb.*, 5th ser., 141, 1087 (4 May 1921); ibid., 142, 1285–6 (2 June 1921).

associated with labour disputes was seen by the police as a public order issue and treated as such. Charges under the Conspiracy and Protection of Property Act 1875 were avoided, perhaps because of the experience in Glamorgan in 1921. Many of the episodes concerned with picketing which occurred in industrial disputes after 1921 reflected badly on both the police and the strikers. In 1922 at South Shields, for example, as a result of a pit-head riot, thirteen men were charged with obstructing the police and behaving in a disorderly manner. *The Times*, reporting the incident, stated that

> thousands of men assembled at the pit-head entrance to prevent other men going to work. Two columns of miners were seen marching towards the police to the cry of 'charge men'. They rushed at the officers who were hopelessly outnumbered.
>
> Mounted police dashed up and a free fight ensued for a considerable time. The police used their batons freely in the darkness. Rioters threw stones, bottles and all sorts of missiles.[30]

At Lincoln, during the engineering dispute in 1922, the chief constable borrowed twelve mounted policemen from the Metropolitan Police on the authorization of the watch committee, to protect blacklegs who were working on non-union wages. Mounted police patrolled the city during the strike and their presence 'allayed the fears of the works managers and general public'.[31] When union men picketed non-union men at Nine Mile Point Colliery in Monmouthshire in March 1923, the chief constable Bosanquet instructed that the ringleaders should be summonsed; seventeen men were served with summonses for riot and unlawful assembly.[32] Again, at Merthyr, in June 1923, the police gave evidence at a series of cases involving intimidation and unlawful assembly, following a disturbance which some alleged to have been stirred up by borrowed police protecting non-union men at Bedlinog earlier in the month. Fourteen men and nine women were charged with unlawful assembly. Five of them were discharged, but eighteen who pleaded not guilty were committed for trial at the assizes.[33]

[30] *The Times*, 12 July 1922.

[31] Report of Inspector of Metropolitan Police for 9 May 1922, MEPO 2/1959.

[32] Chief Constable Bosanquet's report to Home Office, 16 Mar. 1923 (HO 144/4739/442686/5).

[33] Chief Constable Lindsay's report to Home Office, 21 June 1923 (ibid. 11); *South Wales Echo*, 29 June 1923; *The Times*, 2 July 1923.

Mass picketing and particularly violent rioting took place in the anthracite strike in Carmarthenshire in the summer of 1925, after a local dispute over the maintenance of the seniority rule in the anthracite pits around Ammanford. In an attempt to force the men at Rock Colliery at Glyn Neath to stop work in the early hours of the morning of 16 July, a procession started from Seven Sisters a thousand strong. Soon, it increased to 6,000. The demonstrators held a meeting near the pit-head, with the intention of enlisting the support of their employed colleagues. They were then charged by a force of 200 police who had been rushed to the area. The police had their batons drawn and struck out indiscriminately.[34] According to the historian of these events, 'a police whistle blew and all you could hear was the clash of batons on the skulls of miners'. He goes on:

> There were sixteen casualties, including Police Constable Bryn Phillips of Port Talbort, a boxer and international rugby forward, who was badly mauled. One young miner from Cwmtwrch, the sole supporter of a widowed mother and eight children, was so badly beaten by batoning about the head that he spent a long period in hospital and never worked as a miner again. The Policeman responsible was not forgotten. The next occasion he played rugby against one of the Swansea Valley teams he received such leg injuries that he suffered permanent incapacity. . . . The effect of the disturbance was that the Rock miners joined the strike.[35]

This, however, was a mere skirmish compared with what was to follow. The attempt of the mineowners to save their pits by using volunteer pumpsmen and the introduction of police from other counties to protect them caused more disorder. From 28 July serious violence took place. The so-called 'battle of Ammanford' occurred on Wednesday, 5 August. An electrician had covertly entered the colliery. The police were hidden inside the colliery premises when a crowd, said to be armed with staves and other weapons, demanded that the man be removed. They refused to disperse when ordered to do so by the deputy chief constable, and the police on the spot assisted by other police billeted at Gwaun-cae-gurwen Brewery drew their batons and charged. They 'systematically drove the rioters back into the town, batoning everyone in sight'. The 'battle' raged from 10.30 p.m. until

[34] *Daily Herald*, 17 July 1925.

[35] H. Francis, 'The Anthracite Strike and Disturbances of 1925', *Llafur*, 1, 2 (May 1973), 19.

3.0 a.m. with between 50 and 100 people injured. Hywel Francis comments:

More than any other disturbances in the whole inter-war period, those in the Ammanford district in 1925 saw the miners take the offensive in meeting organized police 'violence' with their own violence. . . . One manager while on the way to his colliery was met with a typical comment: 'The only way he'll get through this picket line is on a stretcher.'[36]

There is evidence that, while the Ammanford men were aggressive themselves, the borrowed police from Glamorgan were also prepared to go to extremes. One man formerly in the Leinster Regiment, the Black-and-Tans, and the Ulster Constabulary, who had joined the Glamorgan Police Reserve who were lent to the Carmarthenshire force for the duration of the strike, wrote to Lindsay that 'everything went with a click as forecast'. Although they were ambushed at first,

after that phase, the mob got 'a full dose'. The 'team work' was excellent, and the men were simply splendid. Actually there were tears shed by some who were not chosen to go with the show. . . . I felt very proud to have had the privilege of being amongst those who joined in the battle cry of 'Up Glamorgans' and let the Communist swine see what we were there for.[37]

Conversely, the *Daily Herald* reported that the police had behaved as if 'wild beasts had been let loose'.[38]

Light was thrown on police attitudes by Picton-Phillips, the chief constable of Carmarthenshire. Like Lindsay in Glamorgan, he was extraordinarily ignorant of the mining communities in his county, and their political, social, and cultural characteristics. He attributed the outbreak of the anthracite strike simply to Communist agitators. Although police work and responsibility had increased enormously over the past ten years,

the strongest reason for greater police strength is to be found in the altered character of the Amman Valley which can be attributed largely to the growth of Communism, . . . In the Ammanford and Cross Hands districts there reside 1,000 regular subscribers to 'The Workers Weekly', the principal Communist paper. It can be taken for granted that practically all the regular readers of this Revolutionary paper are in sympathy with the

[36] Ibid., pp. 21, 24.
[37] Colonel V. Haddick to Lindsay, 6 Aug. 1925 (HO 144/6602/481614/12).
[38] *Daily Herald*, 8 Aug. 1925.

sinister purpose and methods of the Communist Party, which stands for the disruption of the British Empire, the end of Constitutional Government, hauling down the Union Jack and hoisting the 'Red Flag' and the setting up of a Soviet Government.

The Amman valley (a stronghold of Welsh-language chapels and eisteddfodic culture), was riddled with sedition, or so he seriously professed to believe.[39] In the event, 198 miners were charged with riot and unlawful assembly at the assizes; fifty-eight of them received sentences varying from one to eighteen months. One of the inspectors of constabulary commented that 'the number of rioters who have been prosecuted . . . bore but a small proportion to those engaged, but, considering the difficulties of the situation, the convictions illustrate the value of the local knowledge possessed by the police'.[40] However, the police were said to have refused to arrest some of the leaders of the strike because they were likely to prove too eloquent in the witness box.[41] Many were confirmed in their belief now that the police in South Wales were engaged in a kind of anti-Communist crusade. Hywel Francis has written that the 'police had made it a practice to acquaint themselves with local political activities, especially in the Rhondda . . . harassment and provocation of "militants" was a long-standing police preoccupation ever since the riots of 1910–11.'[42] This symbolizes the industrial history of South Wales in the early 1920s.

As has been seen, the major strike which the government had been expecting took place in 1926, against a background of lengthy preparations by the forces of the state. In the general strike of 3–12 May 1926, and even more during the prolonged coal strike that followed, mass picketing and intimidation continued to pose severe problems for the police. The state of emergency was declared on 1 May and police powers were again increased dramatically under the Emergency Regulations. Planning for the use of troops, the navy, and the CCR was put into effect, and many special constables enrolled. The Special Branch was active and

[39] Chief constable of Carmarthen's report to Standing Joint Committee, n.d. July 1925.

[40] *Annual Report of HM Inspector of Constabulary*, PP 1926 (2) xv. 211.

[41] Francis, 'Anthracite Strike', pp. 21, 25.

[42] H. Francis, *Miners against Fascism: Wales and the Spanish Civil War* (1984), 145.

army intelligence was reinforced by twelve trained officers from MI5 who mingled with strikers and reported on 'what these chaps are saying and thinking'.[43]

Picketing was not prohibited, but the police were circularized to deal severely with industrial unrest. The term 'peaceful picketing' should be more rigorously interpreted than in the past. Full use should be made of the law to prevent large-scale obstruction such as that which took place in the dock strike of 1924. The circular also redefined the nature of intimidation, which had been narrowly interpreted by some magistrates. It stressed that Section 2 of the 1906 Act, while allowing peaceful persuasion and the obtaining and communicating of information, gave no protection to a person who attended at or near a house or place 'with a view to compulsion' or who intimidated or used 'threats of violence, *actual or implied*'.[44] As in the past, Home Office instructions by circular to the police moved somewhat in advance of the law, serving to increase their involvement and powers in the industrial dispute.

The army, too, now received instructions about the way in which they should handle strikers:

> The strikers misinterpretation of the intentions of the Trade Disputes Act in regard to picketing often creates a difficulty in dealing with crowds and obstructions. . . . It may be found that these pickets, ostensibly present for the purpose of 'peaceful persuasion' are in reality aggressive bodies of men armed with sticks, bludgeons and other weapons. It may therefore become necessary for the strike leaders to be warned that such bodies cannot be recognised as legal pickets . . . and that if the strikers do not limit their pickets to some agreed number and ensure that all pickets wear a distinguishing badge and are unarmed, they will be regarded as unlawful assemblies.[45]

Daily reports on the state of public order in their areas were, as in 1921, sent by chiefs of police to the Home Office, which kept in close touch with provincial forces throughout. It is against this background that the response of police and troops to the general strike must be seen.

Yet, in spite of (or perhaps because of) this large-scale mobiliza-

[43] Jeffery and Hennessy, *States of Emergency*, pp. 116–17; J. Symons, *The General Strike* (1957), 112–13.

[44] PP 1926 [Cmd. 2666] xxiii. 861.

[45] ADM 116/3181, Duties in Aid of the Civil Power (War Office pamphlet, 1923).

tion of the state, the strike was generally peaceful. Although the presence of the military certainly gave added confidence to the police, as was illustrated in London, the army played an indirect role. It was the police aided by special constables who were in the front line of keeping order throughout.

During the general strike, as is well known, many middle-class strike-breakers drove vans and lorries, despite the picketing. As a result, there were collective union efforts in many places to check traffic on key roads. The TUC repeatedly appealed to pickets to confine themselves to their legitimate duties, but this was not always heeded 'on t' field', in Herbert Smith's famous phrase. The police response to picketing of this type was often distinctly restrained. At Ilkeston in Derbyshire it was said by strikers that 'the police were very good and assisted us rather than interfered with us'. The chief constable of Lincoln, as noted above, was thought of as a friend to labour. The famous football match between police and strikers took place at Carstairs, where the chief constable was anxious to keep the temperature down. Dealings between strikers and police were invariably most friendly when they knew one another, while the police were never allowed to act as blacklegs themselves.[46] When the STC proposed that the police should deliver medical supplies, Sir John Anderson of the Home Office argued that such action would contravene the basic principle that the police were impartial in a labour dispute, and his view prevailed.[47]

Picketing, however, did lead to scuffles or worse between police and strikers in more militant areas; on occasion, the police had to retire in the face of superior numbers of mass pickets.[48] On 6 May the Cabinet's attention was drawn to the existence of mass picketing. The *British Gazette* now declared that, although no very serious disorder had occurred in any part of the country, 'Intimidation both by disorderly crowds and picketing has occurred in many places, and may soon occur in many more. His Majesty's Government have directed all authorities to repress and overcome these criminal obstructions.'[49]

Although no official pronouncement from the government had

[46] See Morris, *General Strike*, pp. 54–7.
[47] Wheeler-Bennett, *John Anderson*, p. 106.
[48] Morris, *General Strike*, p. 54.
[49] *British Gazette*, 8 May 1926.

in fact been made, there can be no doubt that these views filtered through to the police authorities. Many of them took tougher measures over picketing during the second week of the strike. The TUC Intelligence Committee assessment noted that 'At the beginning of the strike the attitude of the regular police called for no comment. . . . Towards the end of the first week, however, reports which came to hand indicated some change of attitude of the police.'[50] There were often complaints about police aggressiveness. In many areas, when police violence was complained of, it was actually committed by imported alien police and special constables. In the House of Commons on 10 May George Lansbury claimed that 'the police do seem to be under the impression that no-one has a right to picket' and asked that guidance be issued to the police on this issue. The Solicitor-General replied that public opinion (which he failed to define) believed that the term 'peaceful picketing' had been interpreted 'with undue latitude and moderation'.[51]

Vicious and sustained outbreaks of disorder occurred in working-class districts of Hull, Middlesbrough, Leeds, Glasgow, and Edinburgh as well as London. At Hull a disturbance took place in the city square on 7 May. Five mounted policemen and fifteen foot constables drew their batons and charged, scattering a crowd of 1,000: eight men and one woman were injured.[52] In the north-east picketing, violence, and the flow of transport services were frequently interconnected. Uniquely, this region saw the setting up of a joint strike committee in Northumberland and Durham to co-ordinate strike action in an area corresponding with that of the government's civil commissioners. This strike committee took control of the question of permits for food transport, even though the government let it be known that in no circumstances would it recognize any permit system organized by the local 'council of action'. In one famous episode the future miners' president, Will Lawther, was sentenced to two months' imprisonment for intimidation and interference with food convoys at Gateshead court on 13 May. He had been called out to investigate an inaccurate report of a baton charge on pickets in Blaydon. On the

[50] Report of TUC Intelligence Committee, 15 May 1926, quoted in C. Farman, *The General Strike* (1976), 197.
[51] *Parl. Deb.*, 5th ser., 195, 780 (10 May 1926); ibid., col. 783.
[52] *The Times*, 8 May 1926.

way back, he stopped when he saw two lorries and a number of police outside a public house. He was with the chairman of the Blaydon UDC at the time, and they knew the council had refused a permit to allow the lorries to pass pickets further up the road. After Lawther and Henry Bolton, chairman of the Blaydon UDC, came into dispute with the police outside the public house, Lawther was arrested and imprisoned. Along with him in prison were thirty or forty miners from his own colliery, all pickets.[53]

In some areas the workers formed Workers' Defence Corps to protect themselves, in defiance of TUC instructions. These came into existence at Aldershot, Colchester, Croydon, Selby, Sowerby Bridge, and elsewhere, but no particular conflicts between them and the police resulted. In Willesden, for instance, where a corps of 200 men was formed, there was co-operation between the corps and the police and no arrests were made. A similar state of affairs prevailed in Selby.[54]

By contrast to the vigorous use of police, the CCR, apart from protecting a few convoys, was hardly used in the general strike. They were said to have been looked on as a species of strike-breaker, and so did not, in consequence, give the same confidence to the workers. In attacking them, the strikers 'did not feel they were up against law and order in the same way as with the police'.[55] At Tilbury Docks, for example, it was reported that strikers would allow the mails to go out if regular police guarded them, but that they would break up the CCR.[56] Although they had been created to get away from the use of armed forces, because they were looked on in this way it was necessary to use troops freely in London at least, even after their formation. The strike, therefore, gave new vindication to the more traditional arms of the state.

After the general strike ended on 13 May, the coal stoppage continued its bitter course until the miners gave in at the beginning of November. The daily reports by chief constables in mining areas to the Home Office continued throughout, as did Home

[53] Morris, *General Strike*, pp. 56–7; for file on the Lawther case, see HO 144/12051/494042/10.

[54] Farman, *General Strike*, p. 156.

[55] Report on the general strike as it affected troops in the London District (WO 32/3456).

[56] Ibid.

Office advice to the provincial police about the way picketing should be met. One feature of both the general strike and the miners' strike was the widespread use made by the police of the powers conferred on them under the Emergency Regulations. The value of these regulations was reaffirmed in the House of Commons in ringing tones. Their existence was believed to have prevented disturbances and also to have protected men who returned to work in mining districts from intimidation, and, despite the widespread labour protests, they were renewed until December 1926.[57]

As the return to work began in the coalfields in the summer and autumn of that year, strikers were promised police protection if they resumed work. There was much resultant disorder. In South Wales striking miners now made a determined effort to close all the pits by withdrawing the safety men. Mass meetings were held and picketing intensified. At Pencoed, Glamorgan, in August, when a miner returned from work on a bicycle, he was seized by several women, the wives of locked-out miners, who threw a white shirt over his back and bundled him through the village amid cries of 'blackleg'. Police reinforcements were called in and the women were later fined £10 each. Many other instances of 'white shirting' took place in South Wales during the autumn.[58]

Detachments of police from Devon, Cornwall, Plymouth, and Sussex reinforced the Glamorgans at this time. That these men could be extremely aggressive in the course of the strike cannot be doubted. A graphic description of Chief Constable Lindsay's approach may be seen from one policeman's memoirs:

> In these national emergencies it became the practice of Captain Lindsay . . . to have his Divisional Superintendents together, and to explain to them his own ideas of the different and best modes of action, and such plans as he himself proposed to execute, on falling in with violent action whatever its nature. . . . There was no possible position which he did not take into calculation. . . . The great thing was to gain law and order and then make the best use of it.[59]

The 'Macready formation' of distinct detachments and tight formations of police was again used to break up crowds as it had been previously in 1910 and 1921. At Aldwich-le-Street a baton charge

[57] *Parl. Deb.*, 5th ser., 198, 2509 ff. (30 July 1926); ibid., 199, 731 (26 Oct. 1926).
[58] *Daily Herald*, 13 Aug. 1926, 8 Oct. 1926.
[59] May, *Recollections*, p. 131.

of police took place on 15 September. Although the police had said they would allow two minutes for the crowd to disperse, they charged immediately. The local council protested at the batoning of 'innocent men, women, and children in a most callous and cowardly way' but to no effect.[60]

Joynson-Hicks, the Home Secretary, seemed content merely to defend the police in any action which they took to restore order, however fierce. He declared that:

> where disturbances have taken place during the past month there have been massed baton charges by the police . . . such a thing is inevitable. When you get crowds of 300, 400, 500, 1,500, and sometimes, 2,000 men, armed with sticks and stones . . . a time comes when it is absolutely essential that the disturbance should be ended and massed charges should take place.[61]

Now picketing of workers' homes was intensified. Police initiatives included waking up blacklegs in the early hours of the morning in good time for work and escorting them to and from their homes. In Gateshead, County Durham, on 12 September, the manager and agent of the Fanny Pit met the chief constable and confirmed that the pit would open the next day. None of their own workers had yet volunteered to work but they were in touch with a few men from outside who would be prepared to do so if guaranteed complete protection. This the chief constable promised, but pointed out that 'unless the men were housed on colliery premises incidents of some sort, at their homes or even while in the streets under police escort, were almost inevitable in a district where almost everyone of their neighbours was hotly in sympathy with the miners'.[62] Indeed, reports to the Home Office from many mining areas now indicated that if there was not house-to-house picketing there would be more men at work.[63]

When mass meetings of strikers became more frequent, notably in South Wales, Joynson-Hicks, by an order of 19 October, empowered police chiefs to prohibit meetings without reference to him if they believed they might lead to a breach of the peace: he was also authorized in Cabinet to warn chiefs of police in mining

[60] *Parl. Deb.*, 5th ser., 199, 431 (28 Sept. 1926).

[61] Ibid., 13 (30 Aug. 1926).

[62] CAB 27/334, STC, no. 53; Home Office situation report, no. 133, 12 Sept. 1926.

[63] Ibid., STC, no. 61, 11 Oct. 1926.

areas 'to keep a careful watch in order to prevent the march of large bodies of miners intended to prevent miners from working, since this form of intimidation appeared to have been particularly successful'.[64] This edict from the Home Secretary, together with the increased powers they enjoyed under the Emergency Regulations, acted as a stimulant to chiefs of police to take bolder action. In Staffordshire, for example, the chief constable prohibited a meeting due to be addressed by the Secretary of the MFGB, A. J. Cook, and other speakers. Police officers told the local miners' officials that this meeting had been forbidden. They were threatened with arrest if they attempted to hold the meeting anywhere in Staffordshire. Mounted police in large numbers were sent into the district and it was estimated that 950 police in all were assembled here. Although 15,000 people were gathered together, no one was allowed to address them.[65]

Throughout the coalfields, chief constables were zealous in banning meetings and processions, breaking up groups of miners who picketed in any numbers, and indulging in baton charges. The *Daily Herald* commented that the chief constables were the real rulers of the country. They had been 'invested by the Home Secretary with powers similar in kind if not in degree to those which Mussolini has delegated to his agents in Italy to suppress his critics'.[66] In all, sixty-three meetings were prohibited in England and Wales in the period between the making of the order and 14 November.[67] The issue of the police ban on meetings was raised by Labour members in the House of Commons. The outcry against the Home Secretary's order finally led to its being revoked on 26 November, but by that time the effect had been achieved and the miners were back at work, crushed and embittered.

Clearly, the police were more vigorous in confronting the miners alone than in responding to the general strike in May when they (and the strikers) had been relatively restrained. The concentration and solidarity of the miners in their pit villages made them easier to control. The statistics are eloquent testimony to the energy shown by the police in handling the strikers.

[64] CAB 23/53 54(26), 27 Oct. 1926.
[65] Ibid., 757–60 (26 Oct. 1926).
[66] *Daily Herald*, 17 Nov. 1926.
[67] *Parl. Deb.*, 5th ser., 200, 722 (26 Nov. 1926).

During the general strike itself there were 1,760 charges brought under the Regulations, 1,389 of them for violence and disorder. It is difficult to know precisely where all these occurred, but it is known that 396 prosecutions under the Regulations took place in Northumberland and Durham, and the West Riding of Yorkshire. The Home Secretary thus confirmed that, as could have been predicted, the mining areas provided a larger number of prosecutions and convictions than the other areas. There were in fact twenty-three counties and seventy-one boroughs in which there were no proceedings at all.[68]

One agency of government that looked forward with relish to this supreme confrontation with labour was the Special Branch. Its head, Wyndham Childs, was obsessed with the dangers of Communist infiltration. He was much encouraged by the advent of Joynson-Hicks to the Home Office, 'a man who had the courage and energy to deal with the menace of Communism . . . his enthusiasm almost exceeded my own . . .'[69] As soon as the general strike was over, on 13 May, Childs circularized all chief constables, requesting information on Communist activity and the number of arrests or prosecutions of Communists during the course of the strike. In fact, Childs's information, when it came into the Special Branch in early June, showed a remarkably small number of Communists actually arrested. Of his figures of 1,388 arrests in England, Wales, and Scotland during the general strike, in itself a modest enough figure which disappointed him, only about 11 per cent, or less than 200, were Communist or party members. The attempt by the intelligence services to turn the general strike into a massive anti-Communist crusade had therefore produced only meagre results.[70] Childs's memoirs record his bitter disappointment that in seven years successive governments did not allow him 'to strike one overwhelming and final blow against the Communist organization.'[71]

In spite of Childs's comparative disillusion about Communist arrests, however, the total number of arrests in South Wales during the general strike and coal lock-out was significant. In

[68] Ibid., 196, 822–4 (2 June 1926); Durham provided 183 cases of violence and disorder; Northumberland, 103; the West Riding, 110.

[69] Childs, *Episodes*, p. 210.

[70] B. Weinberger, 'Communism and the General Strike: Documentary Essay', *Bulletin of the Society for the Study of Labour History*, 48 (Spring 1985), p. 32.

[71] Childs, *Episodes*, p. 209.

September miners' leaders were heavily fined at Bridgend Court for taking part in a procession held in contravention of an order made under Regulation 22 by Chief Constable Lindsay. The five leaders had led a procession of 350 towards a colliery where a few miners had returned to work; the police declared this to be intimidatory and took action. Twenty-one miners were committed for trial at Port Talbot on charges of rioting in connection with disturbances in the Afan valley, while court business was much congested at Ystrad and Porth in the Rhondda sessional courts as a result of prosecutions under the Emergency Powers Act. Three hundred people appeared at the Glamorgan Assizes at Swansea on 1 December charged with alleged riot and unlawful assembly. In all, 900 cases of riot and unlawful assembly went to the South Wales Assizes during the whole of 1926.[72] Not only were there many charges of riot. During the general strike and coal strike the number of persons successfully charged with intimidation under the Act of 1875 in courts of summary jurisdiction increased considerably since former years.[73]

It was notable that the government was active in trying to ensure that Labour magistrates did not sit in courts at this period. In July 1926 the Lord Chancellor, Lord Cave, received a letter from the Doncaster and district Trades and Labour Council which declared that 'the savage sentences inflicted during this dispute would not have been given had our magistrates been in attendance'. Cave confined himself to a rebuke to the West Riding

[72] *Daily Herald*, 6 Nov., 2 Dec. 1926; *Parl. Deb.*, House of Lords, 68, 60 (4 July 1927).

[73] *Judicial Statistics for England and Wales* PP 1928 [Cmd. 30551] xxv. More particular details of persons arrested and charged in connection with the general strike and the mining dispute down to 24 January 1927 were given by the Home Secretary early in 1927. Most of the cases were tried at Courts of Summary Jurisdiction. These figures exclude cases not finally disposed of at that date.

Charged (on summons or after arrest) under Emergency Regulations or under the ordinary law	7,316
Charge dismissed or withdrawn	1,175
Discharged or bound over under Protection of Offenders Act	1,067
Bound over otherwise	652
Fined	3,488
Sentenced to imprisonment	900
Sentenced to penal servitude	10
Fines reduced	35
Part of imprisonment remitted	54
Still undergoing imprisonment on 10 February 1927	52

(Parl. Deb., 5th Ser., 8, 202, 263 (10 Feb. 1927))

Labour magistrates in this instance, but he did examine the role of fifty Labour magistrates involved in cases of intimidation or related activity during the general strike. Of these, seven were imprisoned, nine were censured by the Lord Chancellor, and four were eventually removed from duty.[74] By contrast, Conservative magistrates met with warm endorsement. Thus, on 31 May 1926, the General Strike Committee of Northumberland and Durham protested to the Home Office about the attitude adopted by Sir A. Palmer in connection with the prosecution of the Chopwell pickets at the Gateshead County Court. The committee denounced him for 'class bias' and deplored the fact that a magistrate financially interested in the coal trade should sit in judgement in such a case.[75] But Dixon, at the Home Office, commented urbanely that nowhere did the magistrates do their duty more effectively. Joynson-Hicks added that there was no county 'in which the police were more energetic in coping with the activities of the Councils [of Action] or their members'.[76]

During the whole period of May to November 1926 that the Emergency Regulations were in force a total of 7,960 persons were prosecuted: 4,656 for offences under the ordinary law, and 3,304 for breaches of the Regulations. The majority of the charges for contravention of the Regulations concerned offences of damaging property used to produce or maintain essential services and supplies; acts likely to cause mutiny and sedition and disaffection; and obstruction of officers acting in accordance with their duty under the Regulations.[77] The police did indeed find it easy 'to run in anybody who is inconvenient'.[78]

As in the pre-war years, there was little that police authorities in the counties could do about the conduct of the police. In South Wales complaints were made about the behaviour of borrowed police in dispersing a crowd with a violent baton charge at Abercwmboi. On the evening of 9 November police went to the

[74] CAB 24/180 CP 274 (26), memo. by Lord Chancellor on Justices of the Peace, 19 July 1926.

[75] General Strike Committee of Northumberland and Durham to Home Office, 31 May 1926 (Ho 144/12051/494042/8).

[76] Minute by Dixon, and Home Secretary to Sir F. Hall, 18 June 1926 (ibid.).

[77] G. S. Morris, 'The Emergency Powers Acts 1920', *Public Law* (Winter 1979), 340–1.

[78] *Parl. Deb.*, 5th ser., 199, 443 (28 Sept. 1926).

house of a man who was willing to work at the Aberaman Colliery in order to escort him to the pit-head. They were said to have been followed by a crowd of 500 whom they eventually baton-charged. Joynson-Hicks's explanation to the House of Commons was:

> The crowd commenced to stone the police, and as it was feared that they would rush the colliery premises, steps were taken to stop their advance. However, the crowd stoned the police more heavily, and attempted to rush the cordon. . . . I am satisfied that there was no alternative to dispersing the crowd by a charge and I see no reason for any further inquiry into that aspect of the matter.[79]

In fact the Home Secretary now sent Leonard Dunning, an inspector of constabulary and himself an ex-chief constable, to make an inquiry on the spot. He inspected the county police and imported police in the company of the chief constable. The outcome, inevitably, was that Dunning 'afterwards expressed satisfaction at the general conduct of the police'.[80]

This situation in Glamorgan was paralleled by another mining area, Durham, where 'a veritable reign of terror' was said to have been unleashed. There were many complaints about police violence during the general strike and an inquiry was held by the chief constable. When this turned out to be predictably inconclusive, the Labour majority on the standing joint committee urged the Home Office for a further, independent inquiry to be held. But this was refused by Joynson-Hicks on the familiar grounds that the chief constable was solely responsible for the discipline of his force.[81]

In Monmouthshire the Labour majority on the standing joint committee fiercely attacked Victor Bosanquet, the chief constable, for borrowing police during the general strike and the coal strike, and for breaking up meetings and processions. As has been seen, they called for his dismissal. They asked for an inquiry into the conduct of the police at Bedwas in particular, where a violent police attack on pickets had occurred, but this was refused once again on the grounds that the chief constable was solely responsible for discipline in his force.[82] As on countless other occasions, the local authority was simply brushed aside by the central government.

[79] *Parl. Deb.*, 5th ser., 199, 1936 (18 Nov. 1926).
[80] *Police Review*, 10 Dec. 1926.
[81] Inquiries into conduct of police (HO 144/20729/697140).
[82] Monmouthshire Standing Joint Committee Minutes, 23 June 1926.

With the bitter end of the miners' strike in November, the defeat of the trade unions seemed complete. The Baldwin Cabinet now turned its attention to amending the Trade Disputes Act 1906 and introducing a new Trade Union Bill. Since the war, pressure had again been put on the Home Office, to effect the repeal of Section 2 (1) of the Trade Disputes Act of 1906. In 1921 and 1922 attempts were made by a private members bill to repeal this Section of the Act but they received no parliamentary support.[83] Some chief constables had long been in favour of an increase in statutory police powers. In 1922, for example, the chief constable of Sheffield forwarded to the Home Office a copy of a letter he had addressed to the chief constable of Wakefield suggesting that picketing be discussed at the next area meeting of chief constables. He believed that

> the time has arrived when the so called 'Peaceful Picketing' indulged in by gangs of aggrieved persons, accompanied by hooligans etc. should be made amenable to the Law.
>
> In the terms of the 'Trades Disputes Act 1906' . . . this is permitted and is a grave danger to peace and good order.
>
> It is, of course, an 'illusion' in terms for, unless such persuasion is aggressive, it cannot produce ordinarily the desired effect. Moreover, persuasion in the ordinary sense requires no legal backing. . . . In industrial disputes . . . pickets (if permitted at all) should be limited in strength to 4 or 6 persons at the most and certainly processions of persons for any purpose whatsoever during such disputes should be punishable on the part of the ring leaders by imprisonment without the option of fine.[84]

The assistant chief constable of Liverpool wrote to Dixon, at the Home Office, in 1924, suggesting that pickets should be badged, as

> what constantly occurs and is happening actually here today in connection with the attempted seamen's strike, is that the Communists or others take independent and unauthorised action *before* an actual strike starts in order to force the issue, and by establishing pickets of their own often succeed, largely by intimidation, in compelling a stoppage of work.[85]

The Commissioner of the Metropolitan Police, Horwood, told the Home Secretary in 1923 that some magistrates in the metropolis

[83] *Parl. Deb.*, 5th ser., 138, 442 (18 Feb. 1921); ibid., 150, 616 (13 Feb. 1922).

[84] Chief constable of Sheffield to chief constable of Wakefield (forwarded to Home Office), 17 May 1922 (HO 144/5491/212614/56).

[85] Assistant chief constable of Liverpool to Dixon, 27 Aug. 1925 (ibid. 74).

were dismissing cases where people were charged with intimidation when the charge was only supported by police evidence. This rendered 'the difficulties of the police when dealing with strikes or lock-outs well-nigh impossible'.[86]

In October 1925 Sir Douglas Hogg, the Attorney-General, presented to the Cabinet a memorandum on 'The Present Law in Regard to Sedition and Strikes'. He declared that 'it is notorious that "peaceful picketing" in any big strike is in fact used to carry on the most effectual intimidation'. He would like to see the law strengthened, yet this was politically impossible because there would be an outcry from the trade unions.[87] Even Joynson-Hicks, a notorious hardliner, did acknowledge that, if Section 2 of the Act of 1906 were repealed, 'it would be regarded as an attack on trade unionism' and 'might lead to a combination of trade union voters of all shades of opinion against the Government'. In any case, even if this section of the Act of 1906 was repealed, there would be no real answer to the problem since the difficulty of obtaining sufficient evidence for a successful prosecution would remain.[88]

During the general strike mass picketing occurred in many areas and demands were made of the government that picketing be regulated. The London Emergency Haulage Committee was said to have passed a resolution urging that picketing should be made totally illegal.[89] Joynson-Hicks canvassed the possibility of further restrictions than those which had been recommended by the Law Officers and circularized to the police in 1925 to 'assist the police', perhaps by dealing with the matter under the 1920 Emergency Powers Act, but nothing came of it.[90]

On 11 May Dixon, the assistant secretary at the Home Office, told the Protection Sub-committee that many strikers genuinely believed that large-scale pickets fell within the law, whatever the circumstances. The STC agreed that a notice should be drafted to explain that obstruction, intimidation, and besetting by large crowds was illegal.[91] On 13 May the STC approved the issuing of

[86] Commissioner of Metropolitan Police to Home Secretary, 23 July 1923 (MEPO 2/1960).

[87] CAB 24/175 CP 420, 9 Oct. 1925, memo. by Attorney-General on 'Present Law in regard to Sedition and Strikes'.

[88] CAB 27/261 STC (24) 15, memo. by Home Secretary on 'Picketing and Peaceful Persuasion' in Trade Disputes, 28 Oct. 1925.

[89] CAB 27/260 (18), conclusions of STC, 6 May 1926.

[90] Ibid.

[91] Ibid., STC (24), 12 May 1926.

such a notice to the press, and its dispatch to chiefs of police and civil commissioners. The Home Office determined that in any future strike such a notice should be published and broadcast early in the dispute.[92]

When the general strike was called off, there was considerable demand for the repeal of the Trade Disputes Act 1906, especially by the employers' organizations and chiefs of police. Alarmed by the spectacular demonstration of trade-union solidarity shown in the general strike, the National Council of Employers Organizations now sought a modification of the law, so as to curb the powers of the unions and lessen the incidence of strikes. The Commissioner of the Metropolitan Police, Horwood, urged that the public order provisions in the Emergency Regulations should be embodied in the general law of the land. In the absence of the abolition of peaceful picketing altogether, he wanted a statutory limit of two imposed on the number of pickets.[93]

The failure of the strike had also convinced the Conservative Cabinet and leading civil servants that this was an opportune moment to reform industrial relations. Baldwin had previously been reluctant to fire 'the first shot in an industrial war' against the trade unions: he had built up his emollient reputation as the advocate of 'Peace in Our Time'.[94] But he now seemed reconciled to the fact that advantage should be taken to enact sterner forms of trade-union legislation. The politicians were bent on change in the labour law; some were zealous simply for class revenge. The Prime Minister tamely retreated in the face of back-bench pressure at the party conference, and the punitive instincts of the die-hard group in his Cabinet led by Cave, Birkenhead, and Joynson-Hicks.

The Legislation Committee was set up in June 1926 to consider the demand for the repeal of the Trade Disputes Act 1906 and proposals to make strikes illegal.[95] Sir Ernley Blackwell, the legal adviser to the Home Office, and Sir John Anderson, both argued that the police already had adequate powers under the ordinary law to deal with large crowds constituting a picket; intimidation was a problem which could not be solved by changing the law. Blackwell wrote, 'Peaceful picketing, that is to say contraventions

[92] Ibid., STC (26), 13 May 1926; cover note (HO 144/5491/212614/94).

[93] Commissioner of Metropolitan Police to Home Secretary, 1 July 1926 and cover note (HO 144/8014/494552).

[94] *Parl. Deb.*, 5th ser., 247, 417 (22 Jan. 1931).

[95] CAB 24/180 CP 237, 28 June 1926.

of the provisions of section 7 of the Act of 1875, under cover of immunity, supposed or alleged, to be afforded by section 2 of the Trade Disputes Act, 1906, has, I think, been effectively dealt with in the General Strike under the law as it stands.' Many cases of pickets interfering with drivers of vehicles had been dealt with as offences against the Regulations: 'In many cases effective action was taken by the police in dispersing crowds and thus preventing what is called "mass picketing".' Many persons had been charged with obstructing the police in the execution of their duty, using insulting words and behaviour, and assault, and were then sentenced to imprisonment and fines by the courts. However, although some proceedings had been taken under the Act of 1875, intimidation was a problem:

> no doubt there would be many other cases of a similar kind which did not come to light because, as a rule, the person threatened in this way will not complain to the Police. If he does complain and a summons is issued, members of the Trade Union get at him, with the result that when the case comes on he either refuses to give evidence or gives it in such a modified form that conviction does not result.

However, he doubted if any legislation which could be introduced would remedy this state of affairs. He felt that 'There are all sorts of subtle means by which a man can be intimidated without anything being said or done to him which would bring the intimidators within the law.'[96] Sir John Anderson was another voice of calm in the midst of much angry revanchism from right-wing politicians. He told A. L. Dixon on 1 September that there was 'not much to find fault with' in the existing law. With regard to the suggested repeal of Section 2 of the 1906 Trade Disputes Act, he argued that

> a point which is sometimes overlooked is that the right peacefully to persuade is not dependent on the Trade Disputes Act. This is where I think you have gone wrong. Pickets acting on behalf of a union had to be protected, though even this is anterior to the Trade Disputes Act, because otherwise they might be got at for conspiracy. No such question arises where a picket is acting on his own behalf. Such action within proper limits is an exercise of a fundamental right.[97]

Anderson believed that, if any kind of assembly of strikers could be prevented while a strike was in progress, 'it would be a good

[96] Memo. on revision of the Trade Disputes Act 1906 by Sir E. Blackwell, 10 June, 13 Aug. 1926 (HO 144/8014/494552/6).

[97] Anderson to Dixon on the above, 1 Sept. 1926 (ibid.).

thing' and would of course ease the position of the police. He realized that there would be no chance of getting a general prohibition through: 'And anything short of a general prohibition would surely be very dangerous. Every qualification, while it might strengthen the hands of the police in one direction would weaken it in others.' He felt that 'As the law stands . . . the police have the necessary powers to deal with any crowd which seems to them bent on mischief.' But he did urge that house-to-house picketing should be forbidden.[98]

These views were before the members of the Legislation Committee while they were drafting the Trade Disputes and Trade Unions Bill, and were obviously influential.[99] The Committee agreed with Anderson that the Act of 1906 need not be repealed. However, it concluded that the law on picketing did need strengthening. It agreed with the Home Secretary, Joynson-Hicks, that

> the abuses of picketing can best be dealt with by strengthening the executive powers of the police in two respects. (1) it is desirable to emphasise the existing common law right of the police to disperse persons assembled outside works or premises where a strike is in progress, in such numbers as to cause a reasonable apprehension in the mind of any person who may be at work there or who may be willing and ready to go to work. (2) It is essential that the narrow interpretation given by the courts to the word 'intimidation' should be enlarged so as to include threats of loss or damage other than by violence to persons or property.

If this were done, it would go far to prevent the more serious abuse of picketing at a worker's home. Neither Section 7 of the Conspiracy and Protection of Property Act 1875, nor Section 2 (1) of the Trade Disputes and Trade Unions Act 1906 should be repealed. The draft Trade Disputes and Trade Unions Bill was approved by the Cabinet on 15 December 1926.[100]

The Trade Disputes and Trade Unions Act received the Royal Assent in July 1927. Section 3 of the Act concerned the prevention of intimidation. It forbade mass picketing, it widened the meaning of the term intimidation to signify 'to cause in the mind of a person

[98] Ibid. In February 1946, during the debate on the repeal of the 1927 Act, Anderson recapitulated his views at length (*Parl. Deb.*, 5th ser., 419, 389 ff. (13 Feb. 1946)).

[99] CAB 24/181, CP 365, 27 Oct. 1926; CAB 24/182, CP 406, 3 Dec. 1926; CAB 23/53 62 (26), 8 Dec. 1926.

[100] CAB 24/182, CP 406, 3 Dec. 1926; CAB 23/53 62 (26), 8 Dec. 1926.

a reasonable apprehension of injury to him or to any member of his family or to any of his dependants or of violence or damage to any person or property' and it forbade house-to-house picketing which amounted to watching or besetting. The defeat of the unions (and their resultant numerical decline) seemed to have reaped its harvest.

The aftermath of the strike, and particularly the passage of this Act, encouraged a widespread belief in the labour movement that peaceful picketing henceforth would be impossible. It 'made even a crime for which you could be arrested to talk to a blackleg'. Further it was claimed that 'the police could arrest you for "silent contempt" i.e. looking at a blackleg. You had to be mobile pickets, you were only allowed one stationary picket.'[101] Unions in South Wales put up posters attacking the 1927 Act and showing trade unionists locked up behind bars. The local police tore them down. Even one chief constable, A. K. Mayall of Oldham, uttered a note of cautious criticism. He felt 'the General Strike and its consequences to be responsible in some measure for some political feeling which affects the Police. Much legislation was passed as a result which is considered in some quarters to be repressive, and the opinion has grown that the Police are controlled by political elements.'[102] In working-class districts it was credibly believed that 'the police have an absolute right of arrest and search'. 'From that time forth . . . there was a different attitude towards the police. This was the police interfering now with trade union and working class conditions and it was incidents of this description in my opinion, which added even in the village to the idea that the bobby was part of the establishment.' Before this the policeman was described as being 'part of the community' except in times of industrial unrest.[103]

Indeed, although the Act of 1927 conferred no new statutory powers on the police, it did widen the meaning of intimidatory behaviour and created new offences of mass picketing and house-to-house picketing. There can be no doubt that its existence encouraged the police to more vigorous action. During the 1930s

[101] Evidence of Dick Beamish (DB 22) (Transcripts in South Wales Miners' Library, Swansea).

[102] *Report of the Royal Commission on Police Powers and Procedure*, iii. *Minutes of Evidence*, Part II, evidence of A. K. Mayall, p. 577.

[103] Evidence of Len Jeffries (LJ 9) (Transcripts in South Wales Miners' Library, Swansea).

there were frequent demands that the Act of 1927 be repealed. It became a foremost priority for the Labour Party that the work of 1927 be undone, leading to the eventual repeal by the Attlee government in 1946, moved by Ernest Bevin, now Foreign Secretary. Only then did the unions' sense of grievance find redress, twenty years on.

After 1926, trade-union funds ran down, and labour unrest markedly subsided. But widespread industrial troubles continued, nevertheless. The most prolonged disputes in the later 1920s and 1930's again occurred in the mining industry, and especially in South Wales, with Nottinghamshire also a difficult area. The miners now confronted the problem of non-unionism. With the introduction of modern machinery in the mining industry after 1918, there was an increase in the new class of skilled workers who frequently formed separate craftsmen's unions. They made considerable inroads in the membership of the MFGB, especially in South Wales, and the problem of multi-unionism or non-unionism became a key issue. Much friction was caused, and there were often violent clashes between union and non-union men. There was also the phenomenon of the breakaway Spencer Union, powerful in the Midlands and North and South Wales, a virtual company union which sought to break up the federated power of the MFGB.[104]

The police in South Wales particularly played a major part in protecting the non-union men. Again the disputes after 1927 as before proved that picketing could not be regulated by the law. There were many cases of mass picketing, with accompanying police violence, at such places as Nine Mile Point and Bedwas Collieries in Monmouthshire, and Taff Merthyr and Trelewis in Glamorgan. Lindsay was implacably resolved to give 'those who wish to work confidence in police protection'.[105] This often meant bringing in reinforcements from other areas and using the aggressive tactics for which the Glamorgans were legendary and notorious. As in the past, there were cases of Welsh coalowners calling for the drafting in of borrowed police, at their own expense.

In 1929 the county council members of the Monmouthshire Standing Joint Committee demanded an inquiry into the conduct

[104] Francis and Smith. *The Fed*, esp. pp. 308 ff.
[105] Lindsay to Home Office, 13 Mar. 1933 (HO 144/18482/659768/1).

of the police in what even *The Times* described as a vicious and sustained attack by police on unarmed pickets at Nine Mile Point Colliery.[106] A local Labour MP, Charles Edwards (Bedwellty) asked a question in the House, to which the Home Secretary replied (on the evidence of the chief constable) that 'the trouble . . . started with a determined attack by a large crowd on four miners who had been working at the colliery . . . 11 persons, including two constables, received injuries requiring medical attention . . .'.[107] The file on this incident is of much interest. Joynson-Hicks was told of the proposed inquiry by a sub-committee of the standing joint committee into police conduct at Nine Mile Point Colliery on 6 February, and also into two complaints about the behaviour of the force unconnected with this event. The chief constable had made it clear to the committee that 'any disciplinary punishment is a matter for him and that he will not impose any punishment on any member of the Force unless he is satisfied the men deserve it'.[108] The chief constable now telegraphed to Dixon at the Home Office for his view on the matter. Dixon was ambivalent about the role his department should play in the proceedings. He felt that,

> As regards the inquiry into the incidents at Nine Mile Point, the SJC are more within their right than in the other matters, for the Chief Constable was himself present and has taken full responsibility for what happened, though even here the inquiry will doubtless centre mainly round particular incidents of the charge and the action of particular members of the force who were concerned in it.

However, if the chief constable objected to the additional inquiry into the conduct of two officers, as the chief constable of Durham had done in a similar case, the Home Office would be prepared to support him. 'His alternative would be to attend the inquiry and decline to punish or censure his men unless he is satisfied they deserve it, and that he should, of course, have our support.'[109] The proposed inquiry by a sub-committee of the standing joint committee did not, however, take place as the county court judge who was asked to preside over the sub-committee declined to act. The chairman of the standing joint committee, Sir Henry Mather

[106] *The Times*, 7 Feb. 1929.
[107] *Parl. Deb.*, 5th ser., 224, 1948 (7 Feb. 1929).
[108] Minute by Dixon, 15 Feb. 1929 (HO 144/534204/22556/3).
[109] Ibid.

Jackson, now asked the Home Secretary to step in and institute an inquiry. Joynson-Hicks, very surprisingly, was in favour of such an inquiry: 'if a responsible body like the County Council makes definite charges and asks me to hold an inquiry, I think we must do so.' However, there was little support elsewhere in the Home Office: Dixon was firmly against such a course. The quarter session members, headed by the chairman of the standing joint committee, supported the police, while, in any case, the committee had no power to award any punishment.[110] In the event, no action over the proposed inquiry resulted. Nine men were now proceeded against for riot as a consequence of the Nine Mile Point troubles, and seven out of the nine received savage sentences at the assizes. Incidents such as this seemed to prove what one contemporary observer believed: 'that members of the Labour Party or watch committee had no power at all in time of crisis. . . . The real power lay with the police.'[111]

In April 1933 nearly 100 summonses were heard against sixty people, including two women, at Caerphilly Court, arising out of a dispute at Bedwas. The charges, all brought by the police, arose because 500 blacklegs from Glamorgan had been imported and given police protection. They related to besetting, stone-throwing, malicious damage, obstruction, and indecent language.[112] In June 24 defendants were sent to Monmouthshire Assizes accused of riot, but not one civilian witness could be found by the prosecution. It was, therefore, necessary to rely on police evidence alone. After a four-day trial seven men and four women were found guilty of riot and given heavy sentences.[113] The *New Leader* voiced the view on the left at this time: 'it is monstrous that they [the police] should possess the right to consign men and women to prison without corroborative evidence of any kind . . . the power which is placed in the hands of the ordinary constable is self evident.'[114]

However, in South Wales, many local justices were strongly sympathetic to the official SWMF, the beloved 'Fed'. This emerged in 1929, for example, when, after mass picketing in the Garw

[110] Home Office minutes of 18, 23 Feb. 1929 on the Nine Mile Point Colliery Dispute (ibid. 5), *Sunday Worker*, 23 June 1929.

[111] Evidence of Dick Beamish.

[112] *The Times*, 5 Apr. 1933.

[113] Francis, *Miners against Fascism*, p. 55.

[114] *New Leader*, 30 Sept. 1927.

valley, of men from the South Wales Industrial Union (the name of the new Spencer-type body), many charges were brought by the police for unlawful behaviour. These charges were approved by Chief Constable Lindsay and also by the police solicitor, who advised that, in his view, the evidence disclosed serious cases of intimidation, unlawful assembly, and watching and besetting. Accordingly summonses were issued by the police while the strike was still in progress. When the strike ended, however, the local justices—all Labour representatives—declined to proceed with the police charges. Despite an official protest by the chief constable to the Director of Public Prosecutions, no action was taken.[115]

At Bedlinog and Trelewis in 1934, where the new union had been formidably established, more acts of violence were committed against new unionists, and police court proceedings followed. Those charged with riot and unlawful assembly were committed for trial at the county assizes and in November 1934 found guilty by the jury of unlawful assembly. However, without proceeding to act on the verdict of the jury, the judge took the unusual course of instructing the prosecution to annul the verdict so as to enable the defendants to give him an undertaking to be of good behaviour.[116]

These cases show the power both of the judiciary and magistrates: often they were sympathetic to the cause of the 'Fed'. More remarkable was the sympathy sometimes shown by the local police. In 1935, a turbulent year in the South Wales coalfield, the non-union men's spokesmen complained that the police at Bedlinog and Trelewis in Glamorgan were not giving their members adequate protection. The deputy chief constable himself, Colonel F. W. Smith, felt it was undesirable to interfere between the two unions.[117] But Lindsay, the chief constable, characteristically declared that the only question to be considered by the police was one of the maintenance of public order and protecting the constitutional rights of the individual citizen. Smith ignored this warning, so Lindsay took over from his more moderate colleague, and instituted a repressive regime. On 16 October 1935, for example, 150 of the Glamorgans, in a military-style operation, charged a crowd who had refused to disperse outside the Taff Merthyr Colliery at Trelewis. The chief constable had anticipated a 'stay-in' after the morning shift. Since many relatives of the men

[115] May, *Recollections*, pp. 267–70.
[116] Ibid., pp. 279–80.
[117] Ibid., p. 287.

employed at the pit would be involved, there would clearly be a very emotional climate. The police who made the attack were 'well-trained and drilled in light infantry manoeuvring tactics'. It was recorded that 'the whole body with drawn staves went forward full tilt into the mob, left, right and centre, bearing down upon it at close quarters . . .'.[118] Lindsay himself claimed that 'it was the vigorous action of the police, strictly limited to the necessities of the situation, with drawn truncheons, that prevented more serious developments'.[119] This attack by the police triggered off disturbances at Cwmparc, Treorchy, Treherbert, Ogmore Vale, and Blaengarw. A coping-stone was dropped on a ghost train taking non-Federation miners to Nine Mile Point Colliery, and another on the railway track at Trelewis. Lindsay then borrowed additional police from Liverpool, Birmingham, Bristol, and Gloucestershire to give protection, as he saw it. He commented afterwards, 'it was gratifying to observe the influence of the increased police strength on the unruly elements'.[120]

Fifty-seven summonses (fifty-four men and three women) were issued for incidents arising out of the Trelewis episode in October 1935, and charges were served for unlawful assembly and riot. Many in the communities involved believed that the police had deliberately picked out those whom they wished to prosecute. Men who were actually responsible for rolling boulders and toppling coping-stones on to the railway track were not charged at all. Relations between the police and local population were not improved when the judge in the case discounted the alibis provided by the defence, one of which was from the minister of the Pentecostal church at Bedwas. The past record of the accused, including their known political views, were taken into consideration when sentence was passed. Edgar Evans was alleged by the police inspector to have been 'a leader of long standing disruption throughout the district'. Judge Humphreys's sentences were said to have been coloured by the fact that several of the accused had been summonsed for unlawful assembly back in 1934, but had not been prosecuted at that time. Humphreys accused all the defendants and their witnesses of perjury. He praised unreservedly

[118] Ibid., p. 291.

[119] Chief Constable Lindsay's report to Glamorgan Standing Joint Committee, n.d. Dec. 1935 (loc. cit).

[120] Ibid.

the courage of the local police upon whose evidence of identification the prosecution case rested.[121]

This was the biggest mass trial of industrial workers ever held in Britain and took place at the Glamorgan Assizes in Cardiff in March 1936. All those charged were found guilty, fifty-five being convicted of serious riot. Severe sentences were consequently passed, ranging from three to fifteen months' hard labour, which led to widespread indignation. The Glamorgan police were popularly dubbed 'the gloved hand of fascism'. In fact, sentences for riot were more common in South Wales at this period than they had been anywhere in Britain since the eighteenth century. These latest sentences led to a question in the Commons, by Morgan Jones, Labour member for Caerphilly, after which a lengthy and often angry debate took place. The Home Secretary, Sir John Simon, as could have been anticipated, confined himself to endorsing the actions of the police and the verdict of the judge.[122]

A new phase was introduced by the passage of the Public Order Act of 1936. The background and wider significance of this measure will be considered at length in the following chapter. However, it also bore directly upon the theme of the present discussion, since the police themselves, as has been noted, had long been pressing the Home Office for increased statutory powers to deal with picketing and related disorder. Section 5 of the Public Order Act 1936 laid down that any person who in any public place or at any public meeting used threatening, abusive, or insulting words or behaviour with intent to provoke a breach of the peace, or whereby a breach of the peace was likely to result, should be guilty of an offence. A crime of threatening, abusive, or insulting words or behaviour had existed for many years before 1936 as a result of various local enactments, including the Metropolitan Police Act 1839 and the Liverpool Improvement Act 1842. It had been invoked with great regularity by the police over the years, especially over picketing. The effect of Section 5 of the 1936 Act was to extend the operation of threatening, abusive, or insulting words to cover the whole country; to widen the scope of the crime to cover meetings held in a public place or in private premises; and to impose a much more severe penalty.

[121] *Parl. Deb.*, 5th ser., 310, 2537–43 (6 Apr. 1936).
[122] Ibid., cols. 2537–43 and Francis, *Miners against Fascism*, pp. 78–9.

In addition, as will be emphasized in a different context in the following chapter, Section 3 of the 1936 Act gave a chief of police power, where he had reasonable grounds to believe that a public procession might occasion serious disorder, to impose upon those organizing or taking part in the procession such conditions as seemed to him necessary for the preservation of public order. Powers such as these had been exercised under the 1921 and 1926 Emergency Regulations, and unofficially when dealing with industrial disturbances on many occasions since. The Act of 1936, therefore, apart from its effect on marches by the unemployed, to be discussed in Chapter 8, powerfully affected the way the police handled the problem of picketing. The executive now had a far more formidable battery of legal powers to cope with workers who were on strike. The effect of the Public Order Act was not so much to extend police powers, as to legitimize what was already occurring in practice. But it provided a basis for the police to take renewed firm action in future industrial disputes.

During the 1937 Harworth Colliery dispute in Nottinghamshire, the heartland of Spencer unionism, even before the local police had had time to familiarize themselves with the Public Order Act, the chief constable told strike leaders of 'the provisions of Section 5 . . . [and] that the police would make use of the Section if hostile demonstrations were made by the strikers against the men who were working'.[123] Charges were indeed now brought under Section 5 of the Public Order Act. In addition, by 29 April thirty-four people in Nottinghamshire had been charged with intimidation under Section 7 of the Conspiracy and Protection of Property Act 1875. Proceedings were also being taken against many other persons for assault and wilful damage.[124] Many complaints followed about the brutality and violence shown by the police in this dispute.

The newly formed NCCL, led by Ronald Kidd, conducted its own inquiry, based on interviews with local people at Harworth, into police conduct and the associated violence. It was reported that the police had shown partiality between pickets and men who were still working. Many police imported into Nottinghamshire had

[123] Sir J. Simon to F. W. Bellenger, MP, 9 May 1937 (HO 144/20729/697140/10).

[124] *The Harworth Colliery Strike. A Report to the Executive Committee of the National Council for Civil Liberties by the Secretary of the Council* (1937); *Parl. Deb.*, 5th ser., 323, 518–19 (29 Apr. 1937).

actively discouraged peaceful picketing. 'If a picket has approached a non-union worker, the latter has frequently made a complaint to the police, or alternatively, the police have themselves arrested the picket and have alleged insulting language or intimidation.'[125] Meanwhile, the local bench was composed of persons of the same social background as the coalowners, and relied heavily on police evidence. It was notorious that the chairman of the standing joint committee in Nottinghamshire was himself the owner of the Harworth Colliery, creator of the local Spencer Union, and an intimate associate of the chief constable. The entire situation at Harworth was likened to the situation in a mining town in West Virginia.[126] The chief constable of Nottinghamshire himself flatly refused to give evidence to the NCCL inquiry, which was hardly surprising.

The Home Office file on this affair shows that the chief constable's report was the basis for the department's views. Simon, the Home Secretary, concluded that 'Mr. Kidd has allowed his sympathy with the strikers and their cause to cloud his vision.'[127] A Home Office minute stated:

> Mr. Kidd's report does not appear to me to make any serious charges against the police that require investigation. Certain rather sweeping general allegations are made i.e. that the police have exceeded their authority in ordering law abiding people from the streets, that they have adopted a threatening attitude. . . . [they] do not indicate any *serious* and consistent misconduct on the part of police officers, merely an occasional excess of zeal or spasm of ill-temper which is understandable after a strike that has been in progress since November. . . . It is of course natural that the strikers should consider any protection offered by the police to the colliery owners and men still working as evidence of partiality.[128]

After further scenes of violence at the colliery in April 1937, the Home Office noted that Simon might be urged to hold an official inquiry into police conduct during the Harworth strike. In anticipation of this request, precedents were now sought by the Home Office officials for the holding of such an inquiry. A Home Office memorandum followed, noting that, 'where allegations are made

125 *The Harworth Colliery Strike Report.*

126 *Parl. Deb.*, 5th ser., 323, 1179 ff. (5 May 1937).

127 Minute by Home Secretary on Harworth Colliery Dispute, 28 Apr. 1937 (HO 144/20729/697140/10).

128 Home Office minute, 3 Apr. 1937 (ibid., 8).

against the conduct of the police, the matter is one for the disciplinary authority of the Watch Committee in a Borough and the chief constable in a County'.[129] Various Home Secretaries through the years had been pressed to hold inquiries into the conduct of one or other of the provincial forces, but this had consistently been refused. There had not been any case of the Home Office holding an inquiry into the conduct of the provincial police since 1886.[130] Later in 1937 Sir Samuel Hoare, the new Home Secretary, refused an official inquiry, yet again, even though it was said that eighty to a hundred witnesses were prepared to give evidence on behalf of thirty-five defendants brought to trial.[131] Eventually, very severe sentences were passed on twelve of them for riot. Lawyers noted that the political opinions of these twelve were given some emphasis. But so intense was the local outcry that Hoare was ultimately compelled to grant remission at least to some degree.[132] Otherwise public protest against police methods met with the usual negative response in Whitehall.

The conclusion of this analysis must be that, from the outset, the law on picketing was notable for its non-observance and non-enforcement. Picketing was seen by the police essentially as a problem of public order, and treated as such. With the onset of major industrial disputes from 1910 onwards, the Home Office, as has been seen, encouraged the police to take a more vigorous stance towards picketing. This was particularly evident after 1918, when the department was able to co-ordinate the action of the different police forces, and when it also began to popularize the notion of the independence of the constabulary and its accountability to the law alone. It is certainly the case that the major disputes of the post-war period did see the police respond with far more vigorous action towards mass picketing. This policy was facilitated by the passage of the Emergency Regulations, and the increased powers they gave to the police, as seen during events in 1921 and again in 1926. Inquiries into police conduct and methods proved singularly difficult to obtain. Thereafter, the police were

[129] Home Office minute, n.d. Apr. 1937 (ibid., 14).
[130] Ibid.
[131] *The Harworth Colliery Strike Report.*
[132] Kidd, *British Liberty*, p. 175; D. Williams, *Keeping the Peace*, p. 242.

reluctant indeed to relinquish the powers given them under these Emergency Regulations.

For long the police, and others, had pressed for greater statutory powers to deal with picketing and associated intimidation. They were eventually presented with the Trade Disputes and Trade Unions Act of 1927. However, while this measure did widen the meaning of intimidatory action relating to picketing, it gave the police no greater statutory authority. As a result, the police continued to use *ad hoc* methods and the established public order provisions of the ordinary law, as they had done in the past. Where they did prosecute under the Conspiracy and Protection of Property Act 1875, they achieved mixed results. The effect of the later Public Order Act 1936 was basically to give statutory backing to the *ad hoc* public order methods which the police already used to deal with picketing and industrial disorder. Its other consequence was to make the long-established crime of abusive and insulting words and behaviour general for the whole country.

Picketing was, and is, a phenomenon for which it is inherently difficult to define precisely the rights and wrongs required as a basis for legislation. Yet the government, even after introducing measures aimed at curbing working-class protest, still had not succeeded in eliminating intimidation and mass picketing, and the disorder associated with them. As this chapter has shown, the violence often accompanying picketing and other forms of pressure during industrial troubles continued at regular intervals, especially in the coal-mining industry, between the First World War and the 1930s. The police acquired new powers through regulations and the statutory backing for measures they had long been adopting in handling picket lines. Parallel to this process was a failure to make the police accountable for their actions, locally or nationally. It was this ground swell of growing police initiative and irresponsibility that was to reassure the orthodox, but to alarm civil libertarians and organized labour alike, in the years to come.

8

The Police and the Unemployed Marches, 1918–1939

ANOTHER major aspect of the police response to labour troubles was that of the control of public order during meetings and processions, particularly those of the unemployed. Its consequences were far-reaching and sometimes violent. It first arose with particular acuteness as a result of the emergence of mass unemployment from mid-1920 onwards. Hunger marches and other protests by working-class people, using direct action to try to enforce their demands, posed new problems for the provincial and Metropolitan police authorities, particularly the latter. National protest marches tended to make for London, and the capital, therefore, had a lengthy history of association with meetings and processions. Demonstrations by unemployed people, including the so-called 'hunger marchers', took place throughout the 1920s and 1930s, reaching a climax of bitterness with the police response to the hunger march held in the autumn of 1932.

These alarming events generated vigorous debate within the Cabinet, the Home Office and other government departments, and a number of police authorities, as to the most effective techniques of controlling marches and demonstrations. By 1934 the Cabinet was turning to consider the alternative policy of statutory prevention rather than operational control of working-class demonstrations. The current threat posed by Fascist marches in the East End of London, and also in the provinces, with their uniforms, military style, and atmosphere of racial incitement added a new dimension to the debate. The outcome was the Public Order Act of 1936 which gave the police statutory powers to deal with marches and demonstrations. The Public Order Act has commonly been seen in relation to the threat from British Fascism. In fact, as will be shown in this chapter, it had more profound implications for labour and its right to meet, march, and protest.

As soon as the war ended the problem of unemployment was

intensified because of the large number of ex-servicemen seeking work. It was gravely exacerbated by the collapse in the economy through loss of international markets from June 1920 onwards. Unemployment mounted alarmingly and Lloyd George's 'dole' scheme was extended in 1920 by the Unemployment Insurance Act, intended to cover all the working population. The unemployment problem grew worse. Many of the unemployed ceased to be passive, and became organized, mounting a challenge to the authorities. The men who helped bring about this change were frequently associated with the newly formed Communist Party. Leaders like Tom Dingley, a discharged shop steward in the Amalgamated Engineering Union (AEU), and Wal Hannington, an unemployed engineer, organized groups of the unemployed and urged them to unite after the war.

The unemployed movement was most active in the early 1920s, when there were many ex-servicemen seeking work, and then during the years when unemployment was at its height between 1926 and 1936. The year 1922 saw the first national hunger march; five more were held between 1929 and 1936. Each of these marches culminated in a huge demonstration in Hyde Park, followed by a week at least of activity in London involving further demonstrations. In addition to these nationally organized episodes, many other marches by unemployed people took place throughout the country. Glasgow, Merseyside, and Manchester, and other provincial towns and cities, as well as London, were scenes of vigorous confrontations between the police and the unemployed. The activities of the hunger marchers are familiar from the writings of Wal Hannington himself and the works of several historians.[1] The response of the forces of law and order, by contrast, is not so well known.

The legal basis of public meetings and processions was long established. Although there was no express statutory right to hold such meetings on public highways, it was recognized by the common law that they were not illegal if their object was lawful and the conduct of those taking part orderly. The existing provisions of the criminal law, dealing with meetings and processions,

[1] For example, W. Hannington, *Why Do They March?* (1936), and id., *Never on our Knees* (1967); P. Kingsford, *Hunger Marchers*; R. Hayburn, 'The Responses to Unemployment in the 1930s with Special Reference to South-east Lancashire Pt I. The Economic and Social Background' (University of Hull, Ph.D., 1970).

applied only where obstruction was caused, or was possible, or where a breach of the peace might reasonably be anticipated. The Home Office and government Law Officers had often considered the difficulties caused by public meetings and processions especially in London. But successive governments had always opposed legislation designed to interfere with the right of holding meetings and processions, simply because in particular circumstances a breach of the peace might result.[2] Even during the war, Herbert Samuel, the Liberal Home Secretary, when speaking about the wartime regulations which restricted public meetings, stated:

> It is a very good thing that public opinion should be sensitive whenever there is any interference with the right of public meetings, even in time of war, for the free expression of opinion is a matter of the greatest importance, and the House of Commons is well advised to watch any measures taken by the Ministry of the day which in any way threaten or impair the right of public meeting.[3]

However, although meetings and processions were not prohibited or circumscribed by law, the police and local authorities exercised widespread discretion in this area. Throughout the nineteenth century there had never been any doubt that the police authorities could issue instructions as to how processions should be policed. In fact, there was widespread discretion exercised by police authorities, especially by the Home Secretary in the special case of London, as to whether processions were to be allowed or prohibited, and, if allowed, as to the route they should take. Twice in the 1880s a commissioner of the Metropolitan Police was dismissed for 'disregarding the statutory provisions which require him to take his instructions from the Home Secretary' in this respect. In the provinces, however, the handling of the problem showed immense local variety. There is no doubt that many instances arose of the police breaking up meetings and processions. As Dingle Foot, then a National Liberal member, was later to point out in 1936, 'the police can practically always prevent a meeting on a public highway if they chose to do so. They can always say, generally with truth, that the meeting does constitute

[2] *Parl. Deb.*, 3rd ser., 330, 1172 (14 Nov. 1888); Law Officers' opinions as to the prohibition and regulation of meetings and processions, 1867–1905 (HO 45/10332/136764).

[3] *Parl. Deb.*, 5th ser., 86, 299 (12 Oct. 1916).

an obstruction . . . and in nearly every case they will be upheld.'[4] But, at least down to 1914, their actions were regarded as a purely local responsibility and concern. What sharply differentiated the situation after the First World War—or, more precisely, after 1922 when the marches and protests of the unemployed came to be more nationally organized—was that the handling of unemployed meetings and marches by the police, as in the case of picketing and related labour disorder, acquired a national dimension. Here again was an area in which a nation-wide challenge appeared to demand a national response. Thus in this context also a new coherence, force, and centralized direction can be detected in the executive activities of the police in dealing with labour troubles. The official reaction to the unemployed marches and demonstrations merged with a wider fear of industrial unrest or revolution after 1918.

As explained above, the police were encouraged by the government to adopt a much more vigorous stance towards labour after the war. A 'post-war mood' was said to have affected them. One aspect of the period was that fear of police militarism was widespread, particularly in the metropolis where all the national hunger marches ended and where many meetings and marches took place. Here the appointment as Commissioner in September 1918 of General Macready seemed to herald a new form of military discipline. His Assistant Commissioner was Brigadier-General Horwood, who had been one of Macready's staff officers during the troubles in South Wales in 1910–11. Later another of Macready's military aides at Tonypandy, Major-General Wyndham Childs, became Assistant Commissioner, while he had as his closest advisers army officers with wide experience of civil disorder and its political ramifications. Macready also appointed Colonel P. R. Laurie to revamp the mounted branch of the Metropolitans and he was said to have been instrumental in raising the mounted branch to a position of second to none in the police forces of the world. It was said that Macready saw his task as 'to bring the discipline of the Metropolitan Police up to the standard of a Guards regiment'.[5] He was succeeded as Commissioner in 1920 by Horwood, who was to be followed by another former soldier, Viscount Byng, in 1928.

Whether these appointments led to the Metropolitan Police

[4] *Parl. Deb.*, 5th ser., 314, 1596 (10 July 1936).
[5] *Parl. Deb.*, 5th ser., 166, 1708 (12 July 1923).

becoming more militarized in character than they had been before the war aroused much anxious debate. Labour MPs condemned the appointment of Byng as Commissioner of the Metropolitan Police in 1928 because of his military background and outlook: 'We cannot dissociate the appointment of a military man from other appointments as chief constables and headships of police which for some time have been, apparently, the settled policy. We believe that there is a growing militarization of the police force.'[6] The Labour Party considered that such a move would be socially disastrous. Joynson-Hicks, however, warmly defended the appointment of Byng and it was claimed by 1931 that he had won the confidence at least of the Metropolitan Police. When he retired early in 1931 the Labour Cabinet and its Home Secretary J. R. Clynes agreed with John Anderson that yet another 'militarist' should follow Byng. This was Lord Trenchard, founder of the Royal Air Force. Trenchard was promised a free hand by MacDonald to revitalize the Metropolitan Police, and he proceeded to act with great vigour. Like Macready before him, he became Commissioner only with extreme reluctance: this helped him to build up his authority all the more powerfully. Trenchard, like his predecessors, came under attack from the left. George Lansbury later bitterly proclaimed that 'during the past 30 years the police have steadily come under the military mind and been turned from a purely civil force into a semi-military force'.[7] In fact, although the appointment of military officers to the higher posts in the Metropolitan Police was no novelty, the authority of both Macready and Trenchard was unusual. The tendency to run the force in the metropolis and elsewhere along military lines was all the more emphatic (and costly) because so many of the recruits were now drawn from the ranks of ex-soldiers. The report of the Desborough Committee in 1919 had pointedly drawn attention to 'the beneficial effects, both physical and mental, which can be derived from a short period of service in the Army'.[8] It is against this background that the police response to the hunger marchers in the 1920s and 1930s must be viewed.

The first major tests for the police in their handling of demonstrations by the unemployed came in London and in the industrial

[6] Ibid., 219, 2264 (11 July 1928).

[7] Ibid., 278, 958 (23 May 1933).

[8] PP 1920 [Cmd. 574], xxii. 545.

north-west in 1920 and 1921. On 18 October 1920 unemployed ex-servicemen marched from various London boroughs, converging on Downing Street, to support fifteen Labour mayors who were seeking government help to relieve the toll of unemployed. Weeks of careful preparation preceded the march. The secretary of the organizing committee, the town clerk of Deptford, had informed the Commissioner of the Metropolitan Police of the assembly point and the time each contingent would set off. The marchers were not to be allowed to enter Trafalgar Square, but were to accompany the mayors as far as the Embankment, where they were to wait until the mayors returned from their interview at 10 Downing Street. The final arrangements were settled between the mayors of Fulham and Shoreditch, the London County Council, and the Commissioner.[9]

The Commissioner of the Metropolitan Police made detailed plans for the policing of the biggest demonstration of the unemployed so far. The miners were due to start a national strike the same day, so there was widespread alarm in government circles. The Coldstream Guards were moved from Aldershot to London and 1,300 foot police and 100 mounted police were ordered out for 18 October to control the procession in Whitehall and along the route.[10]

The marchers, said to number 20,000, reached Victoria Embankment safely and the mayors were ushered into 10 Downing Street, while the columns waited on the Embankment. Much resentment was caused when a dozen fire engines were driven through the waiting crowd and when the police dispersed an allegedly hostile demonstration outside New Scotland Yard. Contrary to the agreed arrangement, the columns of the unemployed then moved off the Embankment towards Whitehall, and a disturbance broke out between police and marchers at the Whitehall end of Downing Street. Both police and marchers' leaders denied that they had given the order for the crowd to move from their position on the Embankment, but what is certain is that a mêlée ensued. Wal Hannington, who led the column of marchers, gives a graphic, though inevitably partisan, description of the events of that day:

[9] Memo. on preparations for demonstration of ex-servicemen, 9–17 Oct. 1920 (MEPO 2/1958).

[10] Kingsford, *Hunger Marchers*, pp. 13–14.

In front of me, across the Whitehall end of Downing Street, stood a strong cordon of police and at no time during the half-hour that we stood there was any attempt made by the demonstrators to break through that cordon. But suddenly some idiot in high police authority must have issued an order to clear Whitehall. Without warning, mounted and foot police drew their batons and began charging into the crowd, pushing and striking the demonstrators indiscriminately on heads, shoulders and backs. It was a merciless and unprovoked attack. The density of the crowd made it impossible for those nearest the police to escape. . . . Instead of the police allowing the demonstrators to get away from the centre of the conflict they now had them surrounded and were using their truncheons to hold them in. So it then developed into a series of fierce battles, in and around Whitehall, leaving dozens of men lying on the roadway . . . battered and bleeding from the brutal police assaults.[11]

The superintendent in charge of the mounted police, however, reported that the order to move from the Embankment had not been given by the police; the police baton charge was in response to crowd violence. Many protests were then made about police action here. The *Daily Herald* commented that 'the manner in which the police in a mad frenzy were ordered to charge up and down Whitehall running down and clubbing men, women and children is only on a par with the sort of outrage committed by the Black and Tans in Ireland'.[12] The Home Secretary, Edward Shortt, was asked to hold an inquiry as to the causes of disorder, but he refused. Shortt claimed he was 'satisfied that the police were justified in drawing their batons and no unnecessary force was used'. A Home Office spokesman in the House of Commons, Sir John Baird, condoned the charge made by the mounted police without warning, and claimed that this activity was never resorted to without due and sufficient grounds.[13]

In the autumn of 1921 police batoned more unemployed workers in a demonstration which took place in Liverpool on 12 October. On this occasion a number of the unemployed tried to take possession of the Walker Art Gallery after a meeting on St George's Hall plateau. About 150 of the crowd got inside the gallery when a cordon of police was drawn across the entrance. The unemployed then refused to leave the building until the

[11] Hannington, *Never on our Knees*, p. 81.

[12] *Daily Herald*, 19 Oct. 1920.

[13] Home Office to Mayor of Fulham, 8 Nov. 1920 (HO 144/1692/410769/4); *Parl. Deb.*, 5th ser., 134, 187–9 (2 Nov. 1920).

authorities allowed them to use St George's Hall for meetings. When the police, who were now in strong force inside the building, were ordered to remove them, a bloody fight ensued. The police used their batons freely and the unemployed were driven into a room and then removed, one by one, and taken to Bridewell in prison vans, many of them with cut faces and heads. Outside the Walker Art Gallery the crowd was dispersed by mounted police and foot constables, and several baton charges were made. One hundred and fifty people were arrested and taken to court. Most unusually, the Recorder who tried the cases condemned police behaviour in this affair. Although he had sat for twelve years in the court, he had always done his best to support the police. However, in this instance, 'He was . . . bound to say that there were features in the cases he had just been trying which to his mind were profoundly disquieting.' He could not conceive of any possible justification for the injuries received by several of the prisoners. He bluntly declared that 'unnecessary violence was used to these men'.[14]

This incident at Liverpool is particularly well documented since many requests were made to the Home Office for an inquiry into police conduct here. Shortt, however, swayed by the Recorder's comments, urged General Atcherley, the inspector of constabulary, to 'visit Liverpool at once and examine the persons concerned in the affair, both the police and those who were injured in the scuffle and . . . report to the Secretary of State fully on the question whether the police were justified in what they did or whether unnecessary violence was used'. The members of the watch committee were in favour of an inquiry if it were of a judicial nature but would not hold one themselves.[15] The chief constable, Caldwell, however, urged the Home Secretary that 'any inquiry . . . would seriously weaken the authority of the police at a time when it needs every possible support'. Many of the police in Liverpool had been dismissed after the police strike in 1919, so a number of the men were new and inexperienced. Caldwell also suspected ideological factors. He felt that the unemployment trouble was 'being used by a gang of extreme Communists (each of them known to Sir Basil Thomson) for the purpose of a propa-

[14] *Daily Herald*, 13 Sept. 1921; *Morning Post*, 3 Oct. 1921.

[15] Minute by Troup, 3 Oct. 1921; minute by Atcherley, 8 Oct. 1921 (HO 45/11032/423878/9).

ganda of violence'.[16] His report to the watch committee denied that the police had rough-handled the demonstrators; these processions of the unemployed were unlawful assemblies, he argued, and he would have been 'fully justified in breaking up these processions by force'. He had since told 'the leaders that no more processions of a similar nature would be allowed'.[17] The inquiry that was demanded did not, in fact, take place. An inquiry such as that requested by the watch committee could only be undertaken as a result of a special act, or by virtue of a resolution of both Houses of Parliament under the Tribunals of Inquiry (Evidence) Act 1921. Troup felt that it did not seem 'that the matter is of sufficient importance to have it debated in both Houses'.[18] When it was raised by Rhys Davies (Labour) in parliament, Shortt refused to sanction an inquiry.[19]

Much resentment had been caused amongst the unemployed by the treatment they experienced in the 'battle of Whitehall' and the formation of a national organization was discussed. In April 1921, therefore, the National Unemployed Workers' Committee Movement (NUWCM) (which became the NUWM in 1929) was set up to campaign for the provision of work for the unemployed by the state, with the alternative of 'full maintenance'. Its leaders were largely skilled engineers; it was intimately connected with the Communist Party. At no time during the inter-war years did it receive official support either from the Labour Party or the TUC although, after the imposition of the 'means test' and the introduction of the new Unemployment Bill in 1934, the movement did receive some unofficial backing from a wider section of trade unionists and Labour MPs in South Wales and other industrial areas.[20]

In the autumn of 1922 the first national hunger march to London took place. The marchers, demanding work or full maintenance at trade union rates, were widely surveilled by the police *en route* for the capital. Although the march ended in demonstrations in Hyde Park on 17 November, and Trafalgar Square the

[16] Chief constable of Liverpool to Home Office, 6 Oct. 1921 (ibid. 11).

[17] Chief constable's report to Liverpool Watch Committee, 11 Oct. 1921 (ibid., 15).

[18] Minute by Troup, 14 Oct. 1921 (ibid. 15).

[19] *Parl. Deb.*, 5th ser., 147, 1935–6 (3 Nov. 1921).

[20] Hannington, *Why Do They March* and *Never on our Knees*.

following Sunday, there was no disorder.[21] However, the marchers were determined to see the Prime Minister, Bonar Law. They planned to send a deputation to Downing Street the day before the opening of Parliament on 23 November, even though they had been told that the Prime Minister was unable to see them, and that they would be received instead by the Ministers of Health and Labour.[22]

These events alarmed the Cabinet. In September 1921 one of Sir Basil Thomson's Special Branch reports claimed that

> The organisation of the unemployed by Communists acting under Russian inspiration is still developing. . . . there is little doubt that the National Administrative Council of the Unemployed is a section of the International Union of Unemployed. . . . this Union takes its orders from Soviet Russia and its object is to prepare the unemployed for the World Revolution. It is clear that the method pursued at present aims at the creation of a state financial chaos which it is thought may facilitate a revolution.[23]

Thus forewarned, at the request of a conference of ministers on 20 November, it had been arranged for publicity to be given to 'the Communist character and record of the leaders of the unemployed marchers'. It was also decided that it would be 'inadvisable' to prosecute those of the speakers at the Trafalgar Square meeting who had used seditious language, since this would unite Labour MPs in the Commons against the government, and give a national advertisement to the Communists.[24] On 22 November all London daily newspapers apart from the *Daily Herald* had published a list of the leading members of the march, with the police record and past activities of each one. To discredit them further, the Special Branch records of the leaders' personal history were obtained by the Prime Minister's office, and issued to the newspapers, many of whom published them verbatim alongside pronouncements about a Communist plot inspired by Moscow.[25]

Still these government actions did not deter the marchers, said to number 50,000. When they reached Waterloo Bridge they came

[21] Kingsford, *Hunger Marchers*, pp. 33–44; Home Office minutes on unemployed marchers, Nov. 1922 and Feb. 1923 (HO 45/11275/438775/4–27).

[22] CAB 23/39; Conference of Ministers, 20 Nov. 1922.

[23] CAB 24/128, CP 3309, report on revolutionary organisations in the United Kingdom, no. 123, 15 Sep. 1921.

[24] CAB 23/39, Conference of Ministers, 20 Nov. 1922.

[25] Kingsford, *Hunger Marchers*, pp. 52–3; *Daily Mail*, 22 Nov. 1922; *Pall Mall Gazette*, 20, 21 Nov. 1922.

up against a police cordon of 'a formidable but otherwise quite unprovocative' kind. Conversation then took place between police officials and the marshals of the procession, and an agreement was reached that a deputation should go on to Montague House to see the Ministers of Health and Labour. But the leaders themselves now refused to put their case and declared that they would call up reinforcements until the government gave in.[26] On 7 January 1923—'Unemployed Sunday'—a huge gathering, including both employed and unemployed workers, demanded parliamentary action. Many more unemployed men arrived in London during the following weeks.

On 23 January the position of the marchers was discussed in Whitehall. The Ministry of Health took a tough line. It had earlier censured the police for their leniency towards the marchers *en route*:

> In the natural desire to get the marchers out of their area without a breach of the peace they have tended to exaggerate the duty and responsibility properly belonging to a board of guardians and must be regarded as at least sharing the responsibility for the success of the march . . .
>
> The crux of the position . . . is the attitude of the police and it will be useless to issue any such instructions (that a tougher policy regarding the maintenance of the unemployed be implemented by the Board of Guardians) unless the police are also instructed to assist the Guardians in every possible way . . . and to abstain from putting pressure on the Guardians with the object of securing peace in their own area at any price.[27]

Ministry of Health officials thus reiterated the point that these marches were not a matter for the poor-law authority but rather for the police. They were unlawful assemblies, problems of public order rather than social distress, and should be dealt with as such.[28]

An important new dimension of the problem now arose. Hitherto the handling of the hunger marchers had been a matter for the local police authorities and chiefs of police. Now, however, it became caught up in that increasingly centralized direction of law enforcement detectable in government policy towards industrial

[26] *The Times*, 23 Nov. 1922; *Daily Herald*, 27 Nov. 1922.
[27] Note by Francis at the Ministry of Health, 27 Nov. 1922 (MH 57/105).
[28] Kingsford, *Hunger Marchers*, p. 66.

disturbances during strikes and in the treatment of picketing from Edwardian years onwards. The approach towards the control of marching and police executive action changed accordingly. From this time onwards, before every national hunger march chiefs of police throughout the land were circulated and urged to take all necessary steps to prevent disorder or breaches of the peace: marches should be accompanied by a sufficient force of police or else arrangement should be made to have police available, police chiefs should also communicate with the Home Office and with police officers and general inspectors of the Ministry of Health on the route ahead about the numbers, movements, and, if possible, intentions of marchers. In general the Home Office was taking an increasingly stern attitude towards the organized unemployed, and encouraging the provincial police to deal severely with them.[29]

There was, in fact, no more national marching activity by the unemployed between February 1923 and January 1929. But there can be no doubt that these instructions to the police were widely interpreted. Provincial demonstrations were often dealt with severely; many marches were prevented outright. When they did occur, baton charges by foot and mounted police often resulted.[30] Members of the Special Branch frequently attended meetings of the unemployed, or of the Communist Party, to discover if any 'revolutionary sentiments or revolutionary projects' were being discussed, and informed the Home Secretary accordingly.[31]

As noted previously, the Regulations made under the Emergency Powers Act 1920 increased police powers during the major strikes in 1921 and 1926. During the general strike of 1926, and the prolonged coal lock-out which followed, the police made use of their powers under the Emergency Regulations relating to the preservation of public order, for example under Regulations 21 and 22. Regulation 21 related to acts likely to cause sedition, and Regulation 22 to public meetings and processions. The latter provision in particular was of supreme importance:

> Where there appears to be reason to apprehend that the assembly of any persons for the purpose of the holding of any meeting or procession will

[29] Home Office circulars in HO 158, e.g. HO 158/26 (516, 773/10), 26 Jan. 1929; HO 158/27 (516, 773/24), 2 Apr. 1930; HO 158/28 (653, 963/2), 29 Sept. 1932.

[30] Bowes, *Police*, p. 26; *The Times*, 9 Feb. 1926, and many press reports.

[31] *Parl. Deb.*, 5th ser., 185, 2779 (2 July 1925).

conduce to a breach of the peace and will thereby cause undue demands to be made upon the police, or will promote disaffection, it shall be lawful for a Secretary of State, or for any mayor, magistrate or chief officer of police who is duly authorised by a Secretary of State, . . . to make an order prohibiting the holding of the meeting or procession, and if a meeting or procession is held or attempted to be held in contravention of any such prohibition it shall be lawful to take such steps as may be necessary to disperse the meeting or procession or prevent the holding thereof.

In practice the Regulation was extremely controversial as it seemed to give the police the licence to behave as they liked towards meetings and processions. In June 1926 in Poplar, for example, when a meeting was held in the town hall and another was going on outside, a lorry load of police drove through the meeting at the rate of 10–12 m.p.h., and then proceeded to baton people. The Home Secretary was pressed to hold an inquiry into police conduct here, but refused.[32]

In another episode, thousands of miners in South Wales marched from Risca, Cross Keys and Machen, from Bedwas, Nine Mile Point, and other areas, towards Newport, to urge the local Guardians to be more generous by way of relief. They were refused admission to Newport. When they arrived at Bassaleg, where the valleys converge, they were met by the Newport police, who read out a notice prohibiting the demonstrators from going any further.[33] Overall, it must be concluded that the general effect of the Emergency Regulations was to give the police wide powers, which appeared to be as elastic as the police desired to make them, and which they were reluctant to relinquish once the strike ended.

After the petering out of the national miners' strike in November 1926, the NUWCM resumed its activity in 1927. New, lower scales of unemployment benefit came into operation along with the 'not genuinely seeking work' clause. In addition, the proposal to abolish Boards of Guardians because they were sometimes too responsive to local feeling and too generous in handing out relief (as in Poplar, Chester-le-Street, and Bedwellty), and to transfer their responsibilities to new committees of the county councils and borough councils, to be christened Public Assistance Committees, caused renewed activity. The NUWCM saw that this proposal

[32] *Parl. Deb.*, 5th ser., 197, 1521 (2 July 1926).
[33] *Daily Herald*, 22 May 1926.

would remove poor relief further away from the pressure of public opinion. It now launched a campaign of opposition; however, the reform took effect in the Local Government Act 1929. A second and third national hunger march now took place in 1929 and 1930. Unlike the first march of 1922, those of 1929 and 1930 occurred at a time when unemployment as an issue dominated the minds of both the government and the electorate; in 1922 it had still been seen as a temporary phenomenon which might disappear when pre-war industrial conditions returned. Sid Elias and Wal Hannington, both of whom had been prominent in 1922, were among the leaders of the march in January 1929. This march of 1,000 volunteers received much public sympathy *en route*. However, some disturbances occurred, perhaps because of the Home Office circular encouraging stern action by the police. In Birmingham, for example, when the marchers' contingent rejected the accommodation they were offered, the police, 'who had undoubtedly been held in readiness, rushed upon us and a serious conflict ensued. Several of our men were injured and we were finally overpowered by the force of the police and locked in the workhouse for the night, with the police also remaining.'[34] Although the official hostility of the TUC and the Labour Party frustrated the marchers' efforts to meet government ministers, there was no trouble with the police during their stay in London.

The third national hunger march in the spring of 1930 consisted of only 350 people: there was still hope of measures from MacDonald's Labour government to tackle unemployment, while the knowledge that they could not expect much welcome from Labour organizations along the way, and that the Poor Law regulations would be strictly enforced, deterred many from taking part. When the marchers reached London, the Prime Minister, MacDonald, refused to receive a deputation, so the marchers' council resolved to force its way into the House of Commons, while the main contingent distracted the police in Hyde Park. This contingent occupied the Ministry of Health for one hour. A struggle with the police resulted as it tried to rush into the House of Commons; it failed to do so, and by 8 May most of the marchers had left London. But clearly the hunger marchers had become a real problem for the authorities, local and metropolitan. Ministry of Health officials blamed the failure of the policy of repression on the police. One

[34] Quoted in Kingsford, *Hunger Marchers*, p. 101.

general inspector in the poor-law division of the Ministry of Health commented sourly towards the end of 1930: 'It is high time something was done by the Government to stop these people. They are just joy riding at the expense of the public. . . . Of course, the Police are only too kind to the marchers; their only idea is to avoid a breach of the peace and "Pass along please" to the next town.'[35]

Until 1931 it had been difficult to organize the unemployed—who numbered 1,912,000 by this time—into a cohesive body. But the situation changed when the 10 per cent cut in unemployment benefit made by the newly formed national government came into force in September 1931. A renewed zeal now entered NUWM methods of demonstration, since the notorious 'means test' gave rise to a great deal of opposition from all sections of organized labour. Protest meetings and marches were held throughout the country in the autumn of 1931 and the police often responded vigorously to them. For example, the NUWM (whose membership was now 37,000) sponsored a march by some South Wales unemployed miners to the TUC Congress at Bristol.[36] The chief constable, Charles Maby, through use of a large police cordon, stopped this march, led by Wal Hannington, from entering the city. The marchers rushed the barricade and were then attacked by police and stewards of the TUC.[37] On 7 October a crowd of unemployed, numbering more than 20,000, fought with the police in the centre of Manchester, where the chief constable had banned the proposed route. The marchers attempted to break through the police lines, violence erupted, fire hoses were turned on the crowd; mounted police charged. Six people were injured and thirty-eight arrested.

On 1 October there was a major disturbance in Salford, where demonstrators protesting against the reduction in unemployment benefit were confronted by a large body of police in the front of the town hall. There was a pitched battle in the square. The mounted police drew their batons and urged their horses forward into the throng to drive back the demonstrators. Many men were pushed

[35] Note by one of the general inspectors in the poor-law division of the Ministry of Health, 28 Nov. 1930 (MH 57/99).

[36] D. Williams, *Keeping the Peace*, p. 100; Hannington, *Never on our Knees*, pp. 234–6.

[37] Hannington, *Never on our Knees*, pp. 235–6.

over and trampled by the crowd; others clung to police horses until they were shaken off. The chief constable, Major Godfrey, said he was attempting, by use of police, to prevent the demonstrators from invading Bexley Square, at the far end of which a council meeting was being held.[38] In Cardiff in the second week of October, when a procession formed before a meeting of the unemployed, the police 'numbering about 60 endeavoured by tactful persuasion to disperse it'. However a number of the unemployed resisted and a baton charge followed. The most serious threat was in London. On the day parliament reassembled, the unemployed marched to Westminster and conflict between them and the police ensued in Whitehall. Eighteen men were arrested, several of whom were sentenced to a month in prison.[39]

These events, coinciding as they did with unrest in the police force because of proposed pay cuts and the Invergordon Mutiny in the navy, caused widespread alarm in government circles. They prefaced the appointment to the commissionership of the Metropolitan Police of Lord Trenchard. As we have seen, the government felt the need for a strong Commissioner. Trenchard, who required much persuasion to take on the job, thus replaced Lord Byng in November 1931. MacDonald had promised him a free hand to restructure the Metropolitan Police, even if it meant turning the force upside down,[40] and Trenchard set about a complete reorganization of the force to make it more efficient. In the area of police deployment and tactics he introduced the practice of plain-clothes policemen going out on a large scale, and the special constabulary in the metropolis, which numbered over 20,000, were now given much more practical training by attachment to divisions, and use on ordinary police duty. A mounted division of the special constabulary was also formed; indeed, Trenchard constantly extolled the virtues of mounted police in crowd control throughout his four-year commissionership. In his report for the year 1932, for example, he argued that, although the strength of the metropolitan mounted police had been reduced because of economic measures in 1931, the continued existence of the mounted branch was justified:

38 *The Times*, 2 Oct. 1931.
39 Ibid., 17 Oct. 1931; Kingsford, *Hunger Marchers*, p. 133.
40 Quoted in Ascoli, *Queen's Peace*, p. 227.

In the marshalling of processions and the control of crowds it is no exaggeration to say that a man on a horse is worth 3 or 4 on foot, whilst, in the case of disturbances, the assistance of this branch is almost indispensable. If the use of force is necessary they are able to employ it with discrimination and efficiency, but their value is even more noticeable in the quiet and systematic dispersal of disorderly crowds, frequently without resorting to any sort of force.[41]

In November 1931 Trenchard issued an order, under the Metropolitan Police Act of 1839, to prevent meetings by the unemployed being held in front of employment exchanges (which were the NUWM's most effective source of recruitment). The order stated that the Commissioner directed that in future no meeting should be held by the unemployed or other persons at any Labour Exchange in the Metropolitan area, whether likely to cause an obstruction or not, as such meetings had been found liable to lead to a breach of the peace.[42] This became known as the 'Trenchard ban'. It was now alleged by Wal Hannington and others that the police in the metropolis were breaking up meetings wherever they were held. The provincial police were also said to have used this ban, and it was now to become 'a regular practice of the police in many districts to announce in advance that certain meetings will be prohibited'.[43]

In general this evidence suggests that the determination to oppose cuts in unemployment benefit, by violence if necessary, was now met by a much more resolute attitude on the part of the police, both metropolitan and provincial. A long spell of conflict between the police and the unemployed in 1931–2 therefore resulted.

The year 1932 witnessed greater clashes between the police and the hunger marchers than in any previous period. Scotland Yard was by now seriously alarmed that very hostile demonstrations might take place. In January the NUWM disregarded the Metropolitan Commissioner's ban on meetings outside labour exchanges. When the police tried forcibly to eject some individuals, there were more serious disturbances. The NUWM called for a

[41] *Annual Report of Commissioner of Metropolitan Police*, PP 1932–3 [Cmd. 4294], xv. 342.
[42] D. Williams, *Keeping the Peace*, p. 128.
[43] *Parl. Deb.*, 5th ser., 314, 1553 (10 July 1936).

'national day of struggle' against the means test on 23 February 1932, and many violent demonstrations took place throughout the country. In London many of the unemployed converged on Parliament Square. Police guarded the entrance to the House of Commons while uniformed and plain-clothes police patrolled the streets and broke up groups of demonstrators.[44] In Bristol there was a violent baton charge after the police had denied the unemployed the right to hold a procession and the council had refused to see a deputation. In April 1932 the chief constable of Bristol, Maby, wrote that the time had come for these demonstrations to be stopped.[45] In this he was voicing the views of many of his counterparts elsewhere. He reported in April to the under-secretary of state at the Home Office that a deputation from the NUWM had been received at the Council House, Bristol, over a request for the use of a council hall for a meeting. While the deputation was inside, a large number of NUWM members assembled nearby, and the police were duly instructed to move them away. Assaults on the police followed: four persons were arrested and thirteen summonses heard in court against members of the NUWM for disorderly behaviour likely to cause a breach of the peace.[46] Again in June, the Bristol police stopped a demonstration of 600 as it was claimed that they tried to use a route different from that previously agreed. The police charged the crowd: the General Infirmary reported treating fourteen people for minor injuries to the head, and two for injuries to the limbs, all the result of blows from constables' batons. Even the chief constable himself reluctantly admitted that it looked as if 'instructions to the police as to the use of their batons may not have been properly adhered to'.[47]

There were further clashes between the unemployed and the police in Merseyside, Manchester, Birmingham, Cardiff, Coventry, Nottingham, Oldham, Porthcawl, Stoke, Wigan, Preston, Bolton, and Belfast at various times in 1932. Many arrests and prosecutions followed. In Birkenhead on 13, 15, and 16 September hundreds of unemployed were arrested and many

[44] *The Times*, 24 Feb. 1932.

[45] Correspondence between chief constable of Bristol and chief constable of Manchester, 11, 12, 13 Apr. 1932 (Bristol Record Office).

[46] Chief constable of Bristol to under secretary of state, Home Office, 21 Apr. 1932 (HO 144/22587/582367/2).

[47] Chief constable's report to Bristol Watch Committee, 20 June 1932; memo. by A. Dixon, 30 June 1932 (HO 144/22587/582367/2).

injured as they fought with the police. Later that month large numbers of police were drafted into the town and, together with the local force, began what some leaders of the unemployed alleged was a virtual reign of terror. Working-class districts were raided; houses entered without warrants; individuals, including women and children, attacked. In all, over 100 civilians were taken to Birkenhead hospital with such severe injuries as broken pelvises, fractured ribs, and broken arms and legs. Ten men were committed to Chester Assizes on 15 September on charges of riotous assembly.[48]

At Liverpool the following week police on motor-cycles charged crowds of unemployed people. The unemployed were not allowed to gather in Islington Square, where they had held daily meetings for many years. Eventually they assembled in Canterbury Square, where the police asked them to disperse. Bricks and other missiles were thrown, and immediately about thirty or forty policemen, including some on motor-cycles, charged down the street. Policemen on the pillions and in side-cars struck out at the legs of the fleeing demonstrators, who were then pursued down side passages. The *Manchester Guardian* recorded how about twenty police were taken from one spot to another in a matter of a minute or two, giving the unemployed no chance to reassemble.[49] The ILP newspaper, the *New Leader*, condemned the 'sheer ferocity' and 'terrorism' of police methods: it reminded its readers that the chief constable of Liverpool was Superintendent Wilson 'of Dartmoor fame'. It added that in parts of Lancashire the police were acting 'like little Mussolinis' in preventing meetings by the unemployed.[50] On 18 October there were further violent clashes in London between police and unemployed marchers outside County Hall, where a deputation from the NUWM was meeting the leaders of the London County Council with demands for more relief. Mounted and foot police attacked the demonstrators, who threw bricks and stones in return. Charge after charge by the police followed, with motor-cycles and side-cars again used to rush groups of police from point to point. Over forty were arrested, and many marchers and police injured.[51]

[48] Bowes, *Police*, pp. 29–30; *New Leader*, 30 Sept. 1932.
[49] *Manchester Guardian*, 23 Sept. 1932.
[50] *New Leader*, 30 Sept. 1932.
[51] *Daily Herald*, 19 Oct. 1932.

This long spell of conflict culminated in the largest ever hunger-march demonstration in London in the autumn of 1932. The Metropolitan and provincial police were both well prepared in advance of this latest demonstration, as were the Ministries of Health and Labour. The march began on 26 September and was due to arrive in London to present the petition on 27 October. The Ministry of Health told its local authorities to pursue a tough line with the marchers, while the Ministry of Labour gave instructions that persons taking part in the march were not to be given facilities to draw unemployment benefit at Unemployment Exchanges which they might pass *en route*.[52] The Home Office primed the local police with details of the march programme, routes, and assembly points. It added, as usual, that 'strict insistence on the conditions attaching to the grant of relief to the marchers may give rise to disorder'. The police must, therefore, prevent any breaches of the peace, especially near casual wards. The Home Office itself had been fully warned, through 'civil security intelligence', about the activities of the unemployed, the Communists, and the League against Imperialism.[53]

The Metropolitan Police made particularly careful preparations for the marchers' arrival and stay in London. In August 1932 efforts were made to ascertain the names of local leaders; subsequently, particulars of the more notorious of them, with photographs and details of any previous convictions, were forwarded to the divisions.[54] Both the Special Branch and police informers were active at an early stage. Several of these had infiltrated the council of the NUWM and NUWM branch meetings. A Sergeant Buckell reported on 14 September to Scotland Yard:

> With regard to the unemployed march on London. On this occasion the marshals will not lead the procession but will be among the rank and file. Dummy leaders will be put forward. Instructions have been received in the districts to make the march as spectacular as possible and to have as many clashes with the police as can be arranged. . . . If the provincial numbers are large enough . . . then London is to concentrate on local

[52] Memo. to General Inspectors of Ministry of Health, 26 Sept. 1932 (MH 57/101); memo. prepared by Sir Russell Scott for submission to Cabinet on question of unemployed marchers, 1 Nov. 1932 (MEPO 2/6269/2A).

[53] HO 158/28 (653, 963/2), 29 Sept. 1932; Home Office booklet, 1933 (PRO 30/69/598).

[54] Note on hunger march to London, Oct.–Nov. 1932, 30 Jan. 1934 (MEPO 2/3071).

demonstrations in order to keep as many police employed as possible in the suburbs whilst the main demonstration forces its way to the Houses of Parliament.[55]

In addition, informers revealed that the NUWM officials had decided upon tactics to be used wherever there was a demonstration. For example, marchers should not obey police commands that they should form up in the roadway and march four abreast 'but to walk on the pavement . . . so that the police would be unable to discriminate between peaceful and militant citizens'.[56] These and many other reports by informers and Special Branch were sent to Scotland Yard in the weeks prior to the arrival of the march in London.

The Metropolitan Police files show in detail how police arrangements for the mass meeting due to take place on 27 October were well prepared in advance. They also reveal the antagonistic stance adopted by Scotland Yard towards the marchers. The attention of the chief officers of police in the metropolis was drawn to the paragraphs in the Metropolitan Police General Orders, Section 21, relating to meetings and processions. These laid down, for example, that

161 Meetings etc. likely to become dangerous should be carefully watched and the leaders identified if possible with a view to obtaining proof of the same persons acting as ring leaders on various occasions. Notes should if possible be made of the speeches either by uniform or plain clothes constables who will prepare a brief report quoting any inflammatory language used. In special cases authorised by the Commissioner shorthand writers may be employed but not otherwise.

162 Measures must be taken at an early stage to stop riotous behaviour arising out of public meetings. In certain localities inflammatory language may lead to riot and damage to property and it may be necessary to arrest the ring leaders or disperse the meeting or both.

166 In arresting anyone for inciting to public disorder care must be taken that sufficient police are at hand to keep order.

167 Persons guilty of violence or of uttering threats should be at once arrested and charged with one or more of the following offences: Assaulting or resisting or obstructing police on due execution of duty (Offences against the Person Act 1861, Section 38). Using threatening, abusive or

[55] Extract from report submitted by Sergeant Buckell, 14 Sept. 1932 (MEPO 2/3064).

[56] Notes of police informer, 7 Oct. 1932 (ibid.).

insulting words or behaviour with intent to provoke a breach of the peace or whereby a breach of the peace may be occasioned (Metropolitan Police Act 1839, Section 54 (13)). Wilfully obstructing the free passage of any highway (Highways Act 1835, Section 72).

181 Police must deal expeditiously with unlawful assemblies which may very easily develop into riots. Discretion and judgement should be exercised in all cases but police should bear in mind the necessity of taking every step with firmness and preventing public disorder or breach of the peace.[57]

Just before the march Scotland Yard sent out a 'very urgent and confidential' memorandum to officers in charge of districts throughout Britain advising that,

to assist the Commissioner in taking any action he may consider necessary in connection with Unemployed Demonstrations will you please report *as early as possible* the names and addresses of any of the local or other leaders of the Communists or Unemployed against whom you possess evidence of incitement to create disturbance or of participation in disturbances that have occurred.

This met with an immediate response.[58]

The marchers finally arrived in London on 26 October. On 27 October a mass meeting was held to protest about the means test at Hyde Park. There were over 2,000 demonstrators; in addition a crowd of 10,000 had converged from all over London and covered the whole of the surrounding area. A total of 2,600 police, including 136 mounted men, were on duty; this included 758 special constables. *The Times* noted that there were 100 police in Hyde Park itself, consisting of regular officers and the recently recruited special constables. They helped the large force of foot police. It was 'noticeable the higher police officers as well as the mounted men wore helmets in place of their customary cloth caps'.[59] The contingents from various parts of London marched in procession to Hyde Park and no disorder occurred. However, as the procession approached Edgware Road, violence erupted. Nineteen police and fifty-eight demonstrators were injured, and fourteen arrests were made.[60] Some reported that the trouble was started by

[57] Metropolitan Police General Orders, Section 21 (MEPO 2/3039).

[58] R. Hayburn, 'The Police and the Hunger Marchers', *International Review of Social History*, 17 (1972), 629.

[59] *The Times*, 28 Oct. 1932.

[60] Kingsford, *Hunger Marchers*, p. 155.

special constables, who then had to be rescued by mounted police when the situation got out of hand. A confidential document in the Metropolitan Police files by an inspector in charge of special constabulary tends to confirm this suspicion.[61]

In the *Socialist Review*, one eye-witness, James Grant, described the occasion in graphic terms:

> There was a good deal of booing and banter going on between some of the unemployed gathered on the pavements and the police, when suddenly, without the slightest provocation and for no apparent reason, the mounted police started to race up and down the roads flourishing huge staves in their hands, smashing their way in and out amongst the traffic, scattering people gathered on the pavements and even pushing and heaving their horses down upon the innocent citizen who happened to be just going about his ordinary business. From Edgware Road they galloped their horses into the Park, still brandishing their staves at people. . . .
>
> Up to this the marchers and the unemployed had behaved in an orderly manner . . . but it was not to be wondered at that a few of them immediately lost their temper and seized a few branches of trees lying about and flung them at the police. . . . The police immediately lost complete control of themselves and proceeded to sweep their horses into the crowds, slashing out indiscriminately both at spectators and marchers. Their behaviour left a long way behind even the disgusting conduct of the Indian Police, who freely baton down the followers of Mr. Gandhi.[62]

Not surprisingly, the account of the proceedings given by the officer in charge and the Home Secretary differed radically from that given above. The marchers and roughs who had joined the hunger marchers were said to have taken the offensive, and weapons including iron bars were said to have been thrown by the marchers themselves: 'Police mounted and foot were obliged to draw their truncheons and clear the street', at 3.30 p.m. and again at 4.30 p.m., when the marchers 'went into adjoining side streets and again threw staves and bolts'.[63]

The final, violent episode during the 1932 hunger march came on 1 November with the attempt to present the million-signature petition against the means test to parliament. Early in the evening of 1 November the police cleared Parliament Square. They threw

[61] Inspector of Headquarters B Division Special Constabulary to chief inspector at Fulham, 28 Oct. 1932 (MEPO 2/2518).

[62] J. L. Grant, 'The Hunger Marchers and the Police', *Socialist Review* (Winter 1932), pp. 243–4.

[63] Account of the hunger march, 28 Oct. 1932 (MEPO 2/3065).

cordons of foot and mounted police across all approaches, massed their police and military reserves in Scotland Yard and the Horse Guards, and left ordinary police duties in London to the specials, according to the *New Leader*.[64] In all 800 special constables were on service duty. Before the final march began, the police raided the NUWM offices in Great Russell Street, and arrested Wal Hannington. He was charged later in the day at Bow Street court of having attempted, in a speech at Trafalgar Square on 30 October, to cause disaffection among members of the Metropolitan Police. Documents in the NUWM building were also seized.[65]

After this a deputation from a mass rally of the unemployed at Clerkenwell Green went to present the petition to the House of Commons, even though the Sessional Order prohibited all processions while parliament was sitting. A fifty-man deputation, led in the absence of Hannington by two Welshmen, Sid Elias and Emrhys Llewelyn, collected the bundles of the petition which had been left at Charing Cross station. However, the police then closed the station gates and effectively prevented their departure, while confiscating the bundles of petitions. This provoked fighting which spread from Charing Cross to Whitehall and down Victoria Street. A large crowd then assembled in Trafalgar Square and pushed forward to reach Parliament Square, *agents provocateurs* helped further disorder, and the police dispersed the crowd by force.[66] The *Daily Herald* reported how Trenchard had assembled a large force of police to clear a crowd of perhaps 20,000 to 30,000 people in Trafalgar Square. Mounted men swept the roads and pavements; foot police formed a cordon around the Houses of Parliament behind the cenotaph in Whitehall, across Westminster Bridge, across Millbank, in front of the entrance to the House of Lords, and across Victoria Street and Birdcage Walk.[67]

The police now arrested Sid Elias and he was subsequently sentenced on the evidence of documents seized by the police from the NUWM headquarters to two years' imprisonment for 'attempting to cause discontent and disaffection and ill will between different classes . . . and to create public disturbance against the peace.' Hannington himself was sentenced to three

[64] *New Leader*, 4 Nov. 1932.
[65] *The Times*, 2 Nov. 1932.
[66] Quoted in Bowes, *Police*, p. 111.
[67] *Daily Herald*, 2 Nov. 1932.

months. Five days after Elias's trial Emrhys Llewelyn, the NUWM secretary, was also arrested, along with the treasurer, the veteran syndicalist Tom Mann, on charges of being disturbers of the peace and of encouraging others to take part in a demonstration, contravening the Seditious Meetings Act of 1817. On 17 December both men were bound over to keep the peace for twelve months in the sum of £200 each, with sureties of £100 each. Both chose to go to prison for two months.[68] In all a total of 1,432 'workers were prosecuted between 31 October 1931 and 28 February 1933 because of their fight against the Government'.[69]

Many complaints were voiced about the conduct of the police, especially those in the metropolis, in dealing with the hunger marchers. After protests about police behaviour in Bristol in June 1932, the town clerk asked for an inquiry but the watch committee eventually refused to hold one.[70] The annual Labour Party conference moved resolutions protesting about the batoning of the unemployed workers by the police and pressed for an inquiry. Conference urged that the Home Secretary should issue instructions to all local police authorities to grant full facilities for demonstrations of the unemployed to take place.[71] In the Commons, George Lansbury, leader of the Parliamentary Labour Party, accused the police of not permitting peaceful demonstrations as they had done in the past. Another kind of police, it was alleged, was now emerging. In Birkenhead there had been police on motor-cycles charging the crowd; in London horse patrols used long staves to powerful effect. These armed police could take action without the Riot Act being read, or any magistrate being present.[72] The Home Secretary, Sir John Gilmour, who had recently succeeded Herbert Samuel, simply gave a blanket endorsement to the actions of his officers. The police 'behaved . . . with great forbearance. . . . a great part of this difficulty is not caused by the genuine unemployed, but by those who have only one object and that is to create disturbances'.[73] Gilmour was known to be a devoted disciple of Commissioner Trenchard and

[68] D. Williams, *Keeping the Peace*, p. 100; Kingsford, *Hunger Marchers*, pp. 161–2.

[69] D. Williams, *Keeping the Peace*, pp. 14–15.

[70] Chief constable's report to Bristol Watch Committee, 20 June 1932; memo. by A. L. Dixon, 24 June 1932.

[71] *Labour Party Annual Conference Reports* (1931 and 1932).

[72] *Parl. Deb.*, 5th ser., 269, 266 (19 Oct. 1932).

[73] Ibid., 269, 1317 (28 Oct. 1932).

his methods. The events of the autumn of 1932, therefore, which saw the climax of the violence associated with hunger marches, failed yet again to lead to any inquiry into police conduct.

However, a significant development now took place. The Cabinet now began to intervene, to examine the question of the statutory prevention rather than the mere control of hunger marches. The police seemed to possess all the powers they needed to deal with disorder; but, in fact, their statutory powers were not far reaching. They could deal with disorder, but not beforehand; only when it actually arose, could they act. Again, the problem of groups of unemployed people whose conduct was not riotous and who could only with some difficulty be proved to be unlawful assemblies was really beyond the reach of the law. The existing provisions of the criminal law dealing with meetings and processions were applicable only where a breach of the peace resulted, or might reasonably be apprehended. It was true that local authorities had powers to route processions, and that the police, provincial and metropolitan, were able to use *ad hoc* methods to deal with meetings and marches, especially since the enabling provisions of the Regulations introduced under the Emergency Powers Act 1920 in 1921 and 1926. However, if tested in the courts, these methods might be found to have no legal basis, and some firmer statutory foundation was felt to be required. Chiefs of police and successive Commissioners of the Metropolitan Police had long pressed the Home Secretary for increased powers to prohibit meetings and marches. In 1926, for example, Horwood, the Commissioner of the Metropolitan Police, urged that Emergency Regulation 22 (which allowed chiefs of police to prohibit meetings and marches with the approval of the Home Secretary if they feared disorder would arise) be embodied in the general law.[74] In 1932 Trenchard wrote to the Home Secretary:

> I have thought for some time that to allow all and sundry to pass through the centre of London whenever they like was an anachronism in present day conditions quite apart from the question of disorder. I consider that there is a very reasonable case for prohibiting *all* processions (other than ceremonial processions, the Lord Mayor's Show etc.) in the central area at any rate on all days but Saturday and Sunday.[75]

[74] Commissioner of Metropolitan Police to Home Secretary, 8 Oct. 1926 (HO 144/8014/49455/14).

[75] Trenchard to Home Secretary, 27 Oct. 1932 (MEPO 2/6269).

In November 1932 a Cabinet committee was set up to consider the legal position of the hunger marches. It examined a draft Processions (Regulations) Bill which had been prepared as a result of interdepartmental discussions. These discussions had been presided over by Sir Russell Scott at the Home Office,[76] who had concluded that: 'the only means of combatting the mischief is to take power to prohibit the organisation of such a procession and to provide that if the prohibition is disregarded the procession is to be deemed an unlawful assembly which may be dealt with as such.'[77] A draft provision for this purpose was already in existence based on the DORA regulations in force in the 1914–18 period, and the regulations made under the Emergency Powers Acts 1920 in 1921 and 1926. The departments concerned suggested that an Act be passed to make this provision available permanently.

> The events of the last ten days appear . . . to afford ample justification for seeking such power. There can . . . be little doubt that its exercise by the Secretary of State as a means of preventing a recurrence of such events would receive strong support and the necessity of justifying his action in Parliament should be sufficient safeguard against any Secretary of State exercising his power on insufficient grounds.[78]

The proposals were that the Home Secretary should be empowered to prohibit the concentration of persons whether by procession or otherwise outside the areas in which they normally reside if he was satisfied that disorder would result, or that abnormal demands would be made on the poor-law authorities. Powers should also be conferred on local authorities to prohibit processions if they felt disorder would occur. But these proposals foundered on the opposition of the Attorney-General, Sir Thomas Inskip. He told the Cabinet committee that 'the existing provisions of the Criminal Law . . . go as far as is possible in dealing with concentrations or processions where there is reasonable ground to apprehend a breach of the peace'. It would be unwise to ask parliament to pass new legislation based on considerations such as breach of the peace. In addition, the question as to whether the Secretary of State or the magistrates should exercise any new statutory powers was a controversial one. Inskip suggested that, before resorting to new legislation, further trial should be given to

76 CAB 27/497 CP 434 (32), memo. by Sir R. Scott, Nov. 1932.
77 Draft memo. on Processions (Regulations) Bill, 2 Nov. 1932 (MEPO 2/6269).
78 Ibid.

the procedure by which a court of summary jurisdiction may, upon complaint, order any person to enter into a recognizance and find sureties to keep the peace or be of good behaviour.[79]

So at this stage the government did not feel it necessary to acquire new powers by statute, and preferred to rely on traditional procedures in controlling marches. However, Oliver Stanley, under-secretary at the Home Office, assured the Commons in February 1933 that further powers would certainly be sought if the existing methods for controlling processions proved inadequate, and his words were to be borne out, as will shortly emerge.[80]

The rise of Sir Oswald Mosley's British Union of Fascists (BUF), coinciding with renewed hunger-march activity, provided the next stimulus for pressure from chief officers of police and the Home Office for a statutory increase in police powers to deal with meetings and marches. Hunger-march activity was renewed in 1934. As before the police preparations to meet the march were similar to those made to meet an invading army.

In November 1933 the Home Office had been told by the Special Branch that the NUWM was beginning to arrange for a new hunger march to London in 1934. It was to take place at the end of February 1934. The immediate cause of the march was a highly popular one—a protest against the government's Unemployment Insurance Bill, the so-called 'slave bill', which set out to replace the local Public Assistance Committees with Unemployment Assistance Boards (UAB). The latter would implement relief rates which were nationally determined and could not be influenced by local pressure. The grounds for disqualification from payment were to be enlarged, and the means test to be perpetuated. The fury of the labour movement now reached new heights.

The march set off from Glasgow on 22 January 1934. The Home Office issued two circulars in rapid succession to the provincial police saying that they should co-operate fully with the poor-law officials on the route of the march and prevent any disorder, especially near casual wards.[81] The Home Office also instructed

[79] CAB 27/497, memo. by Attorney-General, 2 Dec. 1932; minutes of 3rd meeting of Committee on Hunger Marches, 14 Dec. 1932.

[80] *Parl. Deb.*, 5th ser., 274, 1009 (15 Feb. 1933).

[81] HO 158/28 (668, 992/4), 16 Dec. 1933; HO 158/29 (668, 992/21), 22 Jan. 1934.

chief constables *en route* to submit daily reports to detail each contingent's strength, progress, state of discipline, collections made, and the number of men who had convictions and for what offences.[82] In fact, the Ministry of Health and Home Office were again pursuing a hard line towards the unemployed marchers heading for the capital. In a draft memorandum it was stated that Ministry of Health officials had consulted the Home Office about the proposed hunger march:

> We feel, and they agree, that if only the marchers were firmly handled in accordance with the law at the early stages of the demonstration, the nuisance will be more easily and more completely abated . . . relief shall be given in strict compliance with the Casual Poor Order. . . . The vital point is that the authorities who take these steps should be assured of adequate police protection.

The Ministry of Health general inspectors were circularized accordingly.[83]

At a meeting to prepare his senior officers for the hunger marchers' arrival in London, Trenchard urged the Metropolitan Police to collaborate with the poor-law officials. He reminded his men that the Ministry of Health felt that in the previous year

> the police had not altogether helped them. Senior officers had been told not to provoke conflicts and therefore we had been rather lenient and in order not to provoke a riot some infringements of the law had been allowed to pass . . . Last year some of the police (quite rightly) gave concerts to the unemployed. . . . that sort of thing must not go on during the hunger march.[84]

In the light of its experiences in the autumn of 1932, Scotland Yard had prepared a manual for the Metropolitan Police, 'Notes for the Guidance of Senior Officers in the Case of Large-scale Disturbances'.[85] This was a secret and confidential account of the tactics which the police of the metropolis should use and was adversarial in approach. The police were encouraged to take action to prevent

[82] Kingsford, *Hunger Marchers*, p. 179.

[83] Ministry of Health memo., Jan. 1933; Ministry of Health Circular to general inspectors, 22 Jan. 1934 (MH 57/103).

[84] Note on preliminary meeting on hunger marches held in Metropolitan Commissioner's room, 25 Jan. 1934 (MEPO 2/3071).

[85] Notes for guidance of senior officers in the case of large-scale disturbances, issued 10 Jan. 1933 (MEPO 2/3034).

and break up meetings and marches, and heavy emphasis was placed on the fact that they had enough powers under the common law and existing statute law for this purpose. The booklet gave much detailed information about such factors as deployment of the regular force and special constables, channels of communication, confiscation of weapons, and the marshalling of processions. One dramatic provision which illustrated its tone was: 'Where facilities are available for using fire hoses adjusted to fire hydrants in an enclosed area they should be brought into play if a large crowd refuses to obey police directions.'[86]

Now the instructions in this manual were to come into force, and Trenchard was to ensure that they were given effect. It was stressed that the regular police must be conserved as much as possible for the big demonstration which was to take place in London on Sunday, 25 February, and for the marchers' activities in the metropolis on the days following. Special constables should be used as much as possible to relieve regular police of patrolling, traffic work, and ordinary beat work. Trenchard emphasized that he did not want to employ them in other directions unless it was really necessary: if they were, 'two or three uniform police must be somewhere near in case of an emergency'. A strong mounted contingent of police would also be available. There was no reason why regular officers should not do overtime. The Special Branch should continue with their independent reports and telegrams relating to the different areas, but if they arrested anyone they should hand them over to uniformed police.[87] In addition, the Deputy Assistant Commissioner of the Metropolitan Police had loaned Canada House to him and his staff for the duration of the marchers' stay in London. Here wireless transmission and receiving apparatus was installed for fast communication.[88]

But, although the hunger marchers were to be firmly dealt with *en route*, and Trenchard had made elaborate plans for their arrival and stay in London, Gilmour, the Home Secretary, was far more cautious over the way they should be handled once they reached the capital. He was anxious that the events of 1932 should not be repeated. By this time the popular mood had somewhat changed.

[86] Ibid.

[87] Note on preliminary meeting on hunger marches held in Metropolitan Commissioner's room, 25 Jan. 1934 (MEPO 2/3071).

[88] Note on hunger march of 1934 by Deputy Assistant Commissioner of Metropolitan Police, 8 Mar. 1934 (ibid.).

After the rise of Fascism in Nazi Germany, Labour and TUC sympathy for the Communist-led NUWM was more pronounced. Gilmour emphasized, at a meeting with Trenchard, the Speaker's secretary, and the deputy-sergeant-at-arms on 6 February, that the situation had altered over recent months. There were now at least four MPs in alliance with the movement, and many more on the Labour benches in sympathy. His intention was neither 'to enforce the law to the utmost nor to encourage the marchers'. Deputations of marchers likely to approach members of parliament should be handled by the police with tact and discretion. Trenchard wanted to limit deputations to six persons but had to agree to ten when he was told that that was the regulation number.[89]

Gilmour's wary attitude was reinforced when, a few days before the appearance of the hunger march in London, the NCCL was formed, with Ronald Kidd as its first general secretary. Its seventeen founders included such prominent political and literary figures as Attlee, Laski, Vera Brittain, A. P. Herbert, H. W. Nevinson, Edith Summerskill, and H. G. Wells. Its purpose was to monitor police behaviour at the scene of the hunger marches; its very existence testified to the alarm felt amongst middle-class radicals at the way in which popular demonstrations were being handled at this period.

The marchers arrived in London on 23 February, and in fact the whole of their stay was peaceful, and the march well disciplined. The police adopted significantly different tactics from those of 1932. Although the crowd was said to number at least 50,000, there were now no special constables in sight and no riding by mounted police in crowds. The *Daily Herald* reported how, at Marble Arch, there were police directing the marshals of the crowds and the routes of the demonstrators by means of specially installed telephones. 'Not a single policeman was called on for any duty other than that of escort. It was one of the most orderly demonstrations London has ever seen.'[90]

The Home Secretary's instructions to the Metropolitan Police had obviously been observed reluctantly by Trenchard, after all his

[89] Notes on a meeting of Home Secretary with Lord Trenchard, the Speaker's Secretary and the Deputy-Sergeant-at-Arms, 6 Feb. 1934 (ibid.).

[90] *Daily Herald*, 26 Feb. 1934; Reports on the national hunger march 1934 (MEPO 2/3071); *The Economist*, 15 Mar. 1934; *The Times*, 23 Jan., 9 Mar. 1934.

elaborate forward planning. Perhaps to remind Gilmour where the power really lay, he handed in his resignation to the Prime Minister, Ramsay MacDonald, on 13 March. His value to the Metropolitan Police was then reaffirmed by the King, amongst others, who persuaded him to stay.[91]

The stance generally shown by the police towards the hunger marchers and the unemployed contrasted with that adopted by the police towards the Fascists. The rise of Mosley's Union of Fascists with their provocative uniforms and behaviour aroused the anger of the left; clashes between Fascists and anti-Fascists now became commonplace especially when marches were organized in Jewish areas like the East End of London. This contrast is sharply illustrated by the police response to events at the Fascist rally at Olympia on 7 June 1934, and the Home Office files on this incident are of much interest.

On 9 May 1934 information had been received by Scotland Yard that the BUF was to hold a meeting at Olympia on 7 June to be addressed by Mosley. It was later discovered that the Communists proposed a counter-demonstration. Plans for policing these events were made accordingly and the Special Branch was active.[92] It was agreed that, when the Communist party demonstration was dispersing, the accompanying police 'will infiltrate with them as far as Olympia and will take steps to ensure that under no circumstances is a procession to be allowed to re-form'. It was claimed that many Communists who were going to take part in the counter-demonstration 'will carry missiles and sticks'. The police were to wear helmets and put collar chains on their horses.[93] The anti-Fascist demonstration outside Olympia on 7 June was indeed fiercely dealt with by the police. While this was going on, interrupters inside the hall, during a violent speech by Mosley, were assaulted by stewards and ejected 'with much violence by Blackshirts'. Even the reports of the Special Branch confirm that 'very violent treatment was given to the men removed by the Blackshirts. Two men reached the street minus their trousers and others were bleeding at the face.' There were twenty-three arrests for

[91] Ascoli, *Queen's Peace*, p. 236.

[92] See reports of Special Branch (HO 144/20140/674216/70).

[93] Report on disturbances between the Fascists and Communists at Olympia and preceding preparations by the Metropolitan Police, June 1934 (ibid.).

disorderly conduct, insulting behaviour and obstruction, and assault on the police.[94]

Many protests about events at Olympia were now made. *The Times*, for example, contained a leading article suggesting that 'the interruptions and the violence used against the interrupters seem to have been specially and strenuously preconceived'.[95] In the House of Commons there were many criticisms voiced about police conduct at this meeting.[96] Indeed the growth of the Fascist movement had a major effect on the problem of working-class marches, meetings, and demonstrations in two main respects. First, it was claimed that the police were acting partially by treating the Fascists, with their influential supporters such as Lord Rothermere and his *Daily Mail*, more leniently than the hunger marchers. The police were failing to act in cases of Fascist violence against the left, even after Olympia when police officers had the first-hand evidence of people left bruised and bleeding after being attacked by uniformed Fascist stewards. Secondly, whereas previous complaints about police conduct in this area had had limited support, these latest events aroused the particular fury of the left and of liberal progressives everywhere. For example, in June 1934 a deputation from the National Joint Council of Labour, representing the Labour Party and the TUC, complained to Gilmour:

> If the idea becomes current that the police force on whom one is entitled to rely for the preventing of breaches of the peace have definite and direct knowledge that a breach is being committed and do not interfere, well the moral which will be taken by quite a number of people is that they have to organise to protect themselves because they will not be able to rely upon the law.[97]

The Secretary of the Associated Society of Locomotive Engineers wrote to Gilmour to complain about the pro-Fascist stance of the police. Mosley had boasted after Olympia that he could 'break up any Socialist meeting in this country. The assurance to make that statement can only be based on the fact that he and his trained,

[94] Special Branch report on the Fascist meeting at Olympia on 7 June 1934 (ibid.).

[95] D. Williams, *Keeping the Peace*, p. 135.

[96] *Parl. Deb.*, 5th ser., 290, 1948 ff. (14 June 1934).

[97] Deputation to Home Secretary from National Joint Council of Labour, 26 June 1934 (HO 144/20141/674216/120).

paid thugs will receive some assistance and protection from the police whilst members of working class organisations will get a little less courteous treatment.'[98]

The issue of whether the police had the right to enter public meetings held on private premises was now raised. The usual, though not invariable, practice up to 1934 was for the police not to enter meetings held on private premises unless called upon to do so by the promoters or organizers of the meeting. Many of those who were vocal in protest about Olympia would have preferred to see steps being taken for a much more active part to be played by the police in the control of indoor meetings. With the sympathy of the left on the side of the unemployed and in favour of any seemingly anti-Fascist legislation, Gilmour presented a memorandum to the Cabinet asking for possible legislation to be introduced, to strengthen the powers of the police as to entry into public meetings on private premises where disturbances were anticipated, and to curb the wearing of uniform by political bodies such as the Blackshirts. His proposals for a new Public Order Bill now received broad agreement in Cabinet.[99] However, the scope of the Bill was considerably widened when the Home Secretary consulted chief constables and the Commissioner of the Metropolitan Police. What is most notable is the way in which Gilmour resisted some of the requests from chief officers of police for more sweeping powers, and the manner in which the Cabinet amended his own modifications. Chiefs of police—metropolitan and provincial—had long pressed Home Secretaries for statutory powers to deal with meetings and marches. They had been taking *ad hoc* powers to control or even prevent these forms of demonstration but it was far from clear whether there was any legal justification. In 1934

> Nearly all the chief constables consulted are of the opinion that there should be express statutory provision requiring the prior consent of the chief constable to the holding of an open-air meeting and that the chief constable should be empowered to prohibit such a meeting if he is satisfied that the meeting is likely to cause obstruction or lead to a breach of the peace.

[98] Secretary of the Associated Society of Locomotive Engineers to Home Secretary, 8 June 1934 (ibid. 80).

[99] CAB 24/249 CP 144 (34), memo. by Home Secretary, 23 May 1934; CAB 23/79 24 (34), 13 June 1934.

They also urged that powers be given to the police to prevent riotous seeming processions and that the police and not the local authorities have authority for this.

But Gilmour himself felt that these powers, if granted, would be too far-reaching. He recommended, in addition to his original proposals, that authority should be given to chiefs of police to prohibit meetings held at such times and places likely to clash with other meetings, or to interfere with local authority business; also, chiefs of police should be empowered to prescribe the routes of processions. If the Cabinet decided that steps must be taken to prevent a repetition of the unemployed marches, the Home Secretary should be empowered to prohibit, by order, concentrations of persons outside the areas in which they lived if he felt that they were likely to lead to serious disorder or to the disruption of public assistance services. These additional proposals were much criticized in Cabinet. It was felt that the first would not be popular, owing to the general sympathy with the plight of the unemployed. To include it might endanger the remainder of the measure. The next two proposals would place too much power in the hands of chief constables. The proposals on which there was broad agreement were that the police should be given power of entry into public meetings held on private premises where the chief constable had reason to believe that disorder would occur; that it should be made an offence to be in possession of an offensive weapon when taking part in a meeting or procession, and that it should be an offence for any person, in pursuit of a political objective, to form any body of persons into an organization of a military character.

After discussion, the Cabinet concluded that heads of proposals should be drawn up and discussed by the Home Secretary with leaders of the opposition parties 'without suggesting that the Cabinet had reached any decision on those proposals'.[100] Circumstances did not yet appear to be sufficiently urgent, or the time politically right, for such a measure to be brought forward. However the core of what was later to emerge as the Public Order Act was already in existence in 1934.[101]

[100] CAB 24/250 CP 189 (34), memo. by Home Secretary on Preservation of Public Order, 11 July 1934; CAB 23/79 29 (34), 18 July 1934.

[101] CAB 23/79 31 (34), 31 July 1934.

As we have seen, the furore aroused by the disturbances associated with Fascist meetings had been used to try to bring about a wholesale statutory extension of police powers in relation to indoor and outdoor meetings and processions. The police had not, in fact, gained the increase in their powers which they desired. However, the decisions in three important cases now showed that, if police powers in the area of working-class freedoms were tested in the courts, they would be upheld.

The first, *Elias* v. *Passmore* (1934), raised important questions about the right of the police to search premises in the course of making an arrest on a warrant.[102] Sid Elias, one of the NUWM leaders, was charged in November 1932 with attempts to cause disaffection amongst the police and society generally. This charge was based on documents seized from the NUWM headquarters earlier when Wal Hannington had been arrested. After the prosecution of Elias, civil proceedings were brought because of the way the police had seized documents when arresting Hannington, since no search warrant had been issued to the police. These documents had not been used in Hannington's trial, but they duly led to the arrest of Elias. In *Elias* v. *Passmore*, in January 1934, it was held that it was indeed proper for the police to search a building where someone had been arrested, and seize material which then led to the prosecution of someone else. However, damages were awarded to the plaintiffs for trespass in respect of documents which were used at neither trial, and also for retention of documents in Elias's trial for longer than was necessary. The decision in this important case added significantly to police powers.[103] It recognized, for the first time, the validity, on occasions such as the police making an arrest on a warrant, of searches which resulted in the discovery of documents containing evidence of an offence committed by any person. This would apply even though the search and seizure were illegal in relation to other documents found there. This case made superfluous many of the statutory requirements of a search warrant granted upon application to a police authority. In confronting a working-class body such as the NUWM, the police had acquired legal backing for a formidable instrument of policy.

The second case, that of *Thomas* v. *Sawkins* (1935), held before

[102] [1934] 2 KB 164.

[103] E. C. S. Wade, 'Police Search', *Law Quarterly Review*, 50 (1934), pp. 354–67.

Lord Chief Justice Hewart, established that the police were entitled to be present at meetings advertised as open to the public but held on private premises, if they had reasonable grounds for believing that, but for their presence, seditious speeches would be made, and incitement to violence and breaches of the peace would occur.[104] This newly recognized area of preventable action by the police resulted from an episode concerned with the incorrigible Lindsay in South Wales. At a meeting at Nantymoel workmen's hall in 1934, attended by two local police officers, speeches condemning Lindsay as 'a menace to the liberty of the working class' were made, and there were calls for his dismissal. A similar meeting was held at Caerau library, which was also attended by the police, even though the Public Meeting Act of 1908 laid down that the police should attend only if violence was anticipated or they were called in by stewards. Thomas, one of the organizers of the meeting, took out a summons for assault against Sergeant Sawkins, who had refused to leave the meeting when asked to do so. It was dismissed, but then went to the divisional court which upheld the police view. The wider issue of the right of the police to enter private premises at which meetings were being held then arose when the NCCL sponsored an appeal by Thomas. The law had been quite clear that, if policemen entered such meetings without authorization, they could be asked by the convener or chairman of the meeting to leave. Gilmour had appeared to confirm this in the House of Commons on 26 June 1934 when there were complaints about police failure to enter the Olympia Fascist meeting. He had replied that police could not attend meetings unless they had reason to believe an actual breach of the peace was being committed. If the police were to be armed with further powers, Gilmour added, legislation would be required.[105]

Thomas v. *Sawkins* now reversed Gilmour's view and what had always been understood to be the law of the land. According to L. C. J. Hewart's remarkably flexible interpretation, the police could now enter private premises on far broader grounds—entry based not on the committing of an offence, but mere apprehension in a policeman's mind of some hypothetical offence that might or might not be committed there at some future time. A further gloss on this interpretation was added by Simon, the Home Secretary, in

[104] [1935] 2 KB 249.
[105] *Parl. Deb.*, 5th ser., 290, 1968 (26 June 1934).

1936: 'a policeman, even though he is a policeman in uniform is after all a citizen, . . . if anybody takes a hall and invites the public to come in, he has no right whatever to object to the presence of somebody just because he is a policeman or a soldier, if he likes to come in.'[106]

Thomas v. *Sawkins*, therefore, extended the powers of the police in their right of entry into public meetings. Another major case, *Duncan* v. *Jones* (1936), concerned the power of the police to stop meetings on the highway, in cases where no obstruction or disorder had taken place.[107] On 30 July 1934 Mrs Duncan was advertised to address a meeting against the Incitement to Disaffection Bill. This meeting was held in a *cul de sac* and no obstruction to through traffic could arise. However, the police warned her that she would not be allowed to speak. She was forcibly pulled down from the platform and then arrested. The NCCL sponsored her appeal to quarter sessions. When this failed, it assisted her in taking the case to the divisional court. Mrs Duncan was charged with obstructing the police in the execution of their duty; yet there had been no obstruction and the meeting was orderly. The police view was that she should be prevented from speaking lest at some future time some of her listeners might commit a breach of the peace. The eventual decision appeared to justify the police in prohibiting any meeting at which some speaker might, in the view of the police, say something which might lead someone else to cause a disturbance at some future time. In effect, the police were given the legal power to ban any political meeting in a street or other public place at will.

Previously the police could legally intervene to prevent a meeting being held only when a breach of the peace was at issue. As has been seen, the Trenchard ban of 1931 applied to meetings in front of employment exchanges. People charged with obstructing the police had sought in vain to challenge the Trenchard ban which remained in existence until 1936. The seeds of the *Duncan* v. *Jones* case, indeed, lay in the Trenchard ban, but here was the first ruling in the High Court as to the scope of the preventative power which the police had exercised over meetings for so long. According to Ronald Kidd of the NCCL, the police were set up by the judgment in *Duncan* v. *Jones* as 'the arbiters of what political parties or

[106] Ibid., 317, 1365 (16 Nov. 1936).
[107] [1936] I KB 218.

religious sects shall and shall not be accorded the rights of freedom of speech and freedom of assembly'. They exercised throughout the country their power to

> ban any political meeting in streets or public places at will: no matter that such meetings are held in blind alleys where they cannot interfere with traffic; no matter that they are peacefully conducted; no matter that they are the local people's only means of ventilating their opinions or pressing for redress of grievances.[108]

One authoritative verdict on these events came from the distinguished constitutional lawyer, E. C. S. Wade of Cambridge University. He commented that since *Duncan* v. *Jones*

> the net has closed entirely upon those who from lack of resources or for other reasons, desire to hold meetings in public places. The result is that there is now no assurance, unless police permission is secured in advance, that a meeting can be held anywhere in a public place. . . . We venture to think that had the police sought a general power of this nature from the legislature, no House of Commons in the twentieth century would have been willing to grant it.[109]

At the same time as the police were armed with this new authority through case law, the entire question of the governmental response to public meetings and marches now entered upon a decisive phase. In the latter part of 1934 the Unemployment Assistance Act was passed, with its corollary, the UAB. It rang down the curtain on the Public Assistance Commissioners and the old Poor Law. The new benefit scales which the UAB introduced on 7 January 1935 meant a reduction for many recipients, which led to renewed anger and disorder in the so-called distressed areas. South Wales and South Yorkshire were the most troubled areas, with police baton charges and arrests and prosecutions. In February 1935 there were an estimated 300,000 involved in protests throughout Britain. Even after the government announced its 'stand still order' on the new scale of benefit, demonstrations continued because there was still confusion about the retrospective payment of the old scales. In Sheffield, for example, on 6 February, a demonstration of 35,000 people forced an immediate payment of the increases on the UAB regulation amounts. There

[108] Kidd, *British Liberty*, p. 24.

[109] E. C. S. Wade, 'Police Powers and Public Meetings', *Cambridge Law Journal*, 6, 2 (1937), 179.

was a clash between the police and the crowd outside the town hall with much violence on both sides. Twenty-three workers were arrested and a sub-committee of the watch committee was set up to inquire into allegations against the conduct of the police.[110]

A serious incident took place at Blaina on 21 March 1935, after the Relieving Officer and the Guardians Committee refused to meet a deputation led by a Communist county councillor, Phil Abrahams. On 18 March local leaders had been told by the police that a march and demonstration would be prohibited: nevertheless, they still determined to press ahead. When the procession in Blaina was turned back by the police on the morning of 21 March, the police drew their batons and charged the crowd; fierce fighting then resulted. Altogether 200 civilians and seven police were injured, according to the *New Leader*; eighteen were charged with unlawful assembly and riot.[111] There followed many allegations of police brutality. Yet Mr Justice MacNaughton actually praised police conduct at Blaina: 'The police had merely discharged a plain and urgent duty.' The police evidence for the prosecution recited the political activity of the prisoners.[112] The verdict of the jury showed that they accepted the testimony of the police and heavy sentences were passed at the Monmouthshire Assizes as a result.[113] Eleven of the convicted were gaoled for terms ranging between four and nine months. The whole of South Wales was said to have been roused by the Blaina sentences and a protest meeting of 10,000 workers took place. There was a feeling locally that 'the Blaina trial was not a criminal proceeding but a political prosecution and the beginning of a process which has as its object the denial of workers rights of demonstration'. Letters of complaint were sent to the Home Office about these sentences and police conduct at Blaina, with the usual negative outcome.[114]

In July 1936 the government published the new scales of relief which were to replace the 'stand still' in November. It was stated that they were to govern the relief of all unemployed people

[110] *New Leader*, 7 June 1935.

[111] Ibid., 12, 19 July 1935.

[112] *Manchester Guardian*, 20 July 1935; G. Lansbury to Home Office, forwarding extracts of letter from Monmouthshire Defence Committee, 28 July 1935 (HO 144/20032/684596).

[113] *Manchester Guardian*, 20 July 1935 and reports in HO 144/20032/684596/1.

[114] *New Leader*, 26 July 1935; G. Lansbury to Home Office, forwarding extracts of letter from Monmouthshire Defence Committee.

drawing transitional benefit after 16 November. Severe cuts in benefit would obviously result, and much renewed agitation arose in the depressed areas. Demands for another national march were now heard.

The NUWM was in favour of organizing such a march, even though unemployment had fallen generally and membership of the movement with it. The idea of a march gained much official and unofficial trade-union and labour support. Other marches to protest about the means test were being organized from Jarrow and by the National League of the Blind. It was decided that the NUWM marchers should arrive in London on 8 November in order to give the government a week to change its mind before the new regulations were imposed on 16 November.

In July 1936 the Special Branch reported to Scotland Yard: 'The CP and the NUWM have for the past few weeks been considering the prospect of being able to organise a successful hunger march from various parts of the country to London in October or November next. . . . Every effort is to be made to keep in the background the 'Party' character of the march.'[115] As soon as the report was received, preparations got under way for the policing of the march and its reception in London.[116] The provincial police were circularized as usual and warned to take stern measures to prevent disorder.[117]

The Metropolitan Police were now under new management. At the end of 1935 Trenchard had finally resigned and was replaced by a successor of his own choice, Air-Vice-Marshal Sir Philip Game, who had recently been Governor of New South Wales. Game's appointment also coincided with the arrival of Baldwin in Downing Street and Sir John Simon at the Home Office. As usual, the preparations of the Metropolitan Police to meet this march were similar to those which would have been used against an invading army. Arrangements were made by Scotland Yard for securing the names of magistrates who would hold themselves in readiness to read the Riot Act if necessary.[118] The Assistant Commissioner of the Metropolitan Police was reminded of the

[115] Special Branch report on proposed national hunger march 1936, 25 July 1936 (MEPO 2/3091).

[116] Commissioner of Metropolitan Police to Sir G. Cater, 3 Sept. 1936 (ibid.).

[117] HO 158/30 (693, 384/13), 5 Oct. 1936.

[118] Magistrates who will hold themselves in readiness to read the Riot proclamation (MEPO 2/8132).

tactical operations manual, reissued in 1934 under the title 'Meetings, Processions and Demonstrations: Powers and Duties of the Metropolitan Police'. Special attention was drawn to the paragraphs in this booklet concerning the possession of weapons: light walking sticks were to be permitted but 'should a marcher be found in possession of a weapon police will, unless there is some emergency, ask for its surrender. . . . If the contingent leader cannot or will not obtain its surrender the police will act direct.'[119] A permanent reserve of police was to be placed near every institution where hunger marchers were accommodated: 'The duties of this reserve will be to keep in touch . . . with the master of the institution and to be ready to move immediately information is received that their contingent of Hunger Marchers is about to march.'[120]

In spite of all these preparations, the seven marching contingents were peaceful *en route*. In all, 1,463 marchers arrived in London on 6 and 7 November 1936 after gaining much sympathy on the way. Their stay in the metropolis proved tranquil, even though the Metropolitan Police report contained the alarming information that 220 of the members of the seven contingents had been previously convicted. Hannington, in accordance with the extremists' strategy, 'has kept somewhat in the background'. The report admitted that the speeches made at the welcome rally in Hyde Park were 'moderate in tone' and the speakers avoided 'provocative or extremist remarks' but added darkly that, 'there was a "Left" undercurrent amongst the audience'.[121]

The treatment meted out to the hunger marchers by the police again provided sharp contrast to that accorded to the Fascists. There were many instances of inaction by the police when bloody eviction scenes took place at Fascist meetings, while they almost always entered working-class meetings. Selective action by the police appeared to have been given legal sanction by the decision in *Thomas* v. *Sawkins*. The complaints of police partiality towards the Fascists were now to reach a new peak of intensity. For

[119] Telegram to all Area Commanders Metropolitan Police, 6 Nov. 1936 (MEPO 2/3091).

[120] Confidential memo. 6 Nov. 1936 (ibid.).

[121] Special Branch report on the national hunger march and demonstration, Hyde Park, 8 Nov. 1936 (MEPO 2/3053).

example, on 22 March 1936, simultaneously with a large rally addressed by Mosley at the Albert Hall, the police authorities in London refused to allow any counter-Fascist rally by the left within a half-mile radius of the Albert Hall. Thus, when an anti-Fascist meeting was held in Thurloe Square, it was broken up by a police baton charge with many casualties. The NCCL conducted an inquiry into this incident which revealed gross police malpractice; it urged the Home Secretary to hold an official inquiry into police conduct. Sir John Simon, as tradition decreed, gave a negative reply.[122] This episode, followed by further violent incidents at Fascist marches, culminated in an attempted Fascist demonstration in the East End of London in October 1936, the 'battle of Cable Street' on 4 October when Communists fought with Mosley's Blackshirts.

By now the context of the entire problem had changed. General public anxiety about the BUF and serious criticism of the police in the handling of meetings, both of the Fascists and of the unemployed, had led to the introduction of the Public Order Bill. The government now felt that, whereas in 1934 it had seemed likely that Labour and the Liberals would be hostile to public order legislation, the present outcry on the left about the activities of the Fascists had transformed their attitude. Herbert Morrison, a leading Labour spokesman, for example, had declared that he was now in favour of strengthening the law in this respect.[123]

In October 1936 Simon brought forward a memorandum in which he asked the Cabinet to consider introducing public order legislation. He suggested the appointment of a small ministerial committee to consider whether any legislative proposal should be put forward by the government and if so what form it should take. If legislation against uniforms was decided upon, he thought it would be necessary to consider including some legislation about processions also: 'Otherwise the proposals might have the air of being directed against the Fascists only while the rowdyism and disorder created by the political opponents of Fascism remain untouched.' However, a notable change in the Home Office view

[122] *The Thurloe Square Baton Charge: Report of a Commission of Inquiry into Certain Disturbances at Thurloe Square, South Kensington, 22 March 1936*; Home Office to Chairman of NCCL inquiry, 24 Sept. 1936 (MEPO 2/3089).

[123] CAB 27/610, conclusions of first meeting of Committee on Preservation of Public Order, 16 Oct. 1936.

was apparent. Unlike former Home Secretaries, who had resisted police pressure in this area, Simon now argued that 'any new legislation should not confer any additional powers on the Home Secretary as such. . . . express statutory powers placed in the hands of the Home Secretary would facilitate Parliamentary challenges on every occasion . . .'. He believed that what was needed was not an emergency regulation which empowered chief constables when authorized by the Home Secretary to make an order prohibiting the holding of a meeting or procession if a breach of the peace was feared, but rather a strengthening of the ordinary law of the land.

what needs to be considered is legislation which would empower specifically chief officers of police to prohibit in advance processions and demonstrations in the streets if satisfied that they are calculated to lead to disorder and to provide—what the law does not at present—that any persons who organise or take part in a procession or demonstration in defiance of such a prohibition shall be guilty of an offence.[124]

A Cabinet committee on the Preservation of Public Order was now formed and it rapidly came to the conclusion that a public order bill was necessary. However it was not prepared to agree to the far-reaching powers which Simon had proposed for chief constables.[125]

It was no coincidence that the Public Order Bill was eventually introduced in the House of Commons on 9 November 1936, the day after the national hunger-march demonstration.[126] It contained provisions for the prohibition of organizations and wearing of uniforms in connection with political objectives; powers to preserve order on the occasion of processions, and the prohibition of offensive weapons at public meetings. It extended the operation of the crime of threatening, abusive, or insulting words or behaviour, which had existed for many years before 1936 by virtue of various local enactments, to the whole of the British Isles. The crime would now include words or behaviour at a public meeting, in a public or a private place, and a far more severe penalty was to be imposed. The Public Meeting Act 1908 made it

[124] CAB 24/264 CP 261 (36), memo. by Home Secretary on Preservation of Public Order, 12 Oct. 1936.

[125] CAB 27/610, conclusions of second meeting of Committee on Preservation of Public Order, 20 Oct. 1936.

[126] *Parl. Deb.*, 5th ser., 317, 516 (9 Nov. 1936).

an offence punishable summarily with a fine of £5 or one month's imprisonment to act in a disorderly manner at a lawful public meeting: the initiative in prosecution should come from the promoters and organizers of the meeting. Section 6 of the Public Order Bill was designed to give teeth to the statute of 1908. It provided that, if any police constable reasonably suspected any person of committing an offence under the Public Meeting Act, 'he may if so requested to do by the chairman of the meeting require that person to declare to him immediately his name and address, and if that person refuses or fails so to declare his name and address . . . he shall be guilty of an offence'.

The Bill received the formal support of the Labour Party, especially from London MPs like Attlee, Morrison, and Lansbury, when introduced in the Commons. However, it did not meet with the wholehearted approval of the left, who had pressed for a change in the law as to the wearing of political uniforms and the formation of quasi-military organizations. The strengthening of the Public Meeting Act of 1908 was felt to be directed at the left rather than the Fascists. The interrupters at meetings such as Olympia were to be punished while the stewards retained their favoured status under the law. The NCCL had warned that the Act would be used for purposes other than controlling the Fascists, while the far left tended to argue that the Bill contained 'some dangerous provisions': the Marxist, D. N. Pritt, was one who took this view.[127] Critics also noted that the police were now granted additional power to arrest without warrant.

The most controversial part of the bill was Section 3, relating to the control of processions: a chief officer of police may, where he has reasonable ground for apprehending that any public procession may occasion serious public disorder, impose on those organizing or taking part in the procession such conditions as appear to him necessary for the preservation of public order. For example, those conditions might prescribe the route to be followed. This proposal transferred the existing power of the police authorities, to control the route that a procession took, to the chief constable. It significantly increased, therefore, the statutory powers of chiefs of police. Their actions in controlling and routeing

[127] See debates on Public Order Bill, e.g. ibid., 1434 ff. (16 Nov. 1936); ibid., 318, 99 ff. (23 Nov. 1936); ibid., 678 ff. (26 Nov. 1936); D. N. Pritt, 'The Public Order Bill', *New Statesman*, 14 Nov. 1936, p. 761.

processions were now, in effect, subject to no extra-judicial control either through local authorities or police authorities or through parliament itself. Sub-section 2 of Section 3 laid down that, if a chief officer of police is 'of opinion that', because of the circumstances prevailing in any borough or urban district or place, the power of imposing conditions upon processions is insufficient, then he can apply to the appropriate local authority for an order prohibiting all or particular classes of public procession in that area for up to three months. The local authority could make an order with the consent of the Secretary of State. In London the power of making the order was vested in the Commissioner of the Metropolitan Police, subject to the Home Secretary's consent. In all these respects, therefore, the Public Order Act 1936 brought important changes.

The conclusion must be that the Fascist disturbances of the 1930s and the furore caused by their behaviour, was made the occasion for a broad extension of common-law and statutory police powers, which was to have profound effects on the right of working people to meet and process. Although chief officers did not achieve all the powers they had sought by statute, there is no doubt that, by the end of 1936, there had been a notable extension of statutory and case-law provision relating to public order. Civil liberties in relation to marches and meetings had been seriously affected (some felt eroded) as a result. Police riot-control techniques had been improved considerably in the 1920s and 1930s. In addition there had continued to be a decline in accountability, both locally and nationally. This was especially marked in the major centre of processions and marches—London itself. Here the Home Secretary was now disclaiming responsibility for the actions of the Metropolitan Police in the inter-war years, whereas in the nineteenth century he had staunchly defended his right to direct the Commissioner and issue detailed instructions on matters of law enforcement. In 1936, by contrast, Simon's view of the Home Secretary's powers was that 'he does not give the police detailed directions, he only consults with the commissioner in cases of exceptional importance'.[128] This was now broadly the case, although it is notable that, even when an exceptionally powerful

[128] CAB 24/264 CP 261 (36).

Commissioner like Trenchard wished to assert his authority, as in 1934 when dealing with the preparations for the national hunger march, the Home Secretary could impose his views and they were obeyed.

Police strategy in dealing with marches by the unemployed, and the attendant campaign to maintain the right of public meeting, were products of a rapidly changing political context in the 1920s and 1930s. The precise method of dealing with unemployed meetings and marches and similar demonstrations had been seen during the nineteenth and early twentieth centuries as essentially a problem for the local police and their authorities rather than for the central government. There was little official support until the 1920s for a more coercive policy, and scant Home Office pressure to alter the traditional approach to the policing of open-air meetings and processions. The resolve of the police determination to confront the threat posed by the hunger marches was theoretically hedged around with vital constraints.

However, with the advent of national marches by the unemployed, the Home Office encouraged stern action by the police through its use of circulars and other forms of instruction. The outcome was often the kind of vigorous, even violent, police intervention described in this chapter. With Home Office support, the police were assuming new powers and also taking over powers which they would previously have had to seek from justices or local authorities. Finally, the Public Order Act 1936 confirmed a gradual extension of police authority in controlling meetings or marches by labour organizations and others. Important cases involving key aspects of civil liberties had reinforced this process in a way that aroused the fears of leading constitutional lawyers. The conclusion must be, therefore, that in this respect, as in others, the inter-war years saw the balance tilt significantly in favour of the power of the state and the law-enforcement agencies in controlling the activities of working people.

9
Conclusion

In the first four decades of the twentieth century the approach of the police towards labour unrest underwent profound changes. There evolved the concept of a national police force designed to counter either a local or a nation-wide threat from labour. The idea was steadily developed by the Home Office, in association with chief police officers, between 1900 and 1939. This increased centralization was paralleled by an increase of police operational powers. There was a notable extension of riot-control techniques. In addition, there was a broad expansion of police legal powers through case and statute law, culminating in the Public Order Act 1936. The outcome was an extensive redefinition—many felt an erosion—of civil liberties and the decline of police accountability, locally and nationally.

The main features of this process, so central to modern British social history, yet largely ignored by scholars of the period, have been traced in the course of this book. The fundamental cause of change was extreme industrial confrontation, particularly between 1910 and 1926. During the nineteenth century the police had been subject to the control of their various local authorities, which were responsible for maintaining an adequate and efficient force, and were answerable for the administration and conduct of the police in their area. The Home Office had little interest in the provincial police, other than ensuring efficiency in terms of numbers and discipline. It positively encouraged the principle of local control. With the onset of national labour disputes from the turn of the century, however, the preservation of law and order assumed supreme importance. A national response by the authorities seemed to be required; yet no nationally organized police force existed. In the years down to 1914 the Home Office urged local authorities to build up their reserves, to combine through mutual-aid agreements, and to standardize their executive response, but with mixed effects. The use of the armed forces, by the government rather than by magistrates, was now revived, as in Stuart times in the past. They were used as police, with and without requisition of the civil power. This process reached a spectacular climax during Churchill's period at the Home Office in 1910–11.

In the course of the First World War chief constables became used to acting under central direction from Whitehall. After the war, when there was a far more critical industrial situation, the use of troops in meeting industrial unrest continued, in 1919–21 especially. But more significant, perhaps, were pressures from the Home Office, notably from Troup and later Anderson, for the greater central control of police organization. This tendency was much reinforced by the effects of the Police Act 1919, following Desborough, with the enhanced powers for central government that it brought. The fact that the police were now a central arm of the emergency anti-strike apparatus embodied in the Emergency Powers Act 1920 made this pressure for national co-ordination all the more powerful. In the 1921 coal strike, and more especially in the general strike of 1926 and after, the new cohesion of the police, and their ability to dovetail with the military and naval forces employed by the state, were very pronounced. During these crises local police authorities appeared powerless to hold their police accountable for their actions in the face of the independent stance adopted by chief constables, with Home Office encouragement.

In addition to this increase of central direction and the rise of a police force national in spirit if not in form, the executive powers of the police also went through a major transformation in the labour troubles of this period. During the nineteenth century, in the Chartist troubles for example, the police, who had always had much discretion in the field of public disorder, had relied heavily on obstruction laws that were older than the force itself. This approach, as has been seen, continued into the twentieth century. The police were given no new statutory powers to deal with public order. However, with the rise of national strikes from 1910 onwards the situation changed dramatically. During the national stoppages of the 1910–12 period the police were encouraged by the Home Office to extend their powers in relation to intimidation and violence on the picket line. During the war years the police gained further wide powers in the area of public order under DORA, and picketing as such was prohibited. Thus, in the area of police authority, as in so many other respects, the war acted as a significant catalyst. After the war the police, like other bodies, were reluctant to relinquish their new-found powers. The 1919 Police Act conferred much greater power on central government, and the Home Office now urged a much more aggressive police response to labour unrest and issued circulars which had much more authority than previously. At the same time the Home Office began to popularize the idea of the independence of the office of constable, and his accountability to the law rather than to democratically elected local authorities. This approach was reinforced by the introduction of Emergency Regulations during the states of emergency of 1921 and 1926, which themselves conferred wide powers on the police. There were also further statutory innovations. The Trade Disputes and Trade Unions Act of 1927, followed by the Public Order Act in 1936, along with a series of important case-law decisions in the early 1930s, legitimized powers which the police had, in fact, been adopting to deal with industrial protest at least since the end of the First World War.

All these developments made the police a far more formidable instrument for central government, in confronting labour, than could have been foreseen at the turn of the century. They reflected the institutional growth of the police force itself in the metropolis and the provinces. They also followed the deliberate policy of the Home Office that the law enforcement agencies must be nationalized, to counter labour troubles that were themselves nationwide. In the course of this the police should be largely removed from democratic accountability.

In 1939, theoretically, police organization still reflected the localized character it had retained since the Middle Ages. The police were still under local control. However, major changes had taken place, both within the force and in its relationship to the Home Office. In the nineteenth century the idea of a nationally organized police force had always been rejected, mainly on the grounds that. by bringing the police under the control of the executive, their effectiveness would be weakened. Now a skilful and subtle compromise had been worked out. The Home Office had simultaneously encouraged the police to assume new powers, many of which were later given statutory backing, and had also promoted the doctrine of the independent position of the police constable. At the same time, it had strengthened its position in relation to the provincial police. In these circumstances, the effective control exercised by democratically elected representatives inexorably declined.

In the period since 1945 these pressures have been emphatically extended, often to the alarm of the left and champions of civil liberties.[1] Chief constables in the boroughs, traditionally under the direction of their watch committees, were further encouraged to exercise the independence and freedom from accountability associated with chief constables in the counties. The culmination of this process was the Police Act of 1964, passed by the Douglas-Home government and not opposed by the Labour Party to any significant extent. Watch committees were now abolished and replaced by police committees composed two-thirds of councillors and one-third of magistrates. Borough police chiefs were now granted the same powers of appointment, promotion, and discipline over their forces as their counterparts in the counties, and the role of the chief constable was statutorily defined. However, the question whether police authorities can control or influence their chief constables' operational activities remained undefined and a bone of contention between the two in many areas. Satisfactory inquiries into police conduct have continued to be singularly difficult to obtain, while the Home Office, under Labour as well as Conservative governments, has invariably upheld the police viewpoint. As in the past, it has been industrial crises that have thrown the problem of accountability into sharpest relief. During the 1984–5 miners' strike much attention focused on the independence of chief constables, and the ease with which assistance from other police forces could be brought in. Local authorities such as that in South Yorkshire have tried to mount a challenge on financial aspects over paying the cost of the use of outside police, housing, and other details. In general, the relative powerlessness of local councillors in their dealings with central

[1] The Oaksey Committee in 1948 provided the first official pronouncement on the subject when it claimed that the Commissioners of the Metropolitan Police and the City of London forces were in the same position in relation to their police authorities as were chief constables in counties. Although watch committees exercised greater control over their chief officers because the latter had no statutory position, the case of *Fisher* v. *Oldham* had had wide influence. The Oaksey Committee added that the police authority had no right to give the chief constable orders about the disposition of the force or the way in which police duties should be carried out. The chief officer could not divest himself of responsibility by turning to the watch committee for guidance or instruction on matters of police duty. *Report of the Committee on Police Conditions of Service*, PP 1948–9 [Cmd. 7831], xix. 385–6.

government has been further highlighted. The police have been hampered, not by lack of legal powers, but by practical difficulties of enforcement. When serious disorder has occurred, the most effective way of stopping it has been by better organization and new riot-control weaponry and techniques. However, the fears aroused by the Public Order Act 1936 re-emerged in 1985 with the passing of the Police and Criminal Evidence Act and with newly enacted legislation to cover riot, violent disorder, affray, and conduct likely to provoke violence. These would again enhance the powers of the police against pickets and others. The problems identified in this book remained as very much alive in the era of Mrs Thatcher as they were previously in the age of Asquith and Lloyd George.

The conclusion to be drawn depends on the perspective to be adopted. By comparison with the industrial history of many other countries, Britain has coped reasonably well with bridging the gap between an efficient police and democratic accountability. Apart from their use in labour disputes, the police seem to have remained broadly popular with the local community. Despite the deaths at Featherstone in 1893 and at Liverpool and Llanelli in 1911, British labour relations did not experience the habitual violence and loss of life that punctuated the history of the United States from the 1892 Homestead strike to the stay-in strikes at Flint, Michigan, in 1937. The fearful carnage between a paramilitary state police and industrial workers evident in France, Germany, Italy, and many other European countries down to 1939 again found no echo in Britain. Even the use of troops in Britain, while alarming, and damaging for the particular reputation of Winston Churchill, did not approach the experience in France before 1914. Clemenceau and Briand sent on occasion as many as 40,000 troops into mining areas like the Pas de Calais. The French coal strike of 1907–8 resulted in 104 years of prison sentences, 20 killed and more than 600 injured. By this test, the British record is a reasonably humane one, a tribute both to the restraint of the police and the responsibility of labour leaders. After the Second World War in Britain the policeman remained an acceptable figure, a uniformed but unarmed citizen often celebrated in films or television productions. Despite the fierce antagonism evident in ethnic ghettos in Brixton, Toxteth, Handsworth, and elsewhere in the 1980s, it is reasonable to conclude the police retain some of their traditional acceptance from working-class people, even as the older consensus disintegrates.

Nevertheless, the role of the police in dealing with industrial troubles in Britain between 1900 and 1939 remains in many ways a disturbing story, and one which cannot be approached with complacency by champions of civil liberties. The effect of the process that has been described has been to extend centralized government as so frequently exalted by the Liberal and Labour left, in ways potentially ominous for political and social democracy. The left welcomed the welfare state, the growth of government intervention in the economy after the First World War, the use of collectivism to elevate national standards and alleviate the impact of economic decline. In the case of the police, this Fabian imperative of extended centralization has been less obviously beneficial. Power for the police has meant unaccountability, perhaps even irresponsibility. A new stratum of executive officials has come into being, notably the chief constables with extended powers of intruding upon the individual's daily life and influencing powers of free association. The very pressures of nationalization and centralization have heightened the sense of unease about the police, not in a naive Millite sense of hostility to governmental direction, but rather in terms of the independence of the police from constraints that have operated elsewhere in the years since Britain became a democracy. Labour Home Secretaries between 1945 and 1979, especially Ede and Callaghan, have been anxious to emphasize their toughness in dealing with law and order. The years between 1900 and 1939 were a time of redefinition and much strain for the police system amidst unparalleled industrial conflict in Britain. It was a period from which they emerged physically more effective but at some political and moral cost. The dilemma of reconciling effectiveness and control in the conduct of the law confronts social leaders today with the same urgency, uncertainty, and anxiety as it confronted their predecessors a generation ago.

Appendix

1. *Total number of forces, total establishment, and total population per policeman for census years*

Year	Total no. forces	Total establishment	Total population ('000)	Population per policeman
1861	233	20,488	20,066	979.4
1871	n.a.	26,604	22,712	853.7
1881	224	31,596	25,974	822.0
1891	185	39,198	29,003	739.9
1901	187	44,705	32,528	727.6
1911	188	54,314	36,070	664.1

Source: *Annual Abstracts of Statistics* and *Annual Reports of HM Inspectors of Constabulary*.

2. *Changes in the numbers of police, 1921–1949*

Year	Counties 1921 (18,027) =100	Boroughs 1921 (19,370) =100	London and Metropolitan 1921 (22,121) =100	England and Wales 1921 (59,518) =100
1921	100	100	100	100
1922	96	96	97	96
1923	96	95	93	94
1925	98	97	93	96
1930	102	101	96	99
1931	103	102	97	100
1932	102	101	96	99
1933	102	101	95	99
1935	105	103	92	99
1939	120	115	91	107
1949	140	95	75	101

Source: *Annual Reports of HM Inspectors of Constabulary*.

3. *Population per police constable in England and Wales, 1921–1949*

Year	Total actual strength	Population ('000*)	Population per policeman
1921	59,520	37,887	637
1922	57,350	38,158	665
1923	56,220	38,403	683
1925	57,070	38,890	681
1930	59,250	39,806	672
1931	59,670	39,952	670
1932	59,320	40,201	678
1933	58,900	40,350	685
1934	58,850	40,467	688
1935	59,230	40,645	686
1939	63,980	41,460	648
1949	60,190	43,785	727

* All population totals are estimates given in the Registrar-General's *Statistical Review of England and Wales* with the exception of 1921 and 1931 which are census figures.

Source: *Annual Abstracts of Statistics* and *Annual Reports of HM Inspectors of Constabulary*.

4. *Police income: balance between government support and local rates, 1908–1938*

Year*	Government subsidies (£)†	Balance of costs falling mainly on local rates (£)
1908–9	2,229,082	3,401,155
1919–20	7,710,211	8,215,486
1926–7	9,907,192	10,176,410
1937–8	12,003,702	12,267,056

* In each case, the year covered is from 31 March to 31 March.

† From 1919, the government subsidy was increased to cover nearly half the cost of the police. This involved a large supplementary grant in addition to the basic Exchequer contributions for pay and clothing, and for superannuation.

Source: *Annual Reports of HM Inspectors of Constabulary*.

5. *Number of prosecutions instituted in connection with the mid-Rhondda coal strike, 1910–1911*

Total no. of persons prosecuted	No. of persons convicted for intimidation	No. of persons convicted for assaulting the police	No. of persons convicted for other offences
537	16*	88†	318‡

* Includes 2 committed for trial at assizes for riot.

† Includes 1 committed for trial at assizes for wounding.

‡ Includes 6 committed for trial at quarter sessions for unlawful wounding; 4 committed for trial at quarter sessions for grievous bodily harm; 1 committed for trial at assizes for uttering a forged strike pay ticket.

Source: D. Evans, *Labour Strife in the South Wales Coalfield, 1910–11* (1911), p. 209.

Bibliography

1. MANUSCRIPTS

(i) Public Records

Admiralty: ADM 116 (Aid to Civil Power)
Cabinet: CAB 21 (Registered Files)
CAB 23 (Cabinet Minutes)
CAB 24 (Cabinet Papers)
CAB 26 (Home Affairs Committee)
CAB 27 (Cabinet Committees)
CAB 37
CAB 53 (Committee of Imperial Defence)
CAB 134 (Emergency Committees)
Health: MH 57
Home Office: HO 45 (Home Office Papers: Law and Order)
HO 144 (Seen with Home Office permission)
HO 158 (Home Office Circulars)
Metropolitan Police: MEPO 1
MEPO 2 (Disturbances)
War Office: WO 32 (Aid to Civil Power)

(ii) Police Records

Annual Police Instructions for Birkenhead, Bolton, Liverpool, Manchester, Wakefield.

Birmingham City Watch Committee Minutes, 1900–1939 (Birmingham City Library).

Birmingham City Police: Annual Report of Chief Constable, 1920–1930 (Birmingham City Library).

Cardiff City Watch Committee Minutes, 1900–1939 (Cardiff Central Library).
Carmarthenshire Standing Joint Committee Minutes, 1900–1939 (Carmarthen Record Office, County Hall, Carmarthen).
Denbighshire Standing Joint Committee Minutes, 1900–1939 (County Record Office, Ruthin).
Glamorgan Standing Joint Committee Minutes, 1900–1939 (County Hall, Cardiff; Glamorgan Record Office).
Liverpool City Watch Committee Minutes, 1900–1939 (Liverpool Central Library).
Manchester City Watch Committee Minutes, 1900–1939 (Manchester Central Police Station).
Manchester City Police: Annual Reports of Chief Constable, 1900–1913, 1926–1939 (Manchester City Library).
Monmouthshire Standing Joint Committee Minutes, 1900–1939 (County Hall, Cwmbran).
Neath Borough Watch Committee Minutes, 1900–1914 (County Hall, Swansea), 1917–1939 (Neath Library).
Swansea Borough Watch Committee Minutes, 1908–1939 (Swansea Guildhall).

(iii) Private Papers

Thomas Jones Papers (National Library of Wales, Aberystwyth).
Transcripts in South Wales Miners' Library, Swansea.

2. OFFICIAL PAPERS

Hansard, *Parliamentary Debates*, 3rd, 4th, 5th series.
Annual Reports of HM Inspector of Constabulary, 1900–1939.
Annual Reports of the Commissioner of the Metropolitan Police, 1900–1939.
First Report of the Commissioners Appointed to inquire as to the Best Means of Establishing an Efficient Constabulary Force in the Counties of England and Wales, PP 1839 (169), xix. 1.
Report of a Committee to inquire into and report as to the Original Character of the Disturbances which took place in the Metropolis on Monday the 8th February, and as to the Conduct of the Police Authorities in Relation thereto, PP 1886 [C. 4665], xxxiv, 381.
Report of the Committee Appointed to inquire into the Circumstances Connected with the Disturbances at Featherstone on 7 September 1893, PP 1893–4 [C. 7234], xvii. 385.
Report of the Inter Departmental Committee on Riots (HMSO, 1895).
Report of the Royal Commission on Trade Disputes and Trade Combinations, PP 1906 [Cd. 2825], lvi. 1.

Report of the Select Committee on Employment of Military in Cases of Disturbances, PP 1908 (236), vii. 365.

Report from the Select Committee on the Police Forces (Weekly Rest Day), with Proceedings and Minutes of Evidence, 1908 (353), ix. 679.

Report of the Departmental Committee on the Duties of the Police with Respect to the Preservation of Order at Public Meetings PP 1909 [Cd. 4673], xxxvi. 83.

Colliery Strike Disturbances in South Wales: Correspondence and Report, PP 1911 [Cd. 5568], lxiv. 1.

Employment of Military during Railway Strike: Correspondence between Home Office and Local Authorities, PP 1911 (323), xlvii. 691.

Report by Mr Chester Jones on Certain Disturbances at Rotherhithe on June 11th 1912 and Complaints against the Conduct of the Police in Connection therewith, PP 1912–13 [Cd. 6367], xlvii. 297.

Report of the Committee on the Police Service, England, Wales and Scotland,

—— Part I, PP 1919 [Cmd. 253], xxvii. 709.

—— Part II, PP 1920 [Cmd. 574], xxii. 539.

Minutes of Evidence PP 1920 [Cmd. 874], xxii. 573.

Report of the Committee on the Employment of Women on Police Duties, PP 1920 [Cmd. 877], xxii. 1087.

First and Second Interim Reports of the Committee on National Expenditure, PP 1922 [Cmd. 1581, 1582], ix. 1 and 173.

Report of the Departmental Committee on Crowds, PP 1924 [Cmd. 2088], viii. 225.

Report of the Departmental Committee on the Employment of Policewomen, PP 1924 [Cmd. 2224], xii. 193.

Home Office Circular dated 30 December 1925, Addressed to Chief Constables of England and Wales as to the Provisions of the Law, *Intimidation and Molestation*, PP 1926 [Cmd. 2666], xxiii. 861.

St Helens County Borough Police Force Reports to the Secretary of State for the Home Department, PP 1928 [Cmd. 3103], xii. 49.

Judicial Statistics for England and Wales, PP 1928 [Cmd. 3055], xxv.

Report of the Royal Commission on Police Powers and Procedure, PP 1928–9 [Cmd. 3297], ix. 127.

—— *Minutes of Evidence, Parts I and II* (HMSO, 1929).

Report from the Select Committee on Police Force (Amalgamation), PP 1931–2, (106), v. 123.

Memorandum on the Subject of Certain Changes in the Organization and Administration of the Metropolitan Police, PP 1932–3 [Cmd. 4320], xxi. 649.

Report of the Committee on Police Conditions of Service, PP 1948–9 [Cmd. 7831], xix. 379.

Final Report of the Royal Commission on the Police, PP 1961–2 [Cmd. 1728], xx. 515.

Report of the Royal Commission on Trade Unions and Employers Associations, PP 1967–8 [Cmd. 3623], xxxii. 731.
Report of an Inquiry by the Rt. Hon. Lord Scarman into the Brixton Disorders, 10–12 April 1981 [Cmnd. 8427] (HMSO, 1981).

3. NEWSPAPERS AND PERIODICALS

(i) Newspapers

Clarion
Daily Herald
Daily Mail
Labour Leader (became the *New Leader*)
Manchester Guardian
Merthyr Pioneer (became the *Pioneer*)
Morning Post
Pall Mall Gazette
South Wales Daily News
Sunday Worker
The Times
Western Mail

(ii) Periodicals

Armed Forces and Society
Army Quarterly Journal
Atlantic Monthly
Cambridge Law Journal
Criminal Law Review
Industrial Law Journal
Justice of the Peace
Labour Monthly
Listener
Nation
New Society
New Statesman
Police Journal
Police Review
Police Studies
Politica
Public Administration
Social History
Socialist Review
Solicitor's Journal

Spectator
Workers' Life

4. REPORTS

Annual Reports of the following organizations: Labour Party; Trades Union Congress.
Law Reports: King's Bench.
The Harworth Colliery Strike: A Report to the Executive Committee of the National Council for Civil Liberties by the Secretary of the Council (1937).
The Thurloe Square Baton charge: Report of a Commission of Inquiry into Certain Disturbances at Thurloe Square, South Kensington (NCCL, March 1936).
Times Law Reports.

5. BIOGRAPHIES AND MEMOIRS

Bower, W. Nott, *Fifty-two Years a Policeman* (1926).
Boyle, A., *Trenchard* (1962).
Bullock, A., *The Life and Times of Ernest Bevin*, i (1960).
Butler, Sir H., *Confident Morning* (1950).
Childs, Sir W., *Episodes and Reflections* (1930).
Churchill, R. S., *Winston S. Churchill*, ii (1967).
Citrine, W., *Two Careers* (1967).
Connole, N., *Leaven of Heaven* (1961).
Cross, J. A., *Sir Samuel Hoare* (1977).
Davidson, J. C. C., *Memoirs of a Conservative*, ed. R. Rhodes James (1968).
Gilbert, M., *Winston S. Churchill: Companion Volume IV* (1977).
Hannington, Wal, *Never on our Knees* (1967).
Horner, A., *Incorrigible Rebel* (1960).
Jones, T., *Thomas Jones: Whitehall Diaries*, ed. K. Middlemas (3 vols., 1969–71).
Lloyd George, David, *Lloyd George: Family Letters, 1885–1936*, ed. K. O. Morgan (1973).
Macready, General the Rt. Hon. Sir Nevil, *Annals of an Active Life* (2 vols, 1924).
Marquand, D., *Ramsay MacDonald* (1977).
Masterman, L., *C. F. G. Masterman: A Biography* (1939).
May, W. C., *Recollections and Reflections of a County Policeman* (1979).
Mallett, C. E., *Herbert Gladstone* (1932).
Rhodes James, R., *Memoirs of a Conservative* (1969).
Rose, K., *George V: A Biography* (1983).

Samuel, Viscount, *Memoirs* (1945).
Scott, Sir H., *Your Obedient Servant* (1959).
Taylor, H. A., *Jix, Viscount Brentford* (1933).
Thomson, Basil, *Queer People* (1922).
—— *The Scene Changes* (1939).
Wheeler-Bennett, J. W., *John Anderson, Viscount Waverley* (1962).
Winterton, Earl, *Orders of the Day* (1953).
Young, G. M., *Stanley Baldwin* (1952).

6. OTHER PUBLISHED WORKS

Alderson, J., *Policing Freedom* (1979).
—— *Law and Disorder* (1984).
—— and P. J. Stead (eds.), *The Police We Deserve* (1973).
Allen, V. L., *Trade Unions and the Government* (1960).
Andrew, C., *Secret Service* (1985).
Ascoli, D., *The Queen's Peace* (1979).
Banton, M., *The Policeman in the Community* (1964).
Bailey, V. (ed.), *Policing and Punishment in Nineteenth Century Britain* (1981).
Barnes, D. and E. Reid, *Governments and Trade Unions: The British Experience 1964–79* (1980).
Benewick, R. and T. Smith (eds.), *Direct Action and Democratic Politics* (1972).
Benyon, J. (ed.), *Scarman and After* (1984).
Bordua, D. J. (ed.), *The Police: Six Sociological Essays* (1967).
Bowden, T., *Beyond the Limits of the Law* (1978).
Bowes, S., *The Police and Civil Liberties* (1966).
Brogden, M., *The Police: Autonomy and Consent* (1982).
Brooker, K., *The Hull Strikes of 1911* (East Yorkshire Local History Society Series, 35; 1979).
Bunyan, T., *The Political Police in Britain* (1976).
Bunyard, R. S., *Police: Organization and Command* (1978).
Burns, E. *The General Strike, May 1926: Trades Councils in Action* (1926).
Cain, M., *Society and the Policeman's Role* (1973).
Childs, J., *The Army of Charles II* (1976).
Clegg, H., A. Fox, and A. F. Thompson, *A History of British Trade Unions since 1889*, i. *1889–1910* (1963).
Clegg, H., *A History of British Trade Unions since 1889* (1985).
Clinton, A., *Post Office Workers: A Trade Union and Social History* (1984).
Cowell, D., T. Jones, and J. Young, *Policing and Riots* (1982).
Critchley, T. A., *A History of the Police in England and Wales, 900–1966* (1967).

—— *The Conquest of Violence* (1970).
Deacon, R., *The History of the Secret Service* (1969).
Emsley, C., *Policing and its Context, 1750–1870* (1983).
Evans, D., *Labour Strife in the South Wales Coalfield, 1910–11* (1911).
Evelegh, R., *Peace Keeping in a Democratic Society* (1978).
Farman, C., *The General Strike* (1976).
Foster, D., *The Rural Constabulary Act, 1839* (1982).
Francis, H., *Miners against Fascism: Wales and the Spanish Civil War* (1984).
—— and D. Smith, *The Fed* (1980).
Gatrell, V. A. C., B. Lenman, and G. Parker (eds.), *Crime and the Law* (1980).
Geary, R., *Policing Industrial Disputes, 1893–1985* (1985).
Glasgow, G., *General Strikes and Road Transport* (1926).
Gordon, H., *The War Office* (1935).
Griffin, A. R., *The Miners of Nottinghamshire, 1914–1944* (1962).
Griffith, J. A. G., *The Politics of the Judiciary* (1978).
Grunfeld, C., *Modern Trade Union Law* (1966).
Hannington, Wal, *Why Do They March?* (1936).
Hart, J. M., *The British Police* (1951).
Hasluck, E. L., *Local Government in England* (1948).
Higham, R., *Armed Forces in Peacetime Britain 1918–1940* (1962).
Hikins, H., *The Liverpool General Transport Strike, 1911* (1980).
Hinton, J., *The First Shop Stewards' Movement* (1973).
Holdaway, S. (ed.), *The British Police* (1979).
Holton, B., *British Syndicalism, 1900–1914* (1976).
Hurt, W. W., *To Guard My People: An Account of the Origin and History of the Swansea Police* (1957).
Jefferson, T. and R. Grimshaw, *Controlling the Constable: Police Accountability in England and Wales* (1984).
Jeffery, K. and P. Hennessy, *States of Emergency: British Governments and Strike Breaking since 1919* (1983).
Jones, R. M., *The North Wales Quarrymen, 1874–1922* (1981).
Judge, A., *The First Fifty Years: The Story of the Police Federation* (1968).
Kahn, P., N. Lewis, R. Livock, and P. Wiles, *Picketing: Industrial Disputes, Tactics and the Law* (1983).
Kahn-Freund, O., *Labour and the Law* (2nd edn., 1977).
Keeton, G. W., *Keeping the Peace* (1975).
Kidd, R., *British Liberty in Danger* (1940).
Kingsford, P., *The Hunger Marchers in Britain 1920–1940* (1982).
Kirby, M. W., *The British Coalmining Industry* (1977).
Klugman, J., *A History of the Communist Party in Great Britain*, ii (1968).
Knowles, K. G. J. C., *Strikes: A Study in Industrial Conflict* (1952).
Laurie, P., *Scotland Yard* (1970).
Lee, W. L. Melville, *A History of the Police in England and Wales* (1901).

Lewenhak, S., *Women and Trade Unions* (1977).
Lunn, K., and R. Thurlow (eds.), *British Fascism* (1980).
Lustgarten, L., *The Governance of Police* (1986).
McCord, N., *Strikes* (1980).
McKibbin, R., *The Evolution of the Labour Party, 1910–1924* (1974).
McLean, I., *The Legend of Red Clydeside* (1983).
Manning, P., *Police Work* (1977).
Manwaring White, S., *The Policing Revolution* (1983).
Mark, R., *Policing a Perplexed Society* (1977).
Marshall, G., *Police and Government: The Status and Accountability of the English Constable* (1965).
Martin, J. P. and G. Wilson, *The Police: A Study in Manpower* (1969).
Mather, F. C., *Public Order in the Age of the Chartists* (1959).
Miller, W. R., *Cops and Bobbies: Police Authority in New York and London, 1830–1870* (Chicago 1977).
Morgan, K. O., *Consensus and Disunity: The Lloyd George Coalition Government, 1918–1922* (1979).
—— *Labour in Power, 1945–1951* (1984).
Morris, M., *The General Strike* (1976).
Mortimer, J. E., *History of the Boilermakers Society*, ii. *1906–1939* (1982).
Moylan, J., *Scotland Yard* (2nd edn., 1934).
Newsam, Sir F., *The Home Office* (1954).
Page Arnot, R., *The South Wales Miners: A History of the South Wales Miners' Federation* (1967).
Paul, L., *Angry Young Men* (1951).
Peele, G. and C. Cook (eds.), *The Politics of Reappraisal, 1918–1939* (1975).
Pellew, J., *The Home Office 1848–1914* (1982).
Pelling, H., *Popular Politics and Society in Late Victorian Britain* (1968).
—— *A History of British Trade Unionism* (2nd edn., 1971).
Phelps Brown, E. H., *The Growth of British Industrial Relations* (1959).
—— *The Origins of Trade Union Power* (1983).
Phillips, D., *Crime and Authority in Victorian England* (1974).
Phillips, G. A., *The General Strike* (1976).
Postgate, R. W., E. Wilkinson, and J. F. Horrabin, *A Worker's History of the General Strike* (1927).
Pratt, E. A., *Trade Unionism and British Industry: A Reprint of 'The Times' Articles on the Crisis in British Industry* (1904).
Pribicevic, B., *The Shop Stewards' Movement and Workers' Control, 1910–1922* (1959).
Pritt, D. N., *Employers, Workers, and Trade Unions* (1970).
Punch, M., *Control in the Police Organization* (1983).
Radzinowicz, L., *A History of English Criminal Law*, iv (1968).
Reiner, R., *The Blue-Coated Worker* (1978).
—— *The Politics of the Police* (1985).

Reith, C., *The Police Idea* (1938).
—— *British Police and the Democratic Ideal* (1943).
—— *A New Study of Police History* (1956).
Reynolds, G. W. and A. Judge, *The Night the Police went on Strike* (1968).
Robson, W. A., *The Development of Local Government* (3rd edn., 1954).
Seth, R., *The Specials* (1961).
Scott, Sir H., *Your Obedient Servant* (1959).
Skelley, J. (ed.), *The General Strike, 1926* (1976).
Spiers, E. M., *The Army and Society, 1815–1914* (1980).
Steedman, C., *Policing the Victorian Community* (1984).
Stevenson, J. and R. Quinault (eds.), *Popular Protest and Public Order* (1974).
Sutherland, G. (ed.), *Studies in the Growth of Nineteenth-century Government* (1972).
Symons, J., *The General Strike* (1957).
Thompson, E. P., *Whigs and Hunters* (1975).
Tobias, J. J., *Crime and Police in England, 1700–1900* (1979).
Troup, Sir E., *The Home Office* (1925).
Waller, P. J., *Democracy and Sectarianism* (1981).
Whitaker, B., *The Police* (1964).
—— *The Police in Society* (1979).
Williams, D., *Keeping the Peace* (1967).
Williams, J. E., *The Derbyshire Miners* (1962).
Wrigley, C., *David Lloyd George and the British Labour Movement* (1976).
—— (ed.), *A History of British Industrial Relations, 1875–1914* (1982).

7. ARTICLES

Allen, V. L., 'The National Union of Police and Prison Officers', *Economic History Review*, 2nd ser., 11 (1958–9), 133–43.
Anderson, J., 'The Police', *Public Administration*, 7, 2 (1929), 192–202.
Barnes, T., 'Special Branch and the First Labour Government', *Historical Journal*, 22, 4 (1979), 941–51.
Bean, R., 'Police Unrest, Unionization and the 1919 Strike in Liverpool', *Journal of Contemporary History*, 15 (1980), 633–47.
Beloff, M., 'The Whitehall Factor: The Role of the Higher Civil Service, 1919–1939', in G. Peele and C. Cook (eds.), *The Politics of Reappraisal, 1918–1939* (1975), 209–31.
Bowden, T., 'Guarding the State: The Police Response to Crisis Politics in Europe', *British Journal of Law and Society*, 5 (1978), 69–88.
Carver, Field Marshal Lord, 'The Army and the Police', *Police Studies*, 6, 1 (Spring 1983), 6–12.
Davidson, R., 'Llewellyn Smith, the Labour Department and Government

Growth, 1886–1909', in G. Sutherland (ed.), *Studies in the Growth of Nineteenth-century Government* (1972), 227–62.

Davies, J. L., 'Crowds and Crises', *Atlantic Monthly*, 138 (July 1926), 114–18.

Dennis, P., 'The Territorial Army in Aid of the Civil Power in Britain, 1919–1926', *Journal of Contemporary History*, 16, 4 (Oct. 1981), 706–19.

Desmarais, R. H., 'The British Government's Strike Breaking Organization and Black Friday', *Journal of Contemporary History*, 6 (1971), 112–27.

Dunbabin, J. P. D., 'The Politics of the Establishment of County Councils', *Historical Journal*, 1, 2 (1963), 226–53.

—— 'Expectations of the New County Councils and their Realization', *Historical Journal*, 8, 3 (1965), 353–80.

Ensor, R. C. K., 'The Suppression of County Government', *Politica*, 1, 4 (1935), 425–6.

Fox, K. O., 'The Tonypandy Riots', *Army Quarterly Journal*, 104 (1973–4), 72–8.

Francis, H., 'The Anthracite Strike and the Disturbances of 1925', *Llafur*, 1, 2 (1973), pp. 15–28.

Goodhart, A. L., 'Thomas v. Sawkins: A Constitutional Innovation', *Cambridge Law Journal*, 6, 1 (1936), 22–30.

Grant, J. L., 'The Hunger Marchers and the Police', *Socialist Review* (Winter 1932), 243–4.

Greer, S. C., 'Military Intervention in Civil Disturbances: The Legal Basis Reconsidered', *Public Law* (1983), 573–99.

Griffith, J., 'The Peaceful Picket', *New Statesman* (15 Feb. 1974), 214.

Hart, J., 'Reform of the Borough Police, 1835–1856', *English Historical Review*, 70 (1955), 411–27.

—— 'The County and Borough Police Act, 1956', *Public Administration*, 34 (Winter 1956), 405–17.

Hayburn, R., 'The Police and the Hunger Marchers', *International Review of Social History*, 17 (1972), 625–45.

Henderson, A., 'The Industrial Unrest: A New Policy Required', *Contemporary Review*, 640 (Apr. 1919), 361–5.

Hopkin, D. R., 'The Llanelli Riots, 1911', *Welsh History Review*, 11, 4 (Dec. 1983), 488–15.

Hurd, A., 'The Navy on Active Service', *Fortnightly Review* (July 1926), 88–91.

Jeffery, K., 'The British Army and Internal Security, 1919–1939', *Historical Journal*, 24, 2 (1981), 377–99.

Jones, Inspector W., 'The Scope and Functions of Local and Central Control in Police Administration', *Police Journal*, 5 (1932), 518–43.

Kettle, M., 'The Police and the Left', *New Society* (6 Dec. 1984).

—— 'Reading the Riot Act', ibid. (16 May 1985).

Macfarlane, L. J., 'Hands Off Russia: British Labour and the Russo-Polish War, 1920', *Past and Present* (Dec. 1967), 126–52.

Marshall, G., 'The Armed Forces in Industrial Disputes in the United Kingdom', *Armed Forces and Society*, 5, 2 (Feb. 1979), 270–9.

Mason, A., 'The General Strike in the North-east' (University of Hull Occasional Papers in Economic History, 3; 1970).

Morris, G. S., 'The Emergency Powers Act 1920', *Public Law* (Winter 1979), 330–41.

Parris, H., 'The Home Office and the Provincial Police, 1856–1870', *Public Law* (1961), 230–55.

Price, R., 'The Labour Process and Labour History', *Social History*, 8, 1 (Jan. 1983), 57–75.

Reiner, R., 'Forces of Disorder; How the Police Control "Riots" ', *New Society*, 52 (10 Apr. 1980).

—— 'Is Britain Turning into a Police State', *New Society*, 69 (2 Aug. 1984).

—— 'The Police and Picketing', *New Society* (7 July 1977).

Richter, D., 'The Welsh Police, the Home Office and the Welsh Tithe War of 1886–1891', *Welsh History Review*, 12, 1 (June 1984), 50–75.

Robinson, C., 'Ideology as History: A Look at the Way Some English Police Historians Look at the Police', *Police Studies*, 2 (1979), 35–49.

Rubin, G. R., 'The Strengths and Weaknesses of the Picketing Law', *Industrial Relations Journal*, 4, 2 (1973), 57–64.

Scrutton, T. E., 'The Work of the Commercial Courts', *Cambridge Law Journal*, 1 (1923), 6–20.

Silver, A., 'The Demand for Order in Civil Society: A Review of Some of the Themes in the History of Urban Crime, Police and Riot', in D. J. Bordua (ed.), *The Police: Six Sociological Essays* (1967), 1–24.

Sires, R. V., 'Labour Unrest in England, 1910–14', *Journal of Economic History*, 11 (1955), 258–62.

Smith, D., 'The Struggle against Company Unionism in the South Wales Coalfield, 1926–1939', *Welsh History Review*, 6, 3 (1973), 354–78.

Stevenson, J., 'The BUF, the Metropolitan Police and Public Order', in K. Lunn and R. Thurlow (eds.), *British Fascism* (1980), 135–49.

—— 'Note on the 1932 Hunger March', *Bulletin of the Society for the Study of Labour History*, 38 (1979), 24–7.

Storch, R. D., 'The Plague of Blue Locusts. Police Reform and Popular Resistance in Northern England, 1840–1857', *International Review of Social History*, 20 (1975), 61–90.

—— 'The Policeman as Domestic Missionary: Urban Discipline and Popular Culture in Northern England, 1850–1880', *Journal of Social History* (Summer 1976), 481–509.

Troup, Sir E., 'Police Administration, Local and National', *Police Journal*, 1 (1928), 5–18.

Wade, E. C. S., 'Police Powers and Public Meetings', *Cambridge Law Journal*, 6, 2 (1937), 175–81.

—— 'Police Search', *Law Quarterly Review*, 50 (1934), 354–67.

Watteville, H. de, 'The Employment of Troops under Emergency Regulations', *Army Quarterly Journal*, 12, 2 (July 1926), 783–90.

Weinberger, B., 'Communism and the General Strike: Documentary Essay', *Bulletin of the Society for the Study of Labour History*, 48 (Spring 1985), 31–57.

Whelan, C. J., 'Military Intervention in Industrial Disputes', *Industrial Law Journal*, 18 (1979), 222–34.

Williams, D. G. T., 'Protest and Public Order', *Cambridge Law Journal*, 28, 1 (1970), 96–121.

—— 'The Police, Public Meetings and Public Order', *Criminal Law Review* (1963), 149–58.

8. THESES AND UNPUBLISHED MANUSCRIPTS

Blake, J. D., 'Civil Disorder in Britain, 1910–39: The Roles of Civil Government and Military Authority' (University of Sussex, Ph.D., 1978).

Dixon, A. L., 'The Home Office and the Police between the Two World Wars' (Bramshill Police College Library, 1966).

Edwards, N., 'History of the South Wales Miners Federation' (Nuffield College, Oxford, 1937).

Hayburn, R., 'The Responses to Unemployment in the 1930s with Special Reference to South-east Lancashire' (University of Hull, Ph.D., 1970).

Morris, G. S., 'A Study of the Protection of Public and Essential Services in Labour Disputes, 1920–1976' (Cambridge University, Ph.D., 1979).

Pittam, R., 'The Home Office, 1782–1982' (Bramshill Police College Library, Home Office centenary pamphlet).

Vogler, R., 'The Development of Summary Jurisdiction in Relation to Civil Disorder' (Cambridge University, Ph.D., 1985).

INDEX